Get Out of Our House: Revolution!

A New Plan for Selecting Representatives

Lorie!
I hope you will join the revolution. Together, we will retake our government!

Tim Cox

Get Out of Our House: Revolution!
A New Plan for Selecting Representatives

Tim Cox

Bridgeway Books

GET OUT OF OUR HOUSE: REVOLUTION!: A NEW PLAN FOR
SELECTING REPRESENTATIVES
PUBLISHED BY BRIDGEWAY BOOKS
P.O. BOX 80107
AUSTIN, TEXAS 78758

For more information about our books, please write to us, call
512.478.2028, or visit our website at www.bridgewaybooks.net.

Library of Congress Control Number: 2007934427

ISBN-13: 978-1-934454-03-9
ISBN-10: 1-934454-03-6

This publication is intended to provide competent and reliable information regarding the subject matter covered. However, it is sold with the
understanding that the author and publisher are not engaged in rendering
legal, financial, or other professional advice. Laws and practices often vary
from state to state and if legal or other expert assistance is required, the
services of a professional should be sought. The author and publisher specifically disclaim any liability that is incurred from the use or application
of the contents of the book.

10 9 8 7 6 5 4 3 2

Acknowledgements

This book was made possible with the active input and advice from many friends. I sincerely thank all who participated in the early surveys, attended the focus groups, and reviewed the initial drafts of the text. Sharing your thoughts and listening to mine helped form the plan. When we evict the politicians and see that the course of our nation has been redirected for the better, you should feel proud.

I would like to thank those who served on the editing team, and in particular, Jay Schutawie, Carley Price, and Robyn Conley. I am grateful to Bridgeway Books for their understanding of the seemingly impossible timeline and their get-it-done attitude. A special thank you to the committed patriots who helped build the early version of the Web site and spent countless hours working through the details: Chandar Kamalanathan, Brad Hill, Micah Wiseley, Kent Nagase, Eric Wooten, Ching-Lung Tjiong, Bogdan Odulinski, Chris Ramirez, Kannan Kaliyur, Reva Tolliver, and Steve Cox. This effort could not succeed without your support. You are true American patriots.

To my family, Donna, Traci and Ryan, thank you for your understanding and sacrifice. Your support and patience was absolutely critical in making this happen.

Finally, I want to thank every American patriot who has joined, or is about to join, the revolution. This is our country, and this is your opportunity to change the world. Put your name on the line below if you are ready to commit. It is time for you to step forward.

_____

Charge!

Table of Contents

I Introduction

Our country is in serious disarray. Politicians have taken over our government, and the decline of our once proud nation can no longer be denied. Get Out of Our House explains the causes of America's decline, identifies where we are failing, and most importantly, documents the plan we will use to evict the 435 politicians who have taken over the United States House of Representatives. The men and women who are responsible for our nation's demise should consider this their warning. On November 4, 2008, America will have an opportunity to replace the politicians with true representatives, chosen by the people, and begin the process of restoring our mighty nation.

America needs you to join the revolution and actively engage in the process. This plan will allow you, and almost every other American, to actually run for office yourself. Even if you do not wish to be elected, you are strongly encouraged to participate so the candidate selected in your district will represent your views. If you participate, you will have a say in the selection of your district's nominee. It is critically important that you encourage your spouse, siblings, parents, voting-age children, peers at work, friends at church, next door neighbors, and anyone else you know who is concerned about the direction of our country to get involved. Participation is incredibly easy.

1

For 80 percent of the country it will require nothing more than one evening to answer one hundred or more questions and one Saturday to choose the person who will best represent them in subsequent selection sessions. With proportionate participation from the people in the initial selection stage, the person selected will represent the views of the entire district much better than any politician or party ever could. Without broad participation, those with extreme views will be able to take over the system, and we will be left with one more poor choice to go with the same tired Republican and Democratic candidates we already get. Whether you are ultimately selected as your district's representative or not, I hope you will support this movement of the people with your time, your money, and most importantly, your actions. This is your country. This is your opportunity to make a difference.

Every effort has been made to create an unbiased process. I have strong opinions about the way I believe the country should be run, but the system is designed such that no particular candidate or specific viewpoint is favored, including my own. The opinions I share are not intended to persuade you to see things my way; rather, they are intended to provide information and context about the situation that will help you determine how you would answer a question and on which side of a line you stand. This will become clearer when you get to the questions. Whether you agree or disagree with my opinions, I encourage you to visit our Web site and join the forums where we will be actively debating each and every issue. This is your government. You can no longer afford to be a spectator. It is time for you to engage.

On November 4, 2008, in a national election, we will have an opportunity to vote for 435 American patriots. Regardless of the views these men and women hold, the fact that they will have been selected by the people, without party affiliation or special interest money, offers me comfort. They will have our nation's best interest at heart, something I cannot say about the politicians of either party. These new patriots will lead the effort to restore our great nation and make us once again proud to be an American.

Think of all the men and women who have given their lives to build and protect this great nation. All that is being asked of you is to sacrifice one night, one Saturday (unless you are chosen), and then, if and only if you prefer the nominee that bubbles to the top of our system in your district, to vote for that person instead of the politicians on the ballot. If there are not enough people in America willing to make such a commitment for our country and our grandchildren, we have little hope. It is my belief that the vast majority of our countrymen will understand the importance and make the time. I am certain the candidates we identify will be honorable, trustworthy, committed patriots. Will you be one of them?

Eighty percent or more of the country is on our side. We have the numbers. All we must do is stand up and step forward. I hope you will join me. Let the revolution begin!

When originally written, this book totaled six hundred and sixty pages, much too long to deliver the needed message, and significantly longer than I had intended or imagined. Although I have attempted to consolidate my thoughts, I fear the rush to present this plan to the country did not leave me enough time to perfect the message. Please bear with me.

The chapter "Signs" explains how an extraordinary sequence of events led to the creation of GOOOH. The chapters "The Decline of America" and "The Causes of Decline" initially consumed over two hundred pages; the chapters "Failure" and "Economy" more than three hundred. To manage the length of this book, I have greatly condensed my original thoughts, cutting literally hundreds of stories and facts that left me aghast. I hope I have included enough of them to give you a good feel for the severity of the situation. I did not cut any of the original questions. All are included in the chapter titled "The Candidate Questionnaire." Not all will make the final list for our candidates, but all will be important as you consider your participation.

After the questions, the book offers a detailed explanation of the process Americans will use to select the candidates who will represent us in each of our congressional districts. Finally, drawing upon the words of our Founding Fathers and other patriots, the book closes with why we must act now and calls for you to join the revolution.

I have walked away from a lucrative career in the high-tech world to champion this cause. I cannot, in good conscience, allow the country to deteriorate under the watch of my generation without making any effort to prevent the demise. My goal is to restore our country to greatness, and the only way that will happen is if true Americans, people just like you, will step forward and replace the politicians ruining our country. To get normal, everyday citizens elected, we need normal, everyday citizens to be involved in the selection process. I am counting on you to participate.

II Today

You and I are blessed to live in the greatest country in the world. Of the 6.5 billion people living on this planet, how many do you believe would prefer to be right where you are, standing in your shoes, eating at your table, working at your job, worshiping at your church, sleeping in your bed? Give some thought to how lucky you are to live in America. There are parents around the world who would willingly give their lives if their children could have yours.

But our country is failing. Thirty-four percent of all children are born to unwed mothers, including over 70 percent of all black children.[1] Thirty-seven million people, which is 12.7 percent of all Americans—including most of the children born to single moms— live in poverty according to the National Poverty Center.[2] We have the highest incarceration rate in the world; over 5.6 million people are in our penal system,[3] and 2.25 million children have a parent in jail on any given day.[4] How well do you think those kids will do in life? Over half of high school seniors admit to having used illegal drugs, and 30 percent of all students fail to complete the twelfth grade. Forty-four million Americans do not have health care, and the majority of everyone else can barely afford insurance. Costs are rising with no end in sight. How will we pay for our own care, much less provide the retirement and health benefits we have promised the baby boomers?

We have an $8.7 trillion deficit that increases by more than $1.5 billion each day. Over 40 percent of the population is now excused from paying any income tax while a family that makes one hundred thousand dollars a year sends over fifty thousand dollars of their earnings to the government via income, payroll, property, sales, gasoline, and other taxes; mounting obligations ensure we will be forced to pay even more in the future. Our dependence on the radical Middle East is growing with over 70 percent of the black gold we consume coming from that highly volatile region. Over twenty million Americans now have asthma,[5] an ailment largely attributed to polluted air. Would you dare swim in a river that runs through any major city in our country? As many as ten thousand illegal immigrants are crossing our borders each day. America is suffering. The decay is pervasive. At least the politicians are doing well: over 50 percent of them admit they are multimillionaires, while most of the rest have found a way to hide their money in trusts, shams, or some other out-of-sight mattress.

We all feel the strain. The decline is real; our "leaders" are not. We have big problems and bigger ones looming. If we do not make some changes soon, the greatest country the world has ever known will soon follow in the footsteps of Rome, Britain, and all the great civilizations that came before us. We are not at risk of falling into the great abyss, but we are on course to surrender a status so lofty that it will never be reclaimed and end a prosperity that the rest of the world dreams of but only our nation breathes. If we do not act soon, we will become a broken country ruled by politicians who are more powerful, parties more corrupt, lawyers more controlling, aristocrats more wealthy, and extremists even more extreme. We will soon be a country that is politically correct, morally bankrupt, and financially ruined.

The problem is complex, but the solution is simple. Our country was founded on the premise that a representative government, selected by the people, would serve the people. The concept worked well for many, many years, but few, if any, would argue that it is working today. The root cause of every one of our country's major problems can be traced to the fact that we no longer have representatives of the people in government. Instead, we have pandering politicians who represent their party, special interests, and themselves, and who do what is politically correct, not what is right. The people no longer control our government; politicians and the two parties do. As a result, government is no longer limited.

Our government has three branches: legislative, judicial, and executive. The legislative branch consists of two bodies of lawmakers: the Senate and the House of Representatives. The Senate is intended to include seasoned statesmen experienced in the workings of the country and the process of law, who will ensure the long-term interests of the country are considered and that governmental action is not dictated by the whims of the day. The House is intended to represent the voice of the people, with a trusted local resident from each area of the country working with the Senate to establish the principles and define the laws that govern our citizens. But the House of Representatives no longer speaks for the people. It has become a House of Politicians. The foundation of our House is cracked, severely, and the inhabitants might as well be termites with the most aggressive of dispositions. Even though the cracks are hidden beneath expensive tile and the infestation is masked by stylish wallpaper, the damage spreads daily. Is the foundation about to wash away? Are the walls about to crumble?

The proposed system defines a step-by-step process to initiate the process of repair, inflect the declining trajectory of our country, and assure that our children and theirs will have the same security, freedom, and opportunity that you and I have enjoyed. The first step in taking our country back, in addressing the core problems, is to put people in positions of power who have the interest of our posterity and our country in mind.

This book details the process we will use to replace every single member of the House with true patriots selected by the people, not by the two parties. It is time to replace politicians with Americans who are dedicated, responsible, trustworthy, and honest; with citizens who have proven to be outstanding members of their communities.

It is time to elect people like you, not self-serving aristocrats, and it is time for us to have options, not just a choice between two career politicians. With this plan, the manipulative puppet-politicians who have sold their souls to the lobbyists bankrolling their campaigns, and the parties pulling their strings, will be evicted.

In this system, candidates will document, in advance, exactly where they stand on each important issue of our day by completing a questionnaire that contains one hundred or more questions that must be answered yes or no. They will then commit to voting exactly the way they declared on those issues. Our representatives will address the issues that concern us, not the ones that buy votes, reward contributors, and secure reelection. They will do so without being strapped to the platform of a party or being held hostage by the demands of a lobbyist.

They will have no reason to ignore the issues of controversy that politicians are afraid to confront. Our representatives will no longer feel compelled to cater to the small, noisy factions and the outrageous influence those groups exert. They will bring new cement and hardened timbers to repair the foundation and replace the pillars that sustain our House. They will reinvigorate the principles that should be guiding our country, principles like equality and common sense. They will earn back the respect and admiration of our countrymen and the rest of the world. We will once again be proud to be Americans.

The plan is bold, but it will work. I expect to receive a great deal of input from the citizens of our country on how the plan could be implemented differently or better, and I certainly expect there will be revisions, but I do not expect they will be major. Focus groups have demonstrated that superb candidates will surface in each and every district. The biggest challenge will be getting Americans to participate.

The choices next election will include the same old Democrat and Republican clones that have always been offered, along with our nominees of the people. On election day in November, and only then, America will decide if we want to vote for one of the two-party candidates as we have always done—the ones who have created this mess we are living in—or instead for the people's representatives. Until that day, we should put every ounce of energy we can muster behind this system to prove that we can identify better candidates to run our country than what the two parties offer. There is absolutely nothing to lose by participating in the process.

Those who do not participate have little right to ever again complain about politicians or politics. This system is our chance to retake control of our government. Will you help, or do you have more important things to do?

Author Napoleon Hill said, "Cherish your visions and your dreams as they are the children of your soul; the blueprints of your ultimate achievements." This is my vision of how we can put our country back on track. I am nothing more than a deeply concerned citizen. I am not a political expert with a national platform. I am not a celebrity, whose every controversial word is glamorized by the media. I have left my job and dedicated the last two years of my life to develop this solution that I hope will redirect our country. This is my plan. Jude Wanniski said, "Modern nation states have built into their political frameworks various safety valves that can bring about urgent corrections in the avoidance of violent revolution or war." He added, "A revolution reaches critical mass when the electorate knows that what follows cannot be worse."[6] Revolutions come in different forms, and a bloodless one is beginning to simmer in America. This plan will turn the heat on high. It outlines the process by which we can peacefully make the urgently needed corrections and perhaps avoid a revolution that will involve the blood of our children or grandchildren. But make no mistake; this is a revolution.

GOOOH is for you if you are interested in changing our country, ensuring that we leave it in better shape—stronger—than when we arrived. This is about working within the existing system to identify and then elect true representatives who will honor the desires of the people in their district the way the founders of our country intended. Before our country was formed, writings like *Common Sense* called Americans to action. Thomas Paine wrote, "Who the author of this production is, is wholly unnecessary to the public, as the object for attention is the doctrine itself, not the man. Yet it may not be unnecessary to say, that he is unconnected with any party, and under no sort of influence public or private, but the influence of reason and principle."[7] I have tried to stay true to Paine's vision.

This is my attempt to take an extremely complicated subject and boil it down to something that is easy to understand and easier to implement. I have designed the system so almost every American is allowed to participate—politicians, multi-millionaires, and lawyers are excluded;[8] I believe these groups are disproportionately represented by the two parties. Whether or not we loosen the candidate criteria, such as defining "wealthy" differently or only excluding lawyers who have represented the ACLU or litigated a class-action lawsuit, for example, will ultimately be determined by members of GOOOH.[9] With our representatives once again selected by the people, we will regain control of our government.

Sophisticated authors and pundits with oratory and writing skills far greater than mine, and political and legal practitioners with knowledge far beyond what I possess, may very well critique the simplicity of the approach, my writing, and me, but don't let that interfere with the message. They will insist upon treating politics like a chess game and try to exclude a vast majority of the population from the dialogue, claiming behind our backs that we are too ignorant to play. Watch for the parties' efforts to feed poisoned pawns to the population while they arrogantly play the "Najdorf Sicilian," indirectly trying to force us to back off of what they have claimed as their squares.

They assume we will lose interest or even cower to their threats, that we are too comfortable with our everyday lives to even consider revolting. They are certain we do not have the willpower to seriously challenge their supremacy. They have built a formidable wall, and their power structure is heavily guarded; but the drawbridge is still down, and the gate is open. It is up to us to enter.

To do so, and to make room for true representatives of the people, we must deliver one short and simple message to the politicians living in Washington: Get Out of Our House! It is time for them to *GOOOH!*

III Time to Act

Did you know that if you put a frog into a pot of boiling water, it will leap out right away to escape the danger? But, if you put a frog in a kettle that is filled with water that is cool and pleasant, and then gradually heat the kettle until it starts boiling, the frog will not become aware of the threat until it is too late. The frog's survival instincts are geared toward detecting sudden changes.

Most of us harbor no interest in politics for sensible and obvious reasons. We have busy lives; politics are vile and disgusting. Robert Putnam wrote in *The Beliefs of Politicians*, "Most men are not political animals. The world of public affairs is not their world. It is alien to them…Most men are not interested in politics."[10] It is normal not to be interested, in fact to dislike, politics and politicians, and it is normal to prefer to have nothing to do with either, but we can no longer afford to do so. If we do, it will be at our own peril. George Orwell wrote, "In our age there is no such thing as keeping out of politics. All issues are political issues, and politics itself is a mass of lies, evasions, folly, hatred and schizophrenia." Politics may be uncomfortable, but we can no longer afford to allow others to handle our problems. It is time to get involved.

A famous Chinese proverb claims, "If we do not change our direction, we are likely to end up where we are headed." Politicians tell us if we vote for them, they and their party will fix all that is wrong with America. We know they are lying. If we continue to listen to their lies, to wait for them to address the issues, and to refuse to stand up and take charge, the fate of our endangered nation will soon be sealed. If we don't make some changes soon, the country will end up exactly where we all know it is going.

Without our personal efforts, America will fail. Consider that statement carefully. Our country is falling apart under the watch of our generation. Can you sleep at night knowing that to be true? My deepest concern is that the majority of our citizens have already given up. Are the people willing to put forth the effort to do what we all know must be done, or does the TV have us mesmerized? Can we afford to miss a game or skip a weekend trip to the mall?

We spend fifty dollars for a month of cable, or a ticket to a concert; are we willing to instead spend that money to save our country? Let's face it, getting rid of the politicians and fixing our country is going to cost money and take time. The task will not be easy. Think of all those who came before us and what they sacrificed for our nation. Our founders risked their lives, as did many of our fathers, grandfathers, and many others. The time has come for us to do our part. We must decide what is important. I pray our country will choose to take action.

Thomas Jefferson said, "I am not an advocate for frequent changes in laws and Constitutions. But laws and institutions must go hand in hand with the progress of the human mind. As that becomes more developed...institutions must advance also to keep pace with the times. We might as well require a man to wear still the coat which fitted him when a boy as for civilized society to remain ever under the regimen of their barbarous ancestors."

The quote refers to the days before the American Revolution, and we have advanced immeasurably since that time, but the quote applies more and more every day. It is plain that we have outgrown the ways of politicians and political parties. The way we choose our representatives must change. It is time to free ourselves from the shackles of the parties and the spell of the politicians. It is time to step into the

21st century of representative government. To do so, we need a new plan, an approach that has not existed until now. This is the plan. If we unite and execute, we can retake our government and restore our country. If we do nothing, it will soon be too late.

The work of Madison, Jefferson, and the founders of our country is an incredibly inspiring testament to the capability of mankind. I consider the Constitution, without question, the second greatest literary work of all time. Their efforts have served us exceedingly well for over two hundred years, but the time has come to refine what they wrote, ever so slightly, without sacrificing their wisdom. It is time to reestablish that this nation is our nation. It is time for "we the people" to take our country back. It is time to clarify the foundational principles on which our country is to operate in the century ahead.

This system will show us how to remove the politicians, lawyers, and aristocrats who have claimed the positions of power intended for representatives of the common man. It is a plan to cut all ties with the lobbyists who are so heavily influencing the election process, and bypass the two-party system, returning the government they have confiscated to the people. It will unite our nation, removing the wedge that the politicians have forced between the people. It will allow us to address the issues that must be addressed. It will allow us to repair the failing Social Security, welfare, education, and tax systems.

We will be in a position to intelligently address the core issues that are destroying our country—issues like drugs, crime, the environment, and our dependence on foreign oil. It will allow us to address emotional but critical issues like immigration, gun control, abortion, and homelessness, and enable us to make the needed changes in our out-of-control health, prison, and legal systems. The system will enable us to rebuild our crumbling foundation, clarify our guiding principles, and reset our moral compass. We will put government back in the hands of the people, reign in big government programs, and tame the soaring deficit that could send the world into a depression so great that it will take a generation or more to recover.

We now have a plan that will seize the hands of time and push them forward. We will be able to elect honorable citizens who are committed to serving the people of their district—and nobody else. We will be able to peacefully reclaim every seat in the House of Representatives by electing you or one of your peers in each of the 435 districts. We will elect that person from your office who always makes perfect sense, one of your friends, the teacher who lives down the street, the coach of your daughter's soccer team, your mom or your dad, your aunt or uncle, or you. In one powerful statement, in the election of 2008, we the people will vote out party politicians and vote in citizen representatives, reclaiming every single seat in our House with our selected nominees. We will restore our proud country and put to rest the question of whether or not we will remain the greatest country in the world.

Until today, there has been absolutely nothing we could do. We now have an option. The system that will force change is in place, and you are personally invited to participate.

Mark Twain said, "In the beginning of change, the patriot is a scarce man, and brave, and hated, and scorned. When his cause succeeds, the timid join him..." You can no longer be timid. Now is the time for you to be brave. I need you to join me—now, not later. What will you do? Will you be a patriot or a timid spectator waiting until the hard work is done and the outcome is known? If you do not engage now, will you ever?

Remember the frog story? You and I are the frogs in the politician's kettle. The water is nearing a boil. If we do not jump soon, it will be too late.

IV GOOOH

GOOOH (pronounced "go") is a system that will allow the people of America to identify competent individuals to compete against the Democratic and Republican politicians in the race for seats in the U.S. House of Representatives. It is not a party in the classic sense; there is no national platform. Each member of the House of Representatives must seek reelection every two years, but the outcomes of 95 percent of the races are generally known before the election; that is how often the incumbent wins. This system will allow us to add our candidates to the ballot in each congressional district where they will compete with the politicians. If the people of America truly want change, they will vote for the candidates that we place on the ballot. If we want to continue doing what we have been doing, and allow the country to self-destruct under the watch of our generation, we will again vote for the politicians who have created this ungodly mess.

Let me ask a few loaded questions. Do you know someone who is honest and trustworthy who could do a better job running the country than the politicians we have in Washington today? Could you do a better job? With nothing more than common sense, your ability to learn, and a commitment to the people of your district, would you or someone you know be a better representative of the people? Do you believe there are Americans who could represent us in the way that Madison, Jefferson, Franklin, Washington, and our other Founding Fathers intended?

Do you believe our representatives would be more effective if we took all money out of the election equation? If our leaders were limited to one or two terms, would they be more committed to solving issues and less concerned about reelection? If we identified the best and brightest, non-political members of society and asked them to serve in the House of Representatives, would our government be more responsive to the needs of the people? I expect you answered affirmatively to most, if not all, of those questions.

Unfortunately, the reality that you and I both know is that neither you, nor your friend, are likely to run for office for any of many very good reasons. Like most Americans, both you and your friend probably hate politics and the very essence of what a politician is. You don't have a million dollars to blow, nor do you have any idea or interest in doing what it would take to raise the kind of money needed to support an election bid. You don't know anyone in the system, and you don't have a snowball's chance in hell of ever getting on the ballot, much less elected. We both know it. That leads us to the purpose of GOOOH.

Imagine if someone you know—a friend, colleague, neighbor, coach, teacher, preacher, housewife, boss, John Galt, or perhaps even yourself—who is an intelligent, articulate, charismatic, sincere, trusted, honest, patriotic person went to Washington for a couple of years to represent us in Congress. Further imagine that you or he did not go alone, but went with 434 other representatives possessing the characteristics listed above. Instead of sending 435 career politicians as we repeatedly do, imagine that we send honorable, first-time representatives, just like we did in our nation's first days.

Imagine that the people who express an interest in serving as our representatives have documented exactly how they would vote on the key issues and bound themselves to those positions. Imagine them working together in the House of Representatives to address the problems of our day. Imagine that they only cared about solving the problems we face, and after two years, would return to do whatever it is they are doing today. Do you think our country would be managed a little differently?

This plan allows interested Americans, including you, to have an equal opportunity of being selected to serve in the House of Representatives. The process is open to everyone interested in participating, with a few notable exceptions. The participants will choose, from among themselves, the best candidate, in a controlled, methodical, apolitical way. It bypasses the two political parties altogether. It does not matter how much, or little, money you have, where you live, what you do for a living, or who you know. Instead of being forced to choose between a couple of partisan politicians—choices that often have so little appeal we tend to vote against a candidate or a party more often than we vote for one—we will allow Americans to participate in the selection process, and all who are willing to engage will receive equal consideration.

Once the people of each district have selected their candidate, this system will do the work to have them added to the ballot to compete with the Republican and Democratic politicians. This system will raise all necessary funds and orchestrate the campaign for each of our selected candidates. It will raise money independent of individual candidates, and the funds will be used to support whoever the people select, not whoever promises to repay the financiers with favorable legislation. Our candidates will compete based on voting commitments, not campaign promises.

We have no way, today, to get around the dominance of the two-party system; it has complete control of the government. We have no way, today, to release the anchor of special interest money that so heavily influences our politicians. We have no way, today, to put anyone other than career politicians, on-the-take lawyers, or wealthy aristocrats in office.

This plan removes all of those people from consideration. The plan allows each person in America to have an equal chance of being selected as their district's representative, without requiring a working man to miss work or quit his job unless he is selected by his peers to serve them. This plan does not support any particular view on any specific issue; instead it allows the people of each district to determine the person who can best represent the views of that district. It is a new method to identify independent candidates chosen by members of this system. It will allow us to change the tires on our governmobile while traveling seventy miles per hour down the legislative highway that at this moment appears headed to hell.

The plan details exactly what any interested person needs to do to run for office or participate in the process, and then provides the infrastructure and financing for them to do so. Candidates in the system will not have accepted money from any person or group and will therefore not have to worry about repaying those who funded their election. The hope is that candidates will not view this system as a competition, but rather an opportunity to participate in the democratic process. It will allow candidates to vote their hearts and minds, not a party line. It eliminates the need to badmouth competing candidates. It circumvents the need to make hollow promises that a candidate has no intention of keeping. It terminates the control party bosses have on who appears on the ballot. It removes all of the advantages of incumbency, other than being able to tell the other nine people in your pool that you are their current representative,[11] forcing candidates seeking reelection to start from scratch every election cycle on the exact same terms as every other person in their 660,000-member district. With no need to spend time raising funds for reelection, candidates will be able to focus their time and energy on restoring the nation and fixing the things that are wrong with our government.

In order to identify the best possible candidates to lead our country, some very hard lines will be drawn that will allow us to determine exactly where each candidate stands on issues of importance. Some will argue the line is too far to the left and others that it is too far to the right. Opinions will vary depending on personal beliefs, obviously, so it is recommended you not lose sight of the objective and waste energy debating my personal perspectives. Instead, you are encouraged to focus on determining where you stand on the issue and how important the issue is. The purpose of the line is to identify which candidates stand on the same side as you. There will be a never-ending debate on what questions should be asked and where the lines should be drawn, and that debate will be facilitated by the forums on the GOOOH Web site in the months ahead. It is critically important that you understand that you are unlikely to agree with any person on every issue, so prioritizing which ones are most important, and discounting those you really don't care about, will become critical.

Let me give an example of what I mean by drawing a line. I may ask if you would cut government spending by 5 percent. My right-leaning friends will say 5 percent is not nearly enough and that we should cut by at least 10 percent. My left-leaning friends will say we should not cut at all and, if anything, we should raise taxes and *increase* spending by 5 percent. In this example, the line is being drawn at a 5 percent cut, and it will force potential candidates to declare only on which side they stand: more than 5 percent or less than 5 percent. Determining exactly what number you feel is appropriate is not as critical as specifying on which side you stand. Over time, the line may be modified based on input from the participants in our system, but the initial lines drawn by this author can be seen in the Candidate Questionnaire chapter.

This book will lead you through a high-level discussion on many topics. I will provide data, a few stories, and even make a couple of suggestions that will ultimately lead to a question or two. The most critical questions from each of the topics will be merged into a final Candidate Questionnaire that we will ask each participant to complete. The questions will be straightforward, requiring only a yes-or-no answer. They will be fair questions—some easy, some difficult—but all answerable in a way that will declare your position.

There will be no way to avoid answering even a single question and there is zero wiggle room. Each candidate will be required to declare on which side of every line he stands. The answers will be binding, something that will be explained in more detail later in the text. Beware of those who object to declaring an absolute position; they are the politicians in the crowd, the very ones we need to avoid. If a person is not willing to take a definitive stand on even one issue, I strongly recommend you discard consideration of that person as a candidate. Heed this warning or the results may not be what we want.

A few will find this absolute yes-or-no approach overly constricting, eliminating the opportunity to rephrase the debate in a way more palatable to their position. They will argue that a simple yes-or-no answer is inadequate and campaign for an opportunity to clarify their position. I grant there is some validity to the argument, but counter that politicians have abused the ambiguity permitted in the process for too many years, answering fewer and fewer questions definitively so that we no longer have any way to hold them accountable for their promises. The results speak for themselves. Answers to the questions in this system will be legally binding.

It is important to point out candidates will not be selected solely by their answers. They will also be selected based upon their intelligence, their initiative, and their integrity. They will be judged by their communication, negotiation, and persuasion skills. They will win or lose support based on their looks (yes, looks are a factor) and their personality. Nevertheless, forcing them to answer yes or no in response to direct and specific questions will force them to clearly define where they stand on the core issues affecting our lives. From the aggregate of these responses you will be able to determine each candidate's belief system, values, and views on government. If the candidate's answers are in line with the majority of the people of the district they are hoping to represent, if they have the other intangible skills required, and if they can convince the others in their pools they are the best choice, they will bubble to the top of our system. Focus groups have shown that the people who are selected are stellar candidates.

Each nominee is likely to have taken a position on a few issues that oppose the desires of the majority of the voters in their district. They will not be selected if they disagree on many, but statistically speaking it is likely they will disagree on a few of the issues deemed to be less important. Your candidate may respond no to a question when 90 percent of his district favors yes, or vice versa, but it should only happen on a few issues or he would not have been chosen. To have been selected, the candidate must be in agreement on the vast majority of the most important items.

When there is a difference, it is likely that the other 434 representatives will simply outvote the nominee on the issue in which his opinion differs. He also always has the option of not voting if he knows the way he answered does not represent his district. Further, if a candidate finds himself in a situation where the predominant majority of his district would like him to change his documented position, he can invoke the Override Clause, explained later in the book. You can play out billions of mathematical variations to this scheme, but with so many representatives the voice of the majority will be clear. Those who oppose this system may attempt to make a theoretical point about the possibility of a candidate being "forced" to vote for something his district disagrees with. They will not be able to provide any proof that there will be a problem, but will make a hypothetical statement that it is possible—they will try to scare you. You will know that our revolution has become a threat when you hear the opposition grasping for a straw like this one.

If you know who your representative is (and half the country does not), see if you can determine his answer to each question in the questionnaire. Even better, ask him to answer each and every question and to then commit, in writing, to voting exactly the way he says on every single issue. He will not. I expect politicians will spend the first few months ignoring our plan, then a month or two explaining what a dumb idea it is and why the questions are inappropriate or unanswerable, and then the remaining time attacking a flaw in the process, me, my writing deficiencies, or any one of the number of stupid things I did in the first twenty-one years of my life—and there were many. When they do, you will know they feel the threat.

Before the election, we will request that every Republican and Democratic candidate complete the questionnaire and sign the same legally binding document that our nominees will have signed. I predict that few, if any, will be willing to make such a commitment, claiming "politics" do not work that way. I counter by saying that politics, as practiced by our politicians, do not work at all. The system is broken.

In my surveys I have found that some people may not run for office because they do not want to rehash things they did in high school or college. This process is not about what someone did while growing up. It is about finding outstanding men and women who will document their positions and then stand behind them. In this process, in order to ensure we do not have candidates eliminate themselves because they are afraid of some past spring break incident, we are going to impose a gentleman's agreement that candidates will not discuss anything that occurred in their lives before the age of twenty-five. The recommended answer from all candidates on any question concerning their early years will be the tried-and-true approach the Clintons applied often and well: "I don't remember." Candidates are free to mention their accomplishments, of course, but are not expected to discuss that period of their life.

A most interesting aspect of this process is how it will affect the vote of senators and the president. Imagine that we get all 435 of our nominees elected. Since each of them will have documented their position on the issues of substance, the will of the people will be known. Our representatives will be able to prepare legislation supporting the issues they are in agreement on and the House will be able to approve the laws quickly. The bills will then be sent to the Senate. Imagine the senators who choose to vote against the clear will of the people, or the president vetoing an item that has the overwhelming support of the populace. If we use this system and select true representatives we should be able to get the items that have the unbridled support of the people passed. It is impossible to know at this time what these items will be, but I do list the items I personally hope will appear on that list later in the book. Is there a better way of ensuring that our government knows exactly where the people stand? The concept of voting along party lines, at least in the House, will lose all meaning.

While the people we nominate will have documented their position on one hundred or more issues and legally committed to voting the way they declared, don't overlook the fact that thousands of other issues will arise. The questions are intended to tell us exactly where a candidate stands on specific issues, but more generally, their answers will give us a solid understanding of their philosophical views on government and life. Focus groups indicate that we will be able to accurately deduce how a candidate will vote on whatever issues come up in the future based on the way they responded in the questionnaire. So, while candidates are not locked down on every conceivable item that could ever come up for vote, the expectation is that the citizens we select will vote consistently with the values they exhibited when answering the questionnaire and interacting in the focus groups.

This process will put an end to pork barrel projects and bureaucratic waste. It will rein in out-of-control spending. It will remove lobbyists from the election process and make it significantly more difficult for them to buy special favors afterward. It will not and is not intended to put an end to lobbying altogether, but it will break the link between campaign contributions and legislative payback. Vigilance of those in office will always be required; the magnetic attraction of luxurious perks will always pull on men with power.

I am hopeful that all who read this plan do not first think of the Orwellian line that "a lunatic is a minority of one," but instead see the same things my eyes see and have the same concerns for our grandchildren that I do. This process is not about me in any way. It is about you, representative government, and our country. I hope you will make the time to become part of the solution.

HOW TO BECOME A CANDIDATE: SUMMARY

Let me now provide an overview of how the process will work. Any citizen interested in participating in our process will need to do the six things listed below to become a candidate. All interested Americans will participate through the GOOOH Web site.[12] The six steps are:

1. Become a GOOOH member by registering at our Web site.
2. Pass the Candidate Screening Exam, which requires each person meet all of the Congressional requirements (citizenship, age, etc.), as well as the prerequisites for our system (not "rich," not a politician, not a carpetbagger, etc.).

3. Complete the Candidate Questionnaire. All questions require a yes-or-no answer. Here are a few sample questions:
   a. Will you vote for a presidential line item veto?
   b. Will you vote for House term limits of four years or less?
   c. Will you vote to replace the current tax system with the FairTax as proposed by Linder and Boortz?
4. Sign a "Commitment Letter" that confirms you will vote as you answered in the Questionnaire.
5. Donate one hundred dollars to GOOOH, which will be used to fund the campaign.
6. Finalize your commitment.

A few people have expressed concern with the requirement to make a hundred dollar donation, worried that if they do not like the nominee who emerges they will have supported the wrong cause. I understand the concern but counter that this is the most equitable way to raise the funds needed to get our candidates elected. The money will decrease the number of entrants who enter the process intent on disrupting it, and more importantly, it will free us from relying on special interest group funding. Once the system becomes the established method for identifying candidates, perhaps we can fund them in some other way. In the meantime, the fee should be looked at as an investment in replacing politicians with representatives. If you are not willing to spend such a small amount of money to make the critically needed changes, wish to allow the two parties to maintain their absolute control, and are willing to watch the continued demise of our country, you will get exactly what you pay for—nothing. If you cannot spare the money, ask your family and friends to support your run, or get a second job. One hundred dollars should not get in the way of someone wanting to lead our country.

If you are a conservative and a liberal candidate appears on the ballot, or vice versa, you will of course have the option of voting for the Republican or Democratic candidate. I suspect, however, most of you will like our candidates better than the politicians. For one hundred dollars, you will give the country another choice and more importantly, you will force the parties to take notice, sending them a strong signal that they need to change their behavior. Look at every expense you have, and ask yourself, are they all more important than this chance to effect change?

We will accept larger donations from any person or business in America, but the money will be put into the general campaign fund anonymously. There will be no personal benefit to any candidate who gives more than others, other than the satisfaction they will have in knowing they have done their part to restore our country.

How We Select Our 435 Nominees: Summary

For the election in November, candidates will have until late winter or early spring of that year to complete the six steps—the exact date will be made public by February 15. Once the submission deadline has been reached, all candidates will follow the process summarized below, with one person in each of the congressional districts ultimately bubbling to the top of the system as their district's nominee.

1. Candidates will be randomly assigned into pools of ten participants within their congressional district. There will be as many pools as are needed in each district. All pools will meet simultaneously at predetermined, but unique, locations. If, for example, there are exactly 1,250 participants in each district, there will be 125 pools in the initial round. All sessions will be held on Saturdays.

2. Each pool of participants will select two candidates to advance to the next round, using the process outlined later in the book. Sessions will last approximately five hours and will begin at 9:00 a.m. at a location to be determined.

3. Advancing candidates will be randomly assigned into a new pool within their district. Steps two and three will repeat until there are only ten candidates remaining in each district.

4. With 1,250 participants, there would be four rounds. The actual number of rounds will be determined based upon the number of

participants in each district. There will be a maximum of eight rounds.

5. Before the final round, we are considering having the 4,350 finalists participate in a weekend retreat to ensure they fully understand how the final selection round will work and to confirm they are committed to representing their district if selected. Details will be determined as the time nears.

6. The final ten candidates in each of the districts will select a single nominee to represent their district.

7. The 435 nominees will be placed on the November ballot, in their respective districts, to compete against the Republican and Democratic politicians.

8. The campaign for each of the candidates will be orchestrated by GOOOH, which will provide the necessary funding.

If you would like to help us evict the politicians, we need your help. If you engage, we can vote every single politician out of our House.

GOOOH Is Not...

Now that you understand the plan at a high level, have read how to become a candidate, and have learned how the process works, let me be very clear about a few things the plan is not. It is not a proposal to create a new political party with a common platform, though we may have to create a shell of a party to get our candidates on the ballots in each district. It is not an effort to ensure that people who support my personal views are elected. While I desperately hope my beliefs are the preferred view of the land and that all chosen candidates mirror my views exactly, I'm certain that will not be the case. The plan is not an attempt to shape your views to fit mine. The important thing to look for is whether the candidates in your pool stand on the same side of the line as you on the issues of importance.

Political correctness, one of my pet peeves, has no place in this book. I apologize to those I offend, but there is no way to say what needs to be said while following the guidelines of political correctness.

If you disagree, I urge you to participate in the process and see what the others have to say about your perspective on things. If you are offended that I am not writing gender-neutral throughout the text, get over it. I am using the old-school approach of referring to the male gender throughout because it is simpler. This does not mean I do not believe in or value diversity; rather, I want to make my points as simple and succinct as possible.

I am not attempting to bring groundbreaking new research or hot-off-the-press information to the public for the first time. Most of the information, stories, and facts are public record and have appeared in other writings or on the Internet. Unfortunately, I did not have a vast research team like the ones Bill O'Reilly or Al Franken mentioned in their books, but I've used what I believe are credible sources.

With modern equipment, major league baseball umpires are proven wrong 5 percent of the time. Even with Instant Replay football struggles to get all of the crucial calls right. Is your spouse correct 100 percent of the time? What about the boss or your kids? What about your brother or sister? Do you know any of them who have been correct 100 percent of the time? I think not.

Now, for the harder question, do you think you are right all of the time? I know I am not, but I seldom know when those times are until after the fact. What things could you be wrong about? When you factor in opinions and perceptions, disagreement on issues of substance, like those discussed in the book, should be expected. Always remember that it could be you who is wrong or whose position is out-of-whack. I ask that you not allow your anger to boil in cases where you disagree. Seek a sincere understanding of the other perspective and you may be surprised what you learn.

Let's acknowledge and agree now that we will see some things differently. That is normal and expected. In Mitch Albom's *The Five People You Meet in Heaven*, Eddie meets his captain, the Blue Man, in Heaven. They find themselves on the ravaged battlefield where they had fought together so many years ago. At least that was what Eddie saw. The captain's view, however, was quite different. He lifted his hand and transformed the "smoldering landscape" into "lush green grass" under a "sapphire sky" with "a peach-colored sun" that "reflected in the sparkling oceans." The captain said, "This is what I see."

The scene reminds me of how different our views can be on any given issue, based on our life experiences. Today, when we look at the state of our country and the politicians who are ruining it, I think most of us see something much closer to the war-torn battlefield that Eddie saw, rather than the captain's paradise, which evidently is the politician's perspective. I trust that with some conviction, commitment, and action, paradise can be rediscovered. We have a long way to go to find it, but we can if we have the courage to act.

YOU WILL NOT LIKE THIS PLAN IF:

This plan is not intended to please everyone; in fact, it may make some people fighting mad. Very few things in life are agreeable to all, and this plan will not be an exception. Let me try to identify, up front, those of you who are probably wasting your time reading this book. If you fit into one of the following categories, you are unlikely to agree with what I am trying to accomplish:

1. You are a politician.
2. You believe that politicians are doing a good job.
3. You have a closed mind and are not willing to consider a new paradigm (e.g., you believe that having two parties choose candidates behind effectively closed doors is a good thing).
4. You believe the role of government is to solve your problems.
5. You can take care of yourself just fine, but believe the role of government is to take care of anyone who is unable or unwilling to take care of themselves, regardless of the circumstances or the cost.
6. You ask, "What about me?" when you see what others get from the government.
7. You believe government controls are needed to make the free market work.
8. You believe the government should protect jobs.
9. You are more focused on a specific topic than the country as a whole.

10. You do not mind that the special "rights" of a few stomp on the equal rights of everyone else.
11. You believe your party is going to take control of two thirds of both the House and the Senate, win the presidency, and then fix everything that is wrong with America.
12. You believe your exceptional wealth demands special privileges.
13. You are a lawyer who is more interested in yourself and money than our country. There are far more good lawyers than bad, but way too many have fallen into the American money trap. Far too many have taken positions of power and some are likely to disrupt the process with their legal escapades, so I am excluding lawyers from the initial iteration of this process. I hope the vast majority will understand why and still support the system.[13]

The Goal of the Plan

The goal of the plan is simple, yet grand. It is radical, but practical. It is far from perfect, but will deliver results 435 million times better than the results we get with the current system. It will work!

My hope is that you will read this book and then help spread word of the plan to every person in America. I hope you will consider running for office and get as many like-minded people as you know to do the same. Most importantly, whether or not you choose to run, I hope that you will actively and vigorously support the system. There are leaders among us who can step forward and fix the mess the politicians have created. We need only to create an opportunity for them to do so.

I am reminded of the movie *Field of Dreams* and the line, "If you build it, they will come." I am working with a cadre of colleagues to build the infrastructure that will support this plan. I am confident that once we build it, the modern day incarnations of James Madison, Benjamin Franklin, and Thomas Jefferson will step forward. Could you be one of our movement's founders?

At all times, everyone should keep the key objective of this book in mind: to restore the country for our children and theirs and theirs and theirs. If we do not retake control of our government, we are permitting the destruction of our country as certainly as we know death will one day come for each of us.

The questions I develop in this book form the first draft of the Candidate Questionnaire, but the chapter with that title will include a much more extensive list from which the final questions will be chosen. From the moment the book is published until a few weeks before we begin the selection process, every GOOOH member will have an opportunity to debate and suggest changes to the questionnaire. Candidates will have until two weeks before the first round of selection meetings to finalize their responses. At that point, their positions will become locked until the end of their two-year term.

The plan includes a detailed timeline for the entire country to follow. It will likely be adjusted with time, but the first version documented in this book and on the Web site will give you a good idea of how the process is going to progress. The dates are not expected to change significantly.

Together, we can replace every single politician in the House of Representatives with 435 trustworthy citizens who will represent us with honor and integrity. Will you be one of them?

It's Time to Do Our Part

Have you ever asked yourself, "What have I done to make this country better than when I arrived?" When I ask myself this question, and answer honestly, my answer is much closer to "nothing at all" than "everything possible." If I ask you the same question, what would your answer be? Have you done "nothing at all," "everything possible," or are you somewhere in between? If I were to ask every person in America this question and chart the responses, the graph would not resemble a standard bell curve. The fat part of the graph, we know, would push much closer to the nothing-at-all mark. We have been secure from foreign enemies. We have been afforded a solid education. We have lived in a thriving economy. But few of us have given more than we have taken.

This is not to say we have not contributed at all; some have and some have done even more than others. There are those of you who have served in the military, for example, who have put it all on the line, and to you we are two clicks past grateful. There are also the vast majority of Americans who have done no harm whatsoever to the country. They have contributed greatly to the economy and the nation by simply being honest, hard-working, tax-paying, family-rearing, church-attending members of society, pushing our country forward economically and helping maintain our country's status as the greatest in the world.

For the most part, however, the country has done far more for us than we have done for it. The vast majority of us that were lucky enough to be born in this great land have done little to protect or improve the overall health of our nation. Frankly, we have not been forced to do much, and there really has not been much that we could do even if we wanted. However, it is under our watch that the decline has become obvious, the foundation has revealed its cracks, and the future has been placed in jeopardy. Most of us who are honest with ourselves understand the situation. The time has come for us to do our part, to go to battle and defend our nation—from ourselves.

Almost every American standing on our soil believes that we live in the greatest country in the world. Evidence is provided in the number of us that choose not to leave. Further, almost every other person in the world, except for those who have been shielded from the truth or lied to by their leaders, believes that statement, or at least they used to believe it. The question is will it be true in fifty years?

We can sit by, idly, as we have done for our entire lifetime, and see what happens. Or we can admit openly what we all know, roll up our sleeves, and work together to make the changes that are required.

THIS BOOK

This book explains exactly how we are going to effect change. I suspect you may already understand the seriousness of our country's decline, why politicians will never be able to fix all that is wrong, how badly our systems are failing, and the issues that we must address, but many may not. I would like to discuss the demise in much greater detail than I do, but space does not allow. I will share a few of my thoughts and concerns on the main topics, topics that are significantly impacting the foundation, strength, and future of our country, but only at a high level.

The facts I present are simply that: facts. You may not like them or the way I present them, but they are the cold hard truth. Many should concern you deeply. The stories I share are anecdotes I have come across or events I have lived that together have somehow led me to this point in my life and this plan. Politicians often misuse these stories to play on your emotion and gain either your vote or support for some government program that will inevitably and most assuredly fail. I use these stories to highlight the outrageous impact that government programs and ill-conceived laws are having on society. I expect many of them will either make you mad or sigh in roll-your-eyes disbelief. If more examples are needed, I have another five hundred pages worth of stories in the archives.

On each critical topic, my personal views will likely become clear as I get to the tough questions that each candidate will be required to answer, but my views are irrelevant. What is important is to fully understand the issue—and not only where the line is drawn, but also the implications attached. Each candidate will be required to commit on which side of every line they stand *before* they begin their run for office. As discussed earlier, each question is a yes-or-no question with absolutely no wiggle room. None!

If a candidate is not willing to answer a question, he will not be entered into the process. He cannot become a candidate in this system without answering every question and without legally binding himself to his answers. If he votes against his position, he will be legally committed to resigning from office.

Moving forward, when I entrust my vote to someone, I want to know exactly where that person stands on each issue of importance. I have lived through too many years of politicians saying one thing and then doing another. I no longer want the back door left open so they can trade votes, not for any reason, and particularly not for a favor. Their duty is to represent the people who selected them based on the issues they deemed important. They are not put in a position of power to horse trade for whatever feels right at the moment.

Unfortunately, as we have seen with our present system and our currently employed political zeroes, we cannot trust politicians once they are in power. They refuse to honor their commitments, and they certainly do not serve the people. The candidates we select will be required to stick with their documented positions for the entire two-year term. If a candidate feels compelled to change his stance after he is elected, too bad. He can change the way he will vote in the next cycle and then see if the people agree with his newfound perspective. He will no longer be able to unilaterally change his position after he gets in office.[14]

If the world worked perfectly and politicians had not abused the system to the extent that they have, I would agree that a little wiggle room would be appropriate. But they have so deceitfully abused our trust, particularly over the last fifty years, and have allowed our country to begin deteriorating, that this absolute yes-or-no process is urgently necessary. To turn our country around, we will demand absolutely locked positions on all of the key issues.

Note that if a representative does change his mind, he can always abstain from the vote or resign from office and allow his district to replace him. My guess is that, even with this system, a voluntary withdrawal for such a reason is unlikely. The Override Clause exists to address situations where changing a position is critical.

This book gives us a way to select candidates who will represent us based on personal convictions instead of hollow promises. The process intends to identify people who will serve in the same way preachers, teachers, or policemen are expected to serve society. It intends to identify those who will focus on the public interest first, representing us with honor and integrity. It will identify people who will follow a principled, unwavering, moral compass that is consistent with the views of their district and who emphasize country over power in the way that our founders intended.

My Note to You

It's been a challenge capturing this plan in the form of a book, and it may be a bit more challenging to read than other literary works, but the real challenge is for you to decide whether or not you are going to support the "in" crowd or the "out" crowd. The in crowd will continue to support the current two-party system that allows politicians to further corrupt the government and completely ruin our country. The out crowd will join the revolution and work with us to return the government to the people. The choice is yours.

Surveys show that over 80 percent of the population is dissatisfied with the current political system and politicians. Isn't it odd that we have such a clear majority, yet we have no control? We have allowed a very small 10 percent on the left and 10 percent on the right to take control of our government and run it in a way that very few of us agree with, delivering results that satisfy nobody. We've allowed the two parties and the politicians to manipulate our system to the point that it is virtually impossible for us, the ones in the vast majority, to even have a say in what happens. It is ironic if you think about it, to have complete control but no power, yet that describes our situation exactly. The good news is that we now have a legitimate opportunity to take the power back. All we have to do is engage.

To the readers who are part of the current system, those with the usurped power, I do not understand you. While I recognize that you are American citizens, I do not believe based upon your actions and the corresponding results, that you are patriots. Your vanity is disgusting. Your aspirations are neither honorable nor defensible.

We are prepared for your smear campaign. We expect you to point out the flaws and attempt to discredit GOOOH, not because it cannot work, but because you are clearly more interested in yourself, your power, and your control than you are in our country. You are not expected to acknowledge the true peril of the situation or to accept that you are not able to fix the mess that the two parties have created, because the very act of doing so would be your political demise and mean losing all of the power that you possess. Acknowledging personal failure is exceptionally difficult. Humble pie has never tasted good. If you are a true American, and if you will be honest with yourself if only for a few minutes, you will acknowledge the situation and support the debate that this writing should stimulate. You will encourage dialogue about this system in hopes that our country can be improved, regardless of the personal cost.

Yet it is understandable that you will continue to support the current system as it is, offering whatever minor tweaks you and your colleagues can come up with, and it is understandable that you believe that you personally are best suited to solve the problems our country faces, the ones the government has been unsuccessfully battling for scores of years. You are wrong. You are also too late, because I suspect you are reading this only after the people have been energized. The dam of two-party politics has more holes than you and your conspirators have fingers, and the flood of public outcry is about to wash you and all of your kind out of our House. The people are coming and our message is clear. Get out!

Those of us wanting change must take the time to fully understand and truly appreciate the magnitude of the problem. We will have to turn off *American Idol* and *24*. We will need to skip a ball game or an episode of *Desperate Housewives* and rent one less movie from Blockbuster or Netflix. We will need to stay up past our bedtime reading for the next few weeks. Then, we will need to convince everyone we know to do the same. We will need to discuss politics with our family and friends. We will need to get every single voting-age person in America to vote. As you read about the true state of America, perhaps recognizing the situation for the first time ever, I hope you will begin to understand why you must get involved. The facts should alarm you. The stories should infuriate you. The results should appall you. The predicament should scare the hell out of you. Once you take the time to understand and to see that there is a solution, you must do all that you can to help us get the politicians out of our house!

Let me close this chapter with this 1780 quote from Samuel Adams: "If ever a time should come, when vain and aspiring men shall possess the highest seats in Government, our country will stand in need of its experienced patriots to prevent its ruin."

The time has come. We are the patriots he spoke of. Stand up!

V Signs

The most common question I have been asked over the last year is, "How did you come up with this idea?" It's a great question and one that I initially did not have an answer for. However, after I finished the third draft of the six hundred and sixty page book and began cutting it down to what is included here, the answer appeared, almost magically. This chapter is intended to explain the process that led to the creation of GOOOH and to give you insight into the force I believe is at work behind the scenes. I am convinced I am nothing more than a messenger that has been asked to deliver a critically important message. I failed to see any correlation in the following stories as they occurred. The events spread over years, but as I conceived the system, the events and the connections became clear. It may appear that I am presenting a collage rather than a single painting, but I'll stitch them together before the chapter ends.

REFINERY

Eighteen years old, a week out of high school, and working at one of the refineries lining the Houston Ship Channel in Pasadena, Texas, I hoped to make enough to pay for my first year of college and not have to work while taking classes. I had saved a thousand dollars flipping hamburgers at Wendy's my senior year, and with the intention of renting a house with four friends, calculated I needed about three thousand more to get through year one. Making $5.30 an hour, more than double the minimum wage at the time, I knew the summer days would be long. "Giving it the old college try," is a phrase I would soon fully understand.

From the outside, the plant looked like any of the others I had driven by a hundred times. Assigned with a dozen other college-bound kids to the "clean-up" crew for the summer, I found the pay wonderful and the work hard but bearable. We had various jobs over the summer, but cleaning the sludge from the bottom floor of an enormous sodium factory, a factory that had the look of a prison and the temperament of hell demanded most of our time. The sodium had been collecting on the floor for twenty years, or since the prior summer—we really couldn't tell.

The building itself measured two football fields long, fifty yards wide, and three stories high, with the second floor hosting a hundred or more kettles suspended from above, each the size of a pickup truck bed and boiling a sodium stew. Massive connectors hung from the first floor ceiling, forming a dangerous electrical grid that powered the bottom of the pots, which poked through large holes in the second floor. On occasion, an electrician covered from head to toe in fireproof clothes would use a long wooden oar to engage or disengage the circuit. Just enough space around the sides of each kettle existed so that any excess that boiled over could drip onto the floor below, or on an in-the-wrong-place worker.

Outside, the Texas heat peaked near one hundred degrees each day, but with the air in the building as still as the concrete floor and the heat from the boiling sodium vats, we might as well have been working in hell. On breaks, we would stand by small four-feet-wide and two-feet-high windows that lined the outside walls, each covered with an angled hood so that air could sneak in, but rain, if it ever fell, could not. Sodium explodes when mixed with water, so allowing any moisture in the building would have been like starting a fire in a fireworks factory. The vents in the wall were constructed so the temperature differential ensured that what felt like a cool breeze always blew up and in. A sparkling brown and gray mix of weathered gravel rested on the ground immediately below the window. The hoods blocked whatever view the horizon might have offered and left us admiring the colors of the ground like fine art connoisseurs throughout the summer.

We started work early each morning, and with the Houston humidity were soaked with sweat from head to toe within the first hour. I did not consider the work hard, more like a baseball practice than basketball, but full of the wrong kind of excitement. Electricians would disconnect kettles from the electrical grid as the sodium stew completed cooking. Once the stew had been removed, a handful of us would use shovels, hoes, and picks to break and remove the inches of sodium sludge that had accumulated on the floor.

Our supervisor, Buddy, had the job of keeping us in line and driving a little Bobcat whose bucket we would fill with the boiled-over sodium. We would work full speed for fifty minutes then take a ten-minute break to replenish fluids. The worst part of the job would be when a drip of sodium landed on your back, burning the skin for an hour or more. We all kept towels tucked under our hard-hats and draped over our backs to minimize the number of times we were hit, but the drips always seemed to find the chink in our cotton armor.

Our shift lasted until 4:00 p.m., but those of us who worked hard were almost always asked to stay late and work a double shift. We were paid time and a half after the first forty hours, and working seventy or more hours each week became quite lucrative. I worked eighty-four hours one week, pulling in almost six hundred dollars, and thought I had found a Texas gold mine. The bosses loved us because we worked so hard, even telling us to slow down now and then. But most of us were on the same mission, and we knew if we worked hard they would give us more hours and we could make the money we needed to pay for school. We also knew it would give us a better chance of being rehired the next summer. Finally, we were smart enough to recognize that the quicker we made the money we needed, the sooner we could get out of that hellhole.

After a month or so, we had evidently made a lot more progress than the bosses expected so they began to take a few of us to work in other parts of the plant. A few of the jobs were actually enjoyable, but being a sandblaster's helper was not. Loading eighty-pound bags of sand into a bucket above your head quickly became difficult, and worse, the sand would get inside every crevice in your body as the blaster inevitably and "accidentally" pointed the hose in your direction at least once a day. If you don't know, sand shot from a pressurized blaster goes straight through your clothes and does not feel good.

I weighed a mere one hundred forty pounds at best back then, and grinding welds with a twenty-five-pound grinder as a welder's helper left me completely exhausted by the end of the day. The easiest job was assisting the truck driver. We would load the truck and then ride to a different building and unload it. Life didn't get much easier than that. Occasionally, we would have to load sealed containers marked "Hazardous" into a small dump truck and then sit around and wait for an approved driver to take the truck and dump the load into a pit in some remote corner of the property. I often wonder what it was we were loading and if that pit is now on or should be on the Superfund list.

The second-to-worst day I had at the plant began rather innocuously. I had been assigned to move parts in and out of the second floor washroom, not far from an isolated cell at one end of the building where they took the kettles for intense cleaning. A few of the older guys who worked with the construction company full-time were assigned to the cleaning bay. The jobs, which paid four or five times what we were making, looked to be the easiest ones in the plant, but we would soon learn why we didn't want them. The men wore fireproof suits that covered their entire bodies, and after a large mechanical crane would move a kettle into the clean-room, the men would clean the inside of the big pot. The explosiveness of sodium was clear, and we knew not to get anything that was even the least bit damp anywhere near the chemical. Tools on the second floor were required to be heated before touching the kettles or anything that had come in contact with the chemical. The rule could not have been any clearer, particularly near the cleaning room where warning signs hung on every wall. About fifty yards away and walking toward the room, I saw three workers grab their tools from a heating bin and walk into the room.

A few seconds later I saw what to this day I remember as a Hawaii Five-O sized wave of fire curling out of the room, the top of the wave breaking over the heads of the men as they ran for their lives. It engulfed them just as a wave at the beach would roll over the top of a surfer. Intense pain knocked the workers to the ground as a dozen of us raced toward them with fire blankets, which were placed strategically nearby. Help arrived within seconds. The men rolled on the ground and screamed. I can still hear them.

They were quickly covered and the flames were extinguished, but the damage had been done. I heard through the plant rumor mill that one of the men had third degree burns over most of his head and back. The others fared only slightly better. The suits saved their lives, but evidently not their skin. I can still see the image of the wave of fire rolling over the top of those men as if it happened last night.

That was the second-to-worst day. The worst day is not as vivid, but more personally haunting. I often wonder if I really remember the story accurately, but having lost touch with the guys I worked with and not having any way to get information from the company, I have accepted that I may never know what really happened.

Three of us had been assigned to work at the lead smelter, off and on, for the two weeks prior. On the outside of a long, narrow building, perhaps a quarter of a mile in length, there were thousands of perfectly aligned stacks of lead, each block about the size of a large throw pillow. The blocks were stacked four high, and from a distance looked like tombstones in an overbooked cemetery. One of the main functions of the plant had been to melt the lead that would be added into gasoline, which had not yet been fully phased out.

A few coworkers and I had the job of removing the firebrick that had served its time from the bottom floors of the tall, ten-story smokestacks which rose from the ovens used to melt the lead. After we finished removing the bricks from one smokestack we would begin work on the next; a different crew immediately began laying new brick inside the stack we had just completed. For those who did not have problems with claustrophobia and didn't mind working a twelve-pound jack hammer at a ninety-degree angle twenty or thirty feet up a ladder and inside a pipe three feet in diameter, the job was not that bad.

Three of us would take turns climbing up the ladder, breaking the lowest bricks free, and letting them fall to the ground. We worked as long as our arms would allow us to grip the pounding tool. We would work two days in the leadhouse and then have two days to work elsewhere while we took a blood test to confirm we had not been overexposed. The company restricted the number of hours we could work but, trusting kids that we were, something told us that ten years earlier someone must have worked more hours than his body could stand. I have done many dumb things in my life, and to this day I think working in that building may yet prove the dumbest. I expect at some point to learn that I have lead poisoning, cancer, or some other terrible disease that will somehow be linked to the time I spent in that building.

One Friday night, late in the summer, we agreed to work half of a second shift, declining the request to work until midnight. The weekend beckoned, we were leaving for school in the next week or two, and we had already made more than enough money to get us through the school year. Plans had been made, and we were all anxious to go out after another long week. A shift and a half seemed like a reasonable compromise.

The next day we were back at the plant at 6:30 a.m., waiting on the bus that would transport us from the front gate, likely back to Smokestack #3 to finish removing the bricks. About twenty minutes went by before one of the bosses came and told us in the most somber of tones that we would not be working today. He said there had been an accident.

The story becomes sketchy at this point. I heard later that they had tried to fire the first oven in the leadhouse—the very oven that we had taken the old bricks out of just a week earlier—and that the entire building had been leveled in an explosion. Rumors circulated that multiple people had been killed, though I never heard a definitive count or the full story. My buddies and I who had worked in the building the previous day had left for home just hours before the first oven had been fired. I always wondered if they had intentionally waited until midnight to fire the oven, or if the work had been delayed from earlier in the day for some unknown reason.

To this day I cannot say definitively that the explosion part of the story is true. That Friday ended up being my last day at the plant; we were not needed the next week. I never could confirm a single thing about what happened that night, but admit I never seriously tried. Eighteen and breathing, and as a college-bound kid anxious to get out of "Stinkadena" and on to my new life in Austin, I never looked back.

BASEBALL

A good friend and I skipped work one afternoon to watch a baseball game. During the game, the topic of religion surfaced, and I mentioned that the brother of the kid at the plate had recently passed away. On the very next pitch he hit the ball out of the park, a shot as far as any that I could recall. The young man rounded the bases, crossed home plate, tapped his chest with a fist, and then pointed to the cloudless blue sky stretching endlessly above us.

My friend made the comment that while the concept of God and heaven is comforting, he did not understand how so many people could believe such a wild story. He wondered aloud why so many educated, intelligent people claim to believe in something he found so unbelievable. He suggested that it would have been easy for one very intelligent person to have written all the books of the Bible then find a handful of conspirators to recount rehearsed stories that would lend substance to the mythical powers of the magical man, Jesus. He questioned how we could so willingly accept such ancient stories that to him seemed no different than tales his grandfather told and probably grew just as much each time they were retold. He went on and on with his questions, sharing his doubts, and claimed that, as a man of science, he simply could never believe in something that did not have what he would consider tangible proof, even if he wanted to do so.

He admitted that no scientist has any reasonable explanation on where the material that fed the miraculous "Big Bang" originated, but said, "There are simply too many facts that cannot be ignored." His facts, however, relied on as much faith to accept as any story in the Bible. He saw no flaw in his belief that mud became algae; bacteria became a fish; a fish a lizard; a lizard…a monkey; and a monkey a man. However, he did question how a man could be made from nothing.

Before he could ramble further, I asked my friend if the game of baseball is real. He went on to explain that of course it is real. There are nine uniformed men strategically positioned on the brilliantly groomed field stretching before us. He pointed out how they work in unison, collectively following a set of unwritten procedures in a choreographed dance where the slightest wrong move by either side allows the other to advance. Before he could get religious about his love for the game, I interrupted and made him an offer: "If baseball is real, as you say, I'll give you every penny I have, including every material possession I own, if you can teach your dog the game of baseball."

Jake is a brilliant black Labrador who we had hunted with often, but the problem was obvious. Laughing, he told me that he would like to have my every possession, but we both knew that not even old Jake could ever comprehend a game as complex as baseball. "Why not?" I asked. "We have both agreed it is real. We understand it. If Jake sat here with us, watching the game just as we are, seeing the players, the field, and the fans, you do not think he would understand?"

Not knowing exactly where I was going, my friend replied, "The mind of a dog is incapable of understanding something as complex as baseball." So I asked him, "Is it possible that the mind of a human is incapable of understanding something as complex as God?"

RATTLESNAKES

At the age of twenty-three and barely a year out of college, I had an encounter I can recall as vividly as if it happened yesterday. A beautiful fall morning in Texas had just begun, forty-something degrees on its way to seventy with only a hint of the morning dew left to drip from the season's last blazing red and shimmering yellow leaves, each hopelessly clinging to the oaks scattered across the hillside for a few final days. The fresh smell of cedar filled the air, and the clouds had left the eternal blue sky to itself for the day.

I slid down from the tree I'd hunted from that morning and silently crept along the top of a Texas mesa, one hundred feet higher than the bottom below, working my way through the evergreen shrubs and around scattered, flat stones where a single misstep would break the silence and end the hunt. I had worked my way around a particularly thick cedar, moving slightly to my left and angling downhill. My left foot lifted twelve inches above the ground and advanced forward across a large, holey rock covered with a small cedar log when I spotted trouble.

Three feet in front of my left big toe, and just eighteen inches from its landing spot downhill, coiled the largest snake I had ever seen in my life. For the next two hundredths or two hundred seconds, my life advanced like a slow-motion replay still recorded on my internal Tivo.

I saw an enormous wad of coiled snake with not one but two heads about two inches apart, raised, and pulling back into a well-defined and unmistakable strike position. A rattling noise increased in intensity by the millisecond, and a shaking tail rose above the coil several inches behind the two heads. In my mind's replay, I don't see a second rattle, though I suspect it simply blended into the wad or shook so close to the other that they combined to appear as one. I remember my mind screaming *danger* and being able to slow but not stop my momentum as gravity pulled me down the hill and forward. My unavoidable next step had a known but not-so-happy ending.

I held the stock of the rifle in my right hand near the trigger housing and the barrel in my left, angling from my right hip to about a foot in front of my left knee. The barrel pointed slightly to the left of the wad of snake at an angle most fortunate for me. I instinctively swung it to the right, probably quicker than snake etiquette would suggest I should have, but time to quibble did not exist. The two heads pulled back further, and the noise of the rattle amplified as the gap between my foot and the pile of snake closed. My finger raced to the trigger. It's odd that I don't recall clicking from safety to fire with my thumb, but

I also don't remember taking a breath, feeling my heart beat, or suppressing a scream that would have made any five-year-old proud.

I certainly did not think about it at that moment, and to this day still wonder if I recognized the wad as two snakes mating and expected to kill them both with one shot, or simply thought I had stumbled across one jumbo mutant snake with two heads. I honestly do not know. Nor do I know if I expected to kill it or them or just hoped I would do as much damage to them as they were about to do to me. My best guess is that I knew trouble waited to greet my next step, and the innate, logical, and only thing I had to do was strike first and hope for the best. I knew that I could not stop my momentum and avoid that next step, and I had no question that before the next tick of the clock I would violate the privacy that this beast demanded. I don't recall for certain, but I think my heart skipped three beats. I fired before I could be scared to death.

I did not hear the sound of the rifle as the bullet attacked the snake and reset the situation. My mental video goes to fast-forward from that point on, and I only remember flying uphill and backward, landing at least five feet from a slowly slithering hunk of flesh on the brown and bloody ground. I recall seeing a large broken snake, with one head weakly raised and a rattle still barely shaking under the cedar.

Under any other circumstance, I have no doubt that I would have unloaded every bullet I had until any sign of movement abated and the slithering devil rested as peacefully dead as the dirt itself. However, my memory only has me walking as fast as I could, almost running at times, across the mile of grassy fields and dirt roads back to camp. A little later, my cousin, uncle, a couple of friends, and I went back and found not one two-headed snake but two one-headed monsters. They measured 5'6" and 5'9" respectively, and each had a dozen or so buttons on its tail.

DEATH OF MY MOTHER

After a year-long battle with cancer, my seventy-one-year-old mother passed away in her home with my brother and my wife by her side. I had spent the better part of her last three months traveling back and forth to Houston to stay with her in the hospital and take her to her chemotherapy treatments. She had developed the most wonderful network of friends in her lifetime, including grade school buddies still living in Germany, friends she had made during her travels around the world, work acquaintances, neighbors, and most importantly, church members. The funeral ended as uplifting as funerals can. Everyone in attendance left the church knowing she had led a great life and was comforted by the unquestionable knowledge she had moved to the longest, most important chapter in her life's book.

Speaking to the gathering of family and friends at the ceremony, I described her life using her name like an acronym. I recounted that Edith, my mother's name, would always remind me of the Energizer Bunny, her Determination, her Independence, and her love for Travel. The audience laughed where I hoped they would and listened intently as I described her very full life. I closed with the thought that the last letter in her name, *h*, stood for the destination of her next big trip, Heaven. The audience all nodded in agreement.

We closed with the song "I Can Only Imagine," by MercyMe, and then greeted each other with handshakes, hugs, and tears. All that were present shared the moment, as the Holy Spirit filled the church and everyone inside. She is gone, but she still crosses my mind and taps my heart frequently.

A few months after my mother's death, the stepfather of a young man on a baseball team I coached committed suicide. Trey was in his early thirties, the best friend of every kid on the team, a wonderful father, a talented musician with a vibrant personality and an ever-present smile, and a man who everyone enjoyed being around. He had a troubled past, but in the years I had known him had never once been anything other than a top-notch role model and an outstanding citizen. My heart ached as our team of young men carried his casket from the hearse to the grave. It was a tragic event that I will never understand, an event that left me emotionally empty and mentally drained. Burned out and ready for a break, our family headed to a Florida beach for a vacation.

A shark attacked a surfer days before we arrived, Tropical Storm Cindy (later upgraded to Hurricane Cindy) blew through on day two, and then Hurricane Dennis chased us out of town five or six days later. Believe it or not, I still consider it a great vacation. While in Florida, trapped inside by storms, and kept out of the water by sharks, I stumbled upon a superb book. While the family hung out at the beach (without entering the surf) I took our vehicle to have the air conditioner repaired—yes, we had our run of bad luck. I walked to a nearby bookstore and at the suggestion of a young sales clerk purchased the book *A Brilliant Solution,* by Carol Merkin. The book tells the fascinating story of James Madison and the struggles faced during the development of the United States Constitution. Merkin's book, and my dissatisfaction with politicians, left me deeply interested in learning more about our Founding Fathers.

DEATH OF MY FATHER

When we returned, the baseball season came to a happy end, with the boys claiming the Barrett Fletcher South Texas State Championship. Work, however, became pure drudgery. I had always intended to transition my career and pursue a "fun" job once my children were in school sports and I could no longer coach their teams, and had been saving for years so we could get by on a more meager income when the time came. I knew the time had neared. I began to consider my options for what I would do next. Having been inspired by *A Brilliant Solution,* I began to read every political book I could get my hands on. I came across a wonderful book titled *The Untied States of America,* by Juan Enriquez, and if you are anything like me, you may have misread the second word and thought the title read "United" instead of "Untied." It proved to be a very positive dyslexic mistake. I thoroughly enjoyed the book, thinking deeply now about the future fate of America. Then tragedy struck again.

Hurricane Katrina had wreaked havoc on southern Louisiana weeks earlier, and now Rita, the largest Hurricane on record, had the city of Houston in its sites. I received an early morning call from my dad two days before the storm was predicted to hit, and he anxiously wanted to get out of town, as did the other four million residents of Houston. He planned to pack a few things, secure his house, and drive to Austin that afternoon.

Later that day, while having lunch with a good friend, I received a panicked call from my dad's third wife, who said that my father had fallen over backward in the middle of a sentence. The paramedics had administered CPR once they arrived and they were now in the ambulance racing to a downtown hospital; the local ones had already begun to shut down because of the pending storm. My father had suffered a massive heart attack and would never recover.

I headed for Houston shortly thereafter, visited my unconscious dad, and then spoke with the doctors. They offered little hope. With the storm bearing down on Houston and nothing to do but wait, we were strongly advised to get out of town ahead of the storm.

His wife and I left the hospital at midnight. After a twenty-four-hour drive to Austin that normally takes three, a day of rest, and a withered storm that turned and completely missed Houston, I returned to my dad's bedside. I had them turn off the life-support machines that evening, and he officially passed about three hours later. We hired a man from the funeral home to say a few words, but nobody else spoke. A few family members attended, four old friends he had worked with during his thirty years at NASA and Rockwell, a few neighbors, and a couple of others I didn't know. My youngest brother, for various reasons, did not bother to attend. My father had been a decent, well-educated, friendly man that, as best I could tell, had never seriously offended or caused harm to anyone. He had been a law-abiding, tax-paying citizen who lived his life the way he had chosen to live it. At seventy-two years of age, despite having lived a good life by all earthly accounts, the ending could only be described as sad. The difference in his life and my mother's, and it is a big one, was the absence of God.

As a very young child, before my parents divorced, my dad would pick us up after Sunday school so my mom could stay for church. He would sit in the car reading the paper, smoking a cigarette, not the least bit bothered that he had to drive a few miles to chauffeur us home. He never considered spending a couple of hours of his busy life on something he did not believe in. It was not important to him. He was not opposed, but he simply chose not to spend time with God.

My mother's faith had a profoundly positive effect on her life and the lives of many others. My father's lack of faith had never been an issue to him during his life. I am confident my mother is now in a better place. I remain hopeful for my father, though I suspect he is not.

THE FREEDOM PUZZLE

As I began to think about the founding of our country, I developed a deep sense of admiration for our Founding Fathers and a growing sense of frustration with our current politicians. I had fond thoughts of what it must have been like when our country was being conceived, and disturbing thoughts of what our country had turned into. I had a dream one night, or perhaps what most would call a nightmare, of a puzzle painted on my ceiling somewhere around the year 2050. To call the image disturbing is an understatement. The image I saw is explained a couple of pages hereafter. Working back in time, the description below is what I envisioned the puzzle must have looked like when our country was created.

> Imagine yourself perched comfortably, contently, upon a short stool in a sturdy, candlelit log cabin some 220 years ago. The light flickers merrily, moved by your thoughts and an evening prayer that still echoes. The fresh scent of the season's last flowers float through the air, and the pride of a newly born country holds the moment together. An unlit fire awaits release in a cool, dark corner of the room, with the neatly stacked sweat-stained logs anxious to become coals burning within, warmth that will sustain. The flames, soon to be dancing, will carry us through the years of hard days and dark nights that await us. A yearning, hopefully white and just-built puzzle waits patiently upon an easel, pleading, begging, to be stroked with the knowledge and imagination of unfamed men whose thoughts are pure and actions are honest. Hardened steel, shaped by a swinging hammer and a singing mind, black as silence and

just as free, lines the border of the yet-to-be-painted masterpiece. A pregnant palette holds colors of brilliance with a motherly understanding that dozens of following generations will dull, chip, scrape, and loot, day-by-day, until only the memory and hope of the newborn's first days remain.

A beautiful drawing of a hand-sewn garment begins to appear, magically, on the puzzled backdrop. Reaching from liberal to conservative, stripe-by-stripe and star-by-star, seven wind-blown candy-red stripes take horizontal turns with six pure white ones, foundational highways of the country to come. A royal blue square captures the top left corner and less than a third of the upper seven stripes. Thirteen white stars twinkle intensely while chasing each other round and round the heavenly backdrop. Bold and beautiful, blindingly white, and commanding the prized middle, the word **FREEDOM** stands in chiseled Bodoni letters that are confident and capitalized, blessed by God, numbered seven by luck, and pulsing with the lifeblood of a just-born nation. Circled by hope in the upper left corner rests a stack of precious, sparkling gold coins. A steepled church with three desks lined before a chalk-marked blackboard, and seen through a six pane window, educates on the canvas' opposite upper side. An empty, promising cross stands stately in the bottom right corner—to the left of the cross is a picture of thirteen dining men sharing bread and wine, and to the right, a stone tablet etched with ten rows of wisdom is planted powerfully in the ground. In the bottom left is a shiny black book with a green bookmark holding a page that begins, "In the beginning…" A gentle breeze floats across the image.

Three wanted spirits float down from above, whispering life, liberty, and happiness upon all below. They come on winged stallions, white, black, and brown, and plant the seeds that will in time become our cities and our towns. A young couple, holding hands and sharing dreams, push a laughing child wishfully on a swing that hangs from the lower arm of the letter F, while a baby eagle nests and watches from the circle of the R. Grandparents, sitting on a distant but close bench, watch and smile together.

An enormous, perfectly shaped oak tree, majestic and magnificent, with three powerful branches leading to limbs filled with acorns waiting to drop and begin a life of their own, reaches across the top, offering shade to the letters D and O, and opportunity to those willing to climb. A stately house, painted white, built by the people and for the people, beckons with doors opened wide, unblinded, paneless windows, and roses blooming eastward. An arc of triumph soldiered by two smiling willows stands freshly planted on the newly seeded lawn. Groups are scattered about. A caroler sings, elders debate, children play. Women scurry, laborers labor, businessmen trade. Farmers plant, teachers teach, masons lay. A congregation prays. An atheist strays. Our Father, Peace, Hope, You, Me, and one Holy Spirit are present but unseen.

That is how I envision the day our country began. But admittedly, that is not the image that first came to mind. I had been up reading late one night, and before falling asleep, after my nightly prayer and while in that fading state of consciousness that is usually so relaxing, I found myself thinking about the ungodly mess we are leaving behind for our children, grandchildren, and all who will follow.

A terrible image came to mind; it would not go away. The more I tried to get it out of my mind, the more graphic it became. In the nightmarish trance, I was a much older man, armed with a cane and a head of gray hair. Meticulously painted on my ceiling, or the inside of my eyelids—I couldn't tell which—and reminiscent of the work of Michelangelo in the Sistine Chapel, appeared a sinister, disconcerting picture.

The decaying image of a ten thousand–piece jigsaw puzzle that our Founding Fathers had painstakingly pieced together some 250 years ago hangs from above. It had the word **FREEDOM** scribed across the center in large, bold,

Bodoni letters, each a soiled shade of yellow resembling the teeth of a two-pack-a-day smoker well past his prime.

A flag, draped vertically from bottom to top, lies beneath the letters, with members representing all parts of society trapped like prisoners behind the red and white bars running down and up the flag. There are forty gray stars, none of them twinkling. Empty spaces are left from where ten have fallen; they now reside on the flags of two newly formed and mightily struggling socialist nations.

In the corners, starting in the top left and moving clockwise around the puzzle, are four troubling icons: a shocked Thomas Jefferson, with closed eyes and mouth agape, drops tears on a weathered ten dollar bill that has large bites removed from a little more than a half of the paper; a crumbling brick school house that looks more like a block of holey Swiss cheese; a burned and broken cross, and finally; a shredded Bible with torn pages scattered about. "Luke 23:34*" titles the one page that can barely be read, albeit with drops of blood and an asterisk clearly visible. The flag has just begun to burn.

Four angry men—a politician, an IRS agent, an ACLU lawyer, and the founder of NAMBLA—their absent faces covered by black hoods, swoop down from above on winged horses. The horses, white, red, black, and pale, respectively, are destroying the crumbling Bodoni letters, dropping bombs of voluminous documents filled with regulations, laws, and lawsuits. The horse of the first rider carries saddlebags of money that his lobbyists have filled. The second, a sickle cloned from the Grim Reaper. The third wears boots with menacing spikes, raised to stomp on anyone who thinks otherwise, and the fourth, a crying baby boy who dreads his fate. Inside a bird's nest, hiding inside the letter "R," is a pregnant, runaway teenager holding a screaming baby bald eagle in her ring-less left hand. She leans over a mirror for one last line of cocaine. The reflection she sees in the mirror is not her own, but of her parents looking the other way.

The letter "O" is nearing collapse, with a dented and leaking barrel of oil jammed between the top and bottom of the letter and struggling to prolong the impending collapse. The letter "F" is being pushed over by two hoodlums and is about to land upon an elderly, dignified black man, and a trashy, young, and tattooed white woman playing slot machines. The spinning wheels of the slot machines have stopped, but the windows don't display the cherries and lemons we usually see. In their place one machine has the words, "Red," "tire," and "men," and in the windows of the other "We," "hell," and "fare" appear. Instead of coins spilling out of the bottom, IOUs and handcuffs can be seen piling around and latching onto the two "winners." A dark black smog puffs from the letter "M."

A revised version of Leonardo da Vinci's *The Last Supper* lies broken at the foot of the cross, with a skeleton, choking on a crust of bread, resting on the shoulders of Christ. The diner to the right of the skeleton, in the redrawn and tax-funded painting, is not an apostle but Mary Magdalene, included upon insistence of the American Atheists. On the empty side of the table, facing Jesus, are the backs of two ghostly but headless figures, 90 percent translucent, each seated in armed chairs, with legs not of wood but of a man, a lion, an ox, and an eagle. They hold their heads in their hands. An ancient stone tablet, with three readable lines of text, and seven more lines that have been struck through, lays impossibly crumpled on the ground.

Our military is primed for action, in the middle of the bottom of the puzzle. To the left they are instigating a fight with a gaggle of unarmed old ladies dressed for church but determined to defend themselves. They helplessly throw bullets and empty medicine bottles at the laughing soldiers. To the right, a group of radical, Bible-waving, Christians, Jews, and Buddhists, easily identified by their freshly groomed beards, and the government-mandated red turbans they are now required to wear, march in protest and cry for jihad. Free speech permits them to burn the U.S. flag while waving the colors of Iran, Palestine, and Korea. A platoon of noosed soldiers grudgingly points AK-47s at the kindergarten class that is watching in disbelief as the rights of the people are protected.

A house, freshly painted red, appears in the top center of the puzzle. A large python with a human-sized bulge just behind the neck is slithering out of the upper balcony. The Washington Monument has tumbled onto the west wing, crushing the building and splintering a large and dying oak. It scatters a group of Boy Scouts who had been touring the facility. The all-stone Lincoln Memorial lays upside down in pieces on the back lawn, with beautiful black roses in full bloom in the background.

Just to the right of the house, the Statue of Liberty, sans torch, lays in an open coffin at a ceremony in the Arlington cemetery. The clapper-less Liberty Bell is stuck in the ground, upside down between two unknown soldiers. The crack has widened, the split plainly visible, and the bell looks more like a heart that is breaking than a bell not ringing.

There are two parts of the puzzle that glisten as pristinely as a shiny new penny. One is the Supreme Court, which appears in the top right of the puzzle and is wholly intact. Seen from a distance are nine lounge chairs at one end of a large pool. A party is in progress. Girls with bunny ears serve drinks to those lounging while paralegals huddle around a lawsuit-generating printing press spewing papers and lawsuits into stacks scattered about the yard. The other, on the upper wrong side is the Capitol building, home of the Congress. As with the Supreme Court, everything is in perfect order; the puzzle pieces are all present. There is a buzz in the air as stacks of money move from lobbyists to congressmen and printing machines crank out new bills. Several large helicopters, with destination plates reading Nassau, Switzerland, and The Pacific Beaches, board our elected officials.

My nightmare ended. I asked a few people what they made of the image, but all were too busy bustling off to their daughter's soccer game or their son's baseball practice to spend any time discussing it. My congressman told me to sleep on it.

MONGOLIAN MAN

I traveled to China late last year and experienced things that are difficult to truly appreciate without visiting yourself. We had a blast seeing the sites, tasting the food, and exploring the countryside. The trip proved to be great fun, but there were two particular observations that remain more vivid than the rest. The first was realizing the impact the government ownership of property had on the overall vibrancy, or lack thereof, of a nation; everybody lived in what most of us would consider deplorable slums. The other observation, a memory that will live with me forever, was a young Mongolian man playing an erhu on the overflowing streets of a Beijing hutong. The erhu looked to be a thousand years old and freshly recovered from a Song Dynasty tomb. The tune was a haunting and eerie melody that wailed through the dingy alleys, echoed off the decrepit cinder block huts, and seeped from the rotting sewers. The music flowed like a river, each note tuned as perfectly as the keys on a baby grand. I stopped to throw a few Yuan into the man's case when the music fell silent and the crowd disappeared. My chin fell to the ground. The man had a face with no eyes or nose.

His forehead stopped at the top of his upper lip. I did not see protruding ears, as a normal man has, though I think I could make out the impression of lobes pushing outward from underneath the skin on the sides of his head. My stare was glued to his missing face. My wife grabbed my arm and hastily pulled me away, scolding me like a small child for staring so impolitely. The fact that he could not see that I was staring was lost on my wife; after all, manners are manners. I was intrigued by this man's musical mastery, wondering how someone who obviously couldn't see and possibly could not hear managed to create such a magnificent sound from what looked like the simplest of instruments. What motivated him? I was completely fascinated. In a country so poor, where dollar bills like the ones we hid in the cabbage leaves of a visited farm were worth a month's salary for the lucky harvester, sat this man playing for tips that were likely stolen as soon as they found his jar. His passion, his talent, and his honesty moved me. An hour later, when we came back by his post, the music no longer played. The man was gone, but the image will last forever.

THE SHED

In the original draft of my book, I delayed working on the chapter titled "Religion" until most of the other sections had been completed. There was not any particular reason I had put the chapter aside, other than it was the one I was least comfortable talking about. I have never been one to talk openly about God, and even writing this book made me a little uncomfortable. The chapter had just been completed and a quick break before beginning work on the questions seemed like a good idea. I needed to mend the fence in the kennel that holds our dog, so I headed to the shed to grab my spool of wire and wire cutters. As I glanced at the shelves I did not see what I was looking for; the spool was not where I had thought I left it.

I began searching through some boxes on the ground, and while bending over and looking through a container in the corner, an unsplendidly solid whack smacked the back of my head. A bucket had fallen from the ceiling. It didn't knock me to the ground, but it certainly staggered me. I reached for the back of my head but instinctively jerked away when I first found the gash. Blood covered my hand and began to run down the back of my neck, so I wobbled inside, grabbed a towel, and spent the next fifteen minutes applying water and pressure until most of the bleeding stopped. An hour or so later, my wife came home from another long day of teaching and insisted on taking me to the hospital where they "stitched" the opening with metal staples. Nothing major, just a little freakish.

THE CONNECTION

Hopefully you found a few of those stories interesting, though I am sure it is not clear how they all fit together. It certainly took me a while to see the connection. Let me explain why I believe they are all relevant and related. This plan I have created could be described with many different adjectives. I've heard it called grandiose, wishful, threatening, ingenious, radical, simple, and even brilliant. More important is what I have not heard it called. Not a single person has told me it is not plausible.

The plan is so simple and straightforward that it is completely doable. The common question most of us ask when a new invention appears is, "Why didn't I think of that?" I like to consider myself an inventor, but when people asked how I came up with this idea I had to say I really didn't have a good answer. As I've thought about it, and tried to write this all down, I've reached the conclusion that a series of life events have led me create this system and lay it out for the nation to decide if will be supported or ignored. Will the country find a way to make it work or find a way to pick it apart? Will this be the modern day version of the book I stumbled across at the bookstore in Destin, Florida?

By most accounts, I should be a textbook Republican. I am a middle-aged, white, educated, church-going, pro-business, anti-government American. I live in the suburbs, make good money (or at least I did until I retired to deliver this message and initiate this revolution), have an all-American family, and have lived a good life. But I am by no means a hardcore Republican.

I do not trust business when it comes to the environment or the care of its employees. I believe that unions are absolutely critical in some situations and do not believe in making birth control illegal (technically, the birth control pill causes an abortion). I am also a firm believer in the need for steep estate taxes and believe we need to funnel even more money into our welfare system. I am not a Republican.

However, I am not a Democrat either. I do not believe in mid- and certainly not late-term abortion; I hate the way the party abuses the power to protect endangered species to prevent reasonable use of private property; I disagree strongly with excessively progressive income taxes; and I think it is shameful the way they insist on sneaking their socialist agenda forward at the expense of free enterprise and our republic.

I am also far from a Libertarian because I am strongly opposed to the legalization of marijuana and some of their ACLU-like perspectives on freedom. I think Independents have the right idea, but do not believe they will succeed in their current form. I am stuck in the middle, worried about the decline of America and certain that politicians will never cure our ills. I am frustrated with government and almost every one of the people in charge.

Now, let me try to connect the dots and to point out what why I believe each event is a sign that has been strategically placed in my life, beginning with my job at the chemical plant. While there, I saw firsthand how big business can do some really terrible things to people and the environment. I do not believe they are all intentional, but without unions I suspect many more people would have died from lead poisoning and other such ailments. Businesses are focused on making money, and it is too easy for them to overlook important issues like the environment and their employees' health. We are light years ahead of where we were, but we must remain vigilant. We must look out for our environment. The massive Superfund list is all the proof you need to understand that businesses will destroy our surroundings if we do not watch them like a hawk.

Working at that plant has made me a staunch environmentalist and prevented me from ever becoming a straight-ticket Republican. I wonder at times what would have happened if they had fired that oven on schedule or if it had not been Friday and I had worked a double shift like every other night that week. Would I have been inside the building or would they have evacuated the few dozen workers, recognizing the risk? I consider myself lucky not to know what really happened, or why. I often think of the lead tombstones outside that building, and the men who were inside, and wonder if the incident was a brush with death, an important sign I was intended to see, or both.

I believe the baseball game is a great story. When I have a conversation with someone who has questions about faith, or when I have been asked to write a letter to young men or women going through confirmation at their church, I tell that story. My mother spoke so much about God and religion when I was growing up that it turned me off. There were times, particularly through my college years, where I had doubts, but when those words spontaneously came from my mouth at the baseball game, I think I convinced myself as much as I did my friend. It was an epiphany for me, and it came in an environment where I was comfortable. I have never had a doubt about the existence of God since that day, and I think that is an important part of this story. If I were living just for my family, money, and myself, I would have never dedicated the past year of my life to this effort, or walked away from a profession that has rewarded me so handsomely. I do believe I have been called to deliver this message.

The rattlesnakes may seem like the most disconnected of the stories, but they were important to the innovation of the system. More than anything, that encounter sparked this idea. I'll get back to it in a moment. The death of my mother, and then my friend, left me emotionally exposed. The trip to Florida, the shark, a broken air conditioner, and Hurricane Cindy all somehow conspired to have this young lady recommend a book about the writing of our Constitution. I am a sports fan, a computer guy, and a reader of business books, mysteries, and stuff by Grisham and Koontz. I considered history old news. Why I bought a book about the founding of our country at that vulnerable moment in my life truly escapes me. But I was hooked. I went on to read others by Thomas Paine, Thomas Jefferson, and Ben Franklin. Then I began to read some of the more current writings by or about Armey, Gingrich, Bill Clinton, Hillary Clinton, and George Bush. A fire had been lit. *The Untied States of America*, which I purchased thinking it was *The United States of America*, really got me thinking.

My father died shortly thereafter, and after my twenty-four-hour ride back from Houston, and while wondering about my father's fate, I had the puzzle dream. I admit that I've embellished the puzzle I saw that night, but the timing I think is what is important. Would I have had that dream if the sequence of events had not been exactly as they were? I woke up the next morning convinced our country was falling apart. The fuse was lit. The more I read and the more I conversed with friends, the more I realized our country was self-destructing before our very eyes. We had to do something, but what?

I have lived in Texas my entire life, but have only had two face-to-face encounters with rattlesnakes. The first was the story described above. The second encounter occurred about six months before my mother died and just after we had moved from the city. While at our lake house an electrician was installing some new lighting under our little getaway. We had found that one of the existing switches had failed and needed replacement. I thought I may have a spare in my shed (this is a different shed), so I went to search for one.

The property had this dilapidated metal shed, about fifteen feet wide and fifteen feet deep, sitting on railroad ties. The six-inch gap between the rotting floor and the hidden ground below created a perfect home for rats and snakes. I kept a few boxes in the shed, each about three feet tall, full of miscellaneous building supplies; I never knew what would be broken when we made it to the lake, so keeping spare parts, things like PVC pipe fittings, toilet fixtures, tools, plugs, switches, and gadgets, saved me many trips into town. Whenever I would go to the shed, I would kick the walls to make as much noise as I could before hopping over the rotted floor behind the front door and into the little hut. I always expected to find a snake in that shed, but in fifteen years, never had.

Before entering, I kicked it two or three times as I always did, and then hopped through the front door. I kicked the boxes I was about to search, always mindful of snakes and scorpions, and then bent over, put my head in the box, and started digging through the PVC elbows, tees, caps, couplings, switches, lures, leaders, bobbers, and everything but light switches, when I thought I heard a faint hissing sound. I froze, listened for a good ten or twenty seconds without moving, but heard nothing else.

I recommenced my rummaging when I heard the hissing noise again, but this time it grew loud, echoing off the walls of the little tin shed, maracas mockingly shaking in my ear. I new the tune instantaneously—the snake rattle lullaby—but I had no idea from which direction it came. My head was inside the box, and I didn't dare move. I remained bent over, silent, and motionless for what felt like minutes. The rattle never wavered, and my legs began to tire, shaking ever so slightly.

I called to no avail for my son and the electrician, who were both fifty yards away and inside the cabin. I could not imagine a way out of this predicament. I accepted the bite that was coming, telling myself snakebites are not fatal, moved my hands slowly in front of my face and began to raise my head from the box. I feared the snake was three feet in front of me and anxious to strike my forehead as soon as it was presented. As my eyes climbed high enough to see over the top edge, my legs now quivering like a child exposed in a blue northern, I saw the snake. Coiled directly in front of me, rattle playing, head cocked, and angry, the snake was ready to attack. But there was some good news. The snake waited a good five or six feet away, just beyond striking range. Then I remembered my last encounter.

The rattle continued to shake vigorously, and the head remained cocked in the ready position. The neck slithered back and forth, ever so slightly, and each independent scale on the agitated viper waited to spring forward. I listened intently for a second rattle, but detected only the one. Having seen enough, I sprang backward out the door and probably half the distance to the lake house. I ran up the stairs, grabbed a shotgun, and then raced back to the shed where the snake was still coiled and playing his instrument. Not enjoying the tune, I turned it off, permanently.

While telling this story to a friend I made the comparison between the snake and our politicians. The snake in the shed story led to my mating snake story, and the thought that Democrats and Republicans are nothing more than the male and female gender of the political species (you can decide which is which). I recollected how I had put an end to the mating snakes with one shot, and commented that I wished we could get rid of every poisonous snake in America. I was on the trail to creating this system, which will allow us to get rid of the politicians (not shoot them, but remove them) and replace them all at the same time with representatives of the people, as our founders intended. The idea continued to evolve and eventually became the GOOOH system.

The last two connections are more straightforward. I was reading and taking notes and decided that by February I would write a book to lay out my plan. I began issuing surveys and running focus groups to see if other people had the same thoughts and concerns that I did about the decline of our country, politicians, and the need for change. Every bit of data I collected supported the fact that we all see what is happening, but have no idea what we can do about it. I had a plan forming in my mind.

I had committed to writing this book and was just beginning the process of turning my notes into a story when we took the vacation to Beijing. It was there that I happened upon the Mongolian man. When I look at the politicians running our country today, I see an amazing physical correlation between them and the face of my Chinese erhu player; however, there is a distinct difference in character. I have tremendous sympathy for the erhu player, but only disdain for politicians.

The politicians ruining our country, each and every one, have mouths that dominate every other feature on their face. Their mouths move every waking moment of every day, making promises they have no intention of keeping and deals that benefit the wrong people. Our politicians might as well not have eyes; they do not see what you and I see. They have no need for ears; they cannot hear what our country is screaming. They use only their mouths. As for talent, theirs does not compare; they are masters only of law-twisting, backslapping, money-grabbing, and power-mongering. The politicians ruining our country today no longer represent the people; they represent their parties, those that provide them money, and themselves. If we wish to effect change in America, we must replace politicians with representatives who see and hear the same things the people do.

The Mongolian man put passion in my mission and cemented my decision to leave my job within six months. The writing of what would become a six hundred and sixty page tome shifted into high gear. My family complained that I had become obsessed with this project, and they were correct. Other than attending my son's football and baseball games, sending my daughter off to college, and an occasional night out with my wife or friends, writing the book and developing the plan became my life.

I had almost finished the third draft, one week before I intended to give my notice at work, when the bucket clobbered me on the back of the head. Was that pure coincidence, or was the fact that it happened while I was finalizing the chapter on religion, and just before I wrote the first candidate question, an attempt to make me rethink my decision to quit my job and pursue this endeavor? It sure felt like a devilish attempt to prevent my serendipitous moment. The first question on the list at the end of the chapter on religion is shown here. It existed in draft form when the bucket hit me. It will not be removed. We will ask every candidate to answer this question.

Question: Will you vote to amend the Constitution to specifically affirm that we are a nation under God, that God is welcome in all that we do, but no man can be forced to participate in worship at any time or in any way?

Now go back to the mating rattlesnakes. I put an end to both snakes with one shot from my trusty rifle. I recall squeezing the trigger and ending the situation instantaneously. The speed of the bullet was fortunately quicker than the delivery mechanism of the venom. I believe that incident and all of those included here happened for a reason. We are meant to repeat the story and remove both parties from our House with a single shot—the election of 2008. If we miss, our great country may soon be destroyed.

Looking back at the stories, recounting them here, I now see a series of signs that have appeared in my life. I didn't see them as such at the time, but looking back, I have no question that is what they were. The sequence of events—the lead tombstones, the baseball game, mating rattlesnakes, my move to Liberty Hill, the shed rattlesnake, my mother, my friend, my Florida vacation, my father, the Mongolian Man, the shed—is extraordinary. While I understand some will have a problem considering the sequence anything other than coincidental, I now see the events as signs on my journey to wherever it is that I am going.

As I began writing this book, a title did not become clear until I returned from China, shortly after I stumbled into the Mongolian man. The decline of our country is clear. The root cause, politicians, seems as close to indisputable as anything can be. If we want to solve our problems, the solution is obvious. The answer is to get rid of the politicians. With true representatives in office, I surmise, we will have a chance to reclaim our country and return it to the lofty status we once enjoyed. It is our House, after all. Senators should be seasoned lawmakers, so allowing those in office to remain makes sense to me. But the House of Representatives is intended to represent everyday Americans. The House is where we are off track.

This thought morphed into telling the politicians to Get Out of Our House. The acronym GOOOH fit perfectly. The name was born. More interesting is the thought that came to me shortly after the bucket found my head. In a moment I can't claim to remember, the green GOOOH sign materialized. I had been told everything I needed to know to start this revolution. We need to stop the destruction politicians are causing. It is time for us to tell the politicians to Get Out of Our House. The sign says it is time for them to GOOOH!

When my editor received the initial copy of this book, and before she had read even the first chapter, she sent me an e-mail commenting on the return shipping label; she knew what the book was about and found it most intriguing that I happened to live in the town of Liberty Hill. We had moved to Liberty Hill at the exact same time my mother had been diagnosed with cancer. Was the move yet one more sign? Is the name of the town just one more coincidence?

VI The Decline of America

THE CURRENT STATE

We live in the greatest country in the world. While most of us are unhappy with many things about our country and the people ruining it, few of us question that statement. Our form of government, on paper if not in practice, is second to none. Free enterprise in America successfully drives what has become the global economy. Freedom of speech, the press, and religion, combined with our entrepreneurial spirit and passion to not only succeed but excel has created a culture that most of the rest of the world can only dream of. We have the right to own property and make every one of our life decisions based on personal preferences; we have kept the government at bay for two hundred years, but its encroachment has begun to infringe on our freedoms.

Our health, education, and legal systems, once world-class, are still dependable and functional, but fading. These systems are indicative of how our once-mighty nation has begun to lose its luster. Once number one in the world in education, we are now ranked in the mid-teens by most accounts. Our retirement system is nearing collapse.

Taxes are so complicated the common man can no longer understand the shell game being played. The bottom 40 percent of the population no longer pays income taxes at all, the top 10 percent pay two-thirds of all taxes, and the richest of the rich continue to accumulate the lion's share of the wealth.

The air in our major cities has become so bad that children are finding it increasingly difficult to breathe, as evidenced by the skyrocketing asthma rates. Rivers, lakes, and streams have become so polluted you can neither swim in the waters nor eat the fish (who have no choice).

We incarcerate more people than any other country in the world, in absolute numbers and as a percentage. We have 2.25 million kids who have a parent in jail on any given day.[15] Drugs have become pervasive in our schools. Nearly a third of all children fail to graduate from the twelfth grade. Over one-third of all children are born to an unwed mother, and over 70 percent of all black children. Thirty-seven million people live in poverty, most making under ten thousand dollars per year.[16] Stop and think about these numbers. This is not the greatest country in the world for any of those people.

While you or I may live comfortably, the nation is falling apart for those who have not been as fortunate as we have. The United Nations and the Organization for Economic Cooperation of Advanced Democracies lists the areas where America is the *worst!*[17] Not second or third, but the bottom out of the leading twenty-plus industrialized nations. I added what I believe to be the causes (in parentheses):

- Poverty (drugs, crime, welfare, unwed mothers, education—or lack thereof)
- Economic inequality (education, drugs, unwed mothers)
- Life expectancy (drugs, poverty, crime, lifestyle, unwed mothers, education)
- Infant mortality (drugs, poverty, crime, unwed mothers, education)
- Homicide (drugs, poverty, crime, education)
- Health care coverage (drugs, poverty, health care system, education)

- HIV infection (drugs, promiscuity, poverty, education)
- Teen pregnancy (drugs, promiscuity, poverty, education)
- Personal savings (lifestyle, taxes, education)
- Environment—carbon dioxide emissions (dependency on oil)
- Voter participation (politicians, education)
- Obesity (lifestyle, education)

These are not the things we do "poorly;" these are the things where we are considered the *worst* in the entire the civilized world. Do you see the common theme? Drugs, poverty and a lack of education contribute to almost every one. Do you believe the absence of God is helping the situation? Do you disagree with my conclusions? Have the politicians truly addressed any of these issues? Would effective representatives ever allow us to fare so poorly in so many areas? Think about all the domestic wars our government has started: the War on Drugs, the War on Crime, the War on Poverty, and a dozen others. We are getting killed on every front.

Do you think the next administration, regardless of whether it is Republican or Democrat, is going to suddenly find a silver bullet and magically win these wars? Obesity is the only item on the above list where I cannot make a connection to the government—until now. I recently saw where the city of New York intends to outlaw trans-fats, and I find that concerning. Former Senator Bradley posits we should outlaw them everywhere.[18] I can only imagine the next big war waged by the newest government department: The Department of Food and Trans-fat (FAT). Would you be surprised? Lee Greenwood, are you still proud?

When considering the decline of America, here are some sobering statistics to consider:

- The national debt is 8.7 trillion dollars and increases by over 1.5 billion each day.
- Given that taxes are not paid proportionately, a family of four that makes 75,000 dollars per year owes over one million.[19]

- Half of the families in this country report making less than $46,000 in a year.
- More than 5.6 million Americans are in prison or have served time. [20]
- We spend over $23,000 per year on each federal prisoner.
- We spend over $22,000 per year supporting each person over the age of sixty-five.
- "We spend 8 times as much on seniors as we do per child."[21]
- "To be in the top 10 percent of wage earners, you need to make $75,000 per year, and those 10 percent of the taxpayers pay 62.4 percent of the taxes."[22]
- Thirty percent of students do not graduate from high school.[23]
- "One million teenagers are likely to have a child this year, and only three in ten will be married. Half of all the mothers who have kids in their teens will be poor the rest of their lives."[24]
- By 2050, there will be 86.7 million seniors, or roughly 21 percent of the population.[25]
- "The United States is 139th out of 172 nations in voter turn out."[26]

THE FALL OF EMPIRES

In Edward Gibbon's *The Decline and Fall of the Roman Empire*, written more than two hundred years ago, he claims that nations fail for five reasons:

1. The undermining of the dignity of the home.
2. Higher and higher taxes and the spending of public money for free bread and circuses for the populace.
3. The mad craze for pleasure.
4. The building of great armaments.
5. The decay of religion.

How many of these apply to our great country? Did you catch the statistic earlier about the number of children born to unwed mothers

(34.6 percent)? Men want to marry men, and women want to marry women. "The U.S. Census Bureau reported as recently as 2002 that about 50 percent of all marriages end in divorce."[27] Who hasn't seen children talk back to their parents or disrespect an elder? We even have children suing their parents. In one bizarre case an eighteen-year-old "child" sued her mother so she could collect the child support from her absent father. That sounds like a stable home.

By the time you factor in income taxes, property taxes, sales taxes, payroll taxes, gasoline taxes, and every other tax, people who earn over $75,000 a year send over 50 percent of their money to the government for "free bread and circuses." Despite the 50-percent rate, our government spends hundreds of billions of dollars more than what it collects each year. Do you think taxes are going to go up or down in the future? If you wonder what a present day circus might be, take a look at the stadiums we are building. "From 1990 to 2003 there were 66 major construction and renovation projects for professional sports stadiums and arenas in the United States, costing $17.3 billion....Sixty percent of the funding, or an estimated $10.3 billion, came from the public purse."[28] Thirty-seven million people receive some kind of welfare; is that the "free bread" he was talking about?

Evidence of the mad craze for pleasure is everywhere. Television, Las Vegas, the Internet, and the porn industry are explicit examples.

We have the most expensive and expansive military in the world. "The United States spends nearly as much on defense as the rest of the countries in the world combined."[29]

We can't post the Ten Commandments on a public school wall or say a prayer in the classroom, but organizations like the ACLU will sue for the rights of adult men to advertise to have sex with teenage boys (*Curly vs. NAMBLA*[30]).

We have mixed all the ingredients in Gibbon's recipe for failure. The oven is on and disaster is baking. Will we have a failed nation when the timer sounds?

Empires rise and fall. They do not exist forever. Every empire that has ruled the world has fallen, and the average duration of empires in the twentieth century is only fifty-seven years.[31] We could debate exactly what an empire is, whether or not the United States is one, or when exactly the American empire began, but all technicalities aside, we have been rising for two hundred and thirty years and have spent at least the last seventy at or near the top. The Sumerian, the Phoenician, the Roman, and the British Empires have all fallen. The Chinese empires, shielded from the rest of the world during their existence, have risen and fallen within China just as they have in the free world. The Soviet Union collapsed.

Empires can fail slowly or quickly. There is no rule, but once an empire begins its decline, it falls, and once it falls, it does not rise to the top again. Nobody has written a book on the rise, fall, and second rising of the XYZ Empire. They never will. The Soviet empire lasted less than seventy-five years and is now broken into a dozen interdependent nations. The once-mighty British Empire is now nothing more than wholly independent countries scattered about the globe. America is over two hundred thirty years old, and history suggests that while our decline may not yet be a foregone conclusion, it is looming. We have the ingenuity to stop the demise and extend our run, but not if we sit on our butts and let the politicians continue their ways.

Great powers are not destroyed by other countries; they are destroyed from within. They are destroyed by a cancer that starts without knowledge or fanfare, in a hidden and isolated area. A cancer that grows slowly, day-by-day, as certain as the tides and more powerful than gravity, until it becomes so large and so pervasive that no medicine or surgery can affect the outcome. There is no cure once the cancer spreads. If we do not address the ills of our society today, our children will be left with a *fait accompli.* "Is what we are experiencing the frightening spectacle of a mighty nation committing slow suicide?"[32]

OUR VESSEL

Our hand-crafted vessel, a Picasso meticulously carved from the sturdiest hardwood ever touched by man, was lazily adrift on a magnificently clear, sparkling river that we assumed stretched to eternity. A fresh, soft sky, the deepest shade of heavenly blue only angels could have painted, covered the land just as it had for hundreds of years. Our bellies were full, no jackets were required, and the iced pink lemonade was as refreshing to the palate as the glistening lemon, orange, and lime leaves shimmering on the shoreline were to the eye.

Seated atop feather-soft cushions, our feat propped comfortably, we were oblivious to even the possibility of a negative thought. The silence enveloped us with the most beautiful song our ears had ever heard, as a single, remarkably brilliant bald eagle floated gracefully above and up the river below and behind us. Joy filled our hearts, pleasure our minds, and family and friends our days. Endlessly, we assumed.

The transition from silence to roar comes slowly, advancing imperceptibly in undetectable degree thousandths. We must recognize that silence is now roaring, that lazily drifting is now speeding, and that eternity is not for this world. We are in the twilight of almost-too-late. We must awake from our blissful trance; the most tragically powerful waterfall ever seen by man is looming before us. The waterfall may be awesome and inspiring to onlookers, but it is life-threatening and pending to all afloat.

The choices are obvious: enjoy the ride, if only for a bit longer, or grab an oar.

VII The Causes of Decline

The decline of our country can be attributed to a host of different problems, all interrelated in one way or another. If we wish to inflect the declining trajectory of our nation we need to find a way to address each and every one of these issues. Politicians will at times talk about one problem or another, but for a multitude of reasons they are more likely to ignore or deny them than to confront or even acknowledge they exist. I will discuss each, and ultimately, show how we can elect representatives who will lead us to solutions. The causes of our decline can be segmented into four areas:

1. Foundational Problems
2. Politics
3. People
4. Undermining Issues

The foundational problems are straightforward and, while not trivial to fix, can certainly be corrected. As a country, we have lost our way. We have forgotten that we are a republic; we are not a simple democracy. We have forgotten that our nation was based upon guiding principles, not detailed legalese. We have misplaced common sense, a critical concept in a country intended to operate with limited government. We have completely lost the concept of equal rights for all, somehow creating a nation that grants special rights to most. Finally, we have allowed God to be pushed aside so that we do not offend the atheists who have no problem offending everyone else.

The most vexing of the problems contributing to our nation's demise is politics. The two political parties have made control and power their only priority; those who have different opinions no longer matter. Politicians are now puppets controlled by the parties and special interest groups. The strings have tied them in knots, and their hearts have been stolen. Political correctness has gagged them and forced every ounce of courage from their bodies. Their quest for reelection has turned their brains into straw. Politicians are turning our country into a place as bizarre as Oz.

These spineless politicians, even if they had the desire, will never be able to address our problems because of one catch-22 after another. To address the problems we face, some gut-wrenching decisions must be made and some painful concessions granted, but politics will forever prevent any progress. The only possible solution with a two-party system would be for the party in power to make the needed changes, knowing full well that doing so would result in their being voted out of office in the next election. Let me give an example and explain why that would happen.

Assume for a moment that the politicians in office agree the only way to prevent the collapse of Social Security is to increase the retirement age to seventy-five, and then vote to make that happen. What would their opponents do in the next election? They would attack the party and politicians who voted to increase the age, claiming they have no compassion for the elderly and are going to let seniors starve in the streets. The challengers would promise to reset the retirement age to sixty-eight, sixty-six, or whatever age was necessary to secure enough votes to get elected. Whether or not they actually fulfilled the promise would be irrelevant, as long as the votes of the seniors who lost their handout were received. Most seniors between the ages of sixty and seventy-five, in this example, would vote for the politician promising to improve their personal financial outlook. It's sad, but that's the undeniable way many Americans vote.

The current process is fatally flawed, and the politicians are certainly intelligent enough to understand the situation. Who in the country believes that either party would ever concede their power and vote to increase the retirement age in such a manner, even with the knowledge that doing so was the only way to solve the problem and was the best thing for our country? Conceding to the other party, handing them control of the government, is not something a politician or a party can do, and most of us recognize and even appreciate why. Politics prevents solutions.

Election after election we work to remove a party or a politician from an individual office, but we are fighting the wrong battle in the wrong war. We must recognize that politicians and the two parties are the problem. I am not saying all politicians are bad people. I am simply saying the problem cannot also be the solution. The answer cannot be the same as the question. If a male rattlesnake appears in my path, coiled and ready to strike, and you replace it with a female, also coiled and ready to strike, you have not helped me in any way. That would be a ridiculous thing to do. But that is what we do with politicians. We say this particular politician is the problem, but then we replace him with another politician, albeit of a different stripe.

Regardless of who is in office, the core problems cannot be solved as long as we continue practicing politics in the way we are practicing today. The only way to prevent our demise is to take the politics out of government, and the only way to do that is to elect citizens who will represent the will of the people, not the will of the party.

Third on the list of major contributors to our decline are three groups, who collectively represent less than one percent of the population. Politicians, Lawyers, and Extremists will be discussed in detail, and it is at the end of the sections on these groups where I will begin to identify the questions we would like our candidates to answer before they are selected.

To turn our country around, we must put the right people in place, and to do so, we must first get the wrong people out. We need to redefine the roles of these three groups and adjust the power they have usurped. These three groups have taken control of our country, manipulated our legal system for their own benefit, and set us on a course vastly different from the one we were on when our country was founded. It is a course that contradicts the one 80 percent of us believe we should be on.

I believe if we can rein in these three types of people, limit the influence they have, and ensure they no longer captain the ship they have pirated we will be well on our way to a thriving America like the world has never seen before. Individually, they are no worse than raindrops, but collectively their actions have created a dangerously flooded river, wildly out of its banks and racing to the sea with a force that cannot be stopped. Along the way, the uncontrolled current, pulled by gravity and pushed by abuse, is uprooting our stately principles and undermining the foundational blocks on which our homes, our churches and our Congress have been built. We cannot survive if these people retain control.

A summary of the causes of our decline is provided below. Each item will be discussed in the pages ahead. The text will not always transition smoothly from section to section as I've tried to keep this as brief as possible. Following are the items I believe are causing our decline:

1. Foundational Problems
   a. A (forgotten) Republic: The majority cannot always rule.
   b. Guiding Principles: Detailed laws will never suffice.
   c. Common Sense: A forgotten friend.
   d. Equal Rights: Special rights have become a trump card.
2. Politics
   a. Two-Party System: Control has become the quest.
   b. Special Interest Groups: They only care about themselves.
   c. Puppet Politicians: Controlled by their party and special interests.
   d. Political Correctness: Prevents politicians from doing the right thing.
   e. Political Catch-22: Doing the right thing will get you fired.

3. Three Groups
   a. Politicians: The root cause of every major problem we have.
   b. Lawyers: Abusing the legal system and controlling the legislature.
   c. Extremists: The few control the many.
4. Undermining Issues
   a. Religion: Time to push back.
   b. Drugs: The first step to failure.
   c. Unwed Motherhood: Inviting poverty and failure.
   d. Failing Education System: Almost one-third of our children fail to complete the twelfth grade.
   e. Crime: We have the highest rates in the world.
   f. Oil Dependency: Dependency on foreign oil is a recipe for disaster.
   g. Environment: We must protect our air and water.
   h. Morals: We cannot legislate everything.
   i. Media: Understand it is biased entertainment with an agenda.
   j. Government: An expanding government beckons socialism.

With the right people in the House of Representatives we have a chance to clarify our guiding principles, put some logic and sanity back into the legal system, and reclaim the ground that the extremists have taken. We can address the issues that are destroying our country, not by talking about them, but by enacting specific changes and wiping clean the years of collective dust that are now obscuring the words of our Constitution. We will rebuild the foundation of our country. By clearly identifying the issues and electing candidates who represent our districts and are committed to fixing what is wrong with America, we can put our country back on track for the next one hundred years. We can leave the country in better shape for our kids than it was when we arrived.

Foundational Problems

If a building is built upon bedrock you can rest comfortably knowing that the foundation is not going to shift. If a country is built on solid foundational principles, it will remain strong as long as the principles are followed. If a building is not built on bedrock, its long-term viability will be in jeopardy.

Once a country allows its foundational principles to wane, it becomes at risk. Our Founding Fathers warned of the need for the citizens of our country to remain vigilant. We have not heeded their warnings. The decline of America can largely be attributed to our neglect of principles. We have enjoyed our freedoms and made the utmost of the free market, but we have not tended to the issues of utmost importance. Over the last fifty years, we have allowed the undermining of our foundation. I contend that we have forgotten five key principles:

1. We are a republic; we are not a pure democracy.
2. Guiding principles should be the basis of our legal system, not legalese and technicalities.
3. Common sense should be applied in all legal matters.
4. All men are created equal; special rights should not be considered a trump card.
5. We must recognize and respect the importance of God in our society.

If we do not address these five items, our country has little hope of remaining the greatest in the world.

If you disagree on any of the first four points, you are wasting your time reading further. If you believe that the majority should always rule, irrespective of our Constitution, my proposal is not for you. If you favor written law over guiding principles, you and I will never agree on anything of importance. If you do not believe common sense could settle most disputes, you and I have very different beliefs in the goodness of man and the simplicity of right versus wrong. Those statements do not suggest that we abandon written law, but merely that we consider our guiding principles and apply common sense in every case. If you believe that every faction of society or each minority group in the country deserves special treatment, then you do not understand the concept of equality or the very essence on which our nation was founded.

I separate the fifth foundational principle intentionally; religion will be explored in a section of its own later in this book. While 92 percent of the nation believes in God, nobody is arguing that the government can or should be able to force any particular religion on any individual. However, we have allowed the pendulum to swing too far in the opposite direction. We now cater to the whims of the 5 percent of the population who are atheists and have allowed them to take God out of too many aspects of our lives.

The atheists have chosen, as is their right, to not accept the "self-evident truth" that we are "endowed by our Creator" as the Declaration declared. But they are working to eliminate God from our country, and that is wrong. James Madison, primary author of the Constitution, said, "We have staked the whole future of civilization, not upon the power of government, far from it. We have staked the future of all our political institutions upon the capacity of mankind for self-government, upon the capacity of each and all of us to govern ourselves according to the Ten Commandments of God." The atheists and ACLU members conveniently overlook this very important perspective. There is a sensible middle ground, which we must find. If we do not, the country we love will continue to fall apart.

POLITICS

When considering the decline of America, it is important to understand how politics and the two-party system are contributing to our demise. The current system prevents any other outcome. The root of the problem is that we have two parties who have lost sight of the purpose of government; their focus has become control and power.

Like two mating rattlesnakes, the parties use each other to keep the political species alive. We are safe from them as long as we keep our distance, but they will fight as soon as we enter what they have claimed as their territory. So determined are the parties to gain the upper hand, they will do whatever they must to obtain 50.1 percent of the vote. Once they have it they will behave as if they have a mandate for every issue their party supports. The problem in the approach is obvious to all except those blinded by the power, or on a quest to re-take it. Let me show you why.

Imagine there are only two issues: taxes and welfare. Call them Issue #1 and Issue #2. The two parties give us two choices: we can be for Issue #1 and for Issue #2, or against both. Those are the only two choices we are given. The problem is that there are actually four op-tions, and even then there is some gray:

> For Issue #1 and For Issue #2
> For Issue #1 and Against Issue #2
> Against Issue #1 and For Issue #2
> Against Issue #1 and Against Issue #2

If you are for one and against the other neither party represents the way you feel. In this simple example, if we assume the population is split evenly on the issues, when the party in power pushes Issue #1 and Issue #2 through the system, only 25 percent of the people will be completely satisfied. If there are three issues, the parties still give us only two choices, but simple math shows there are now eight options, each representing 12.5 percent of the vote:

> For Issue #1, For Issue #2, For Issue #3
> For Issue #1, For Issue #2, Against Issue #3
> For Issue #1, Against Issue #2, For Issue #3
> For Issue #1, Against Issue #2, Against Issue #3
> Against Issue #1, Against Issue #2, Against Issue #3
> Against Issue #1, Against Issue #2, For Issue #3
> Against Issue #1, For Issue #2, Against Issue #3
> Against Issue #1, For Issue #2, For Issue #3

In this example, assume one party supports each issue and the other party is against all three. Each party would represent 12.5 per-cent of the possible views. The party in power would not represent 87.5 percent of the choices. If there are four issues there would be sixteen options, but again, the parties would only cover two of them, each representing 6.25 percent of the population. If there are ten issues, there are twenty million possible views. If there are twenty issues there are 200 quintillion options: 200,000,000,000,000,000,000. As you go through this book you will see there are well over twenty topics and more than a hundred different issues. There is no possible way either of the parties can represent even one percent of the population. The two-party system is fundamentally flawed and unquestionably broken. It guarantees disillusionment if the government insists on writing laws for so many issues. The two parties will never satisfy the desires of our diverse population. This is why we are all so unhappy. We need to legislate differently.

But the parties are entrenched in the current system. The leaders have power, and they have no plans to give it back to the people. The parties now compete against one another, and the needs of the people have been forgotten. Nikita Khrushchev, during the Cuban Missile Crisis, talked about the two sides pulling on each end of a rope trying to gain an advantage, forcing the knot in the middle to get tighter, so tight it could never be untied. It must ultimately be cut out. The Republicans and Democrats are doing exactly this. They are pulling the political rope so firmly, particularly for the last fifty years, that we may never be able to untie the knot they have created. If we have to cut it out we will be left with two separate ropes that can never be rejoined. We must step in before the knot becomes too tight.

The parties, however, are not the only reason things are so bad. Creating three or four or ten parties is not the solution. The second compounding political problem, beyond the two parties, is the special interest groups. Like the parties, they have more influence than they should. Politicians need a million dollars to get elected, and unless they have a million dollars of their own money to spend, they must accept money from someone. Where do you think candidates go to get the million dollars needed to run for office? They go shopping for people with deep pockets who need legislative favor. The groups are not shelling out that kind of money because Candidate Wannabe is a nice guy. No, they demand legislation that will help them do whatever they do better or that will protect their market from competitors.

That brings us to the third problem. Politicians are controlled by the parties that put them on the ballot and the special interest groups that funded their campaign. They must support the party at all times, or risk being Liebermanned out of office. If you aren't familiar with the story, let me give you a quick summary.

Senator Joe Liebermann ran into trouble when he did not toe the Democratic Party line on the war in Iraq. He was their vice presidential nominee in 2000. He didn't support the party platform on the war, so the party ran a different candidate against him in the primary, and with all of its support behind the unknown, the senator was beaten handily. Even the best-intentioned politician has no choice but to serve the party.

There is a reason Bush was able to go six years without a single veto; his party voted together on every issue of importance. Individual politicians knew they had to support the party line. If they did not, they would feel the wrath of the party and likely be replaced by relatives of party members or lawyers with influence, men who have rabidly supported the party line for years and who have money, connections, or both.

The system is set up to take even well-intentioned, honorable people who sincerely want to represent us and, from the very first day, force them to begin compromising their standards to serve their two newfound masters. With the agenda largely determined, at least on the main issues, they become puppets. To hide the truth, politicians are forced to find creative ways to show they are productive, and the results are devastating. They write detailed laws that prevent the use of common sense, that ignore or trample foundational principles, and that destroy the concept of equality. And then they make it worse. They create expansive government programs that attempt to solve the most complex problems of our day, and each program they create pushes our country further into debt, destroys the very essence of our republic, and fails miserably. They manipulate the people to get what they want, and they increase the number of people who depend on government to secure more votes, pushing us closer and closer to pure socialism.

There are a few politicians, particularly in their first term, who have the best of intentions. But the political catch-22 snags them every time. To get elected, they first had to agree to support the party. If they do not, they are replaced like Liebermann or gerrymandered like Jim Maloney, Frank Mascara, or a dozen others. The politician must deliver for his special interest group, and to do so he must gain the support of other politicians. To get that support, he must agree to support projects that his constituents could care less about. In the end, you have 435 politicians agreeing to support each others projects so they can get their project approved. Spending goes through the roof, as each individual politician has no choice but to play the game in order to get the project for their special interest approved. Fiscal responsibility is not possible; it is a political catch-22.

The ultimate catch is a politician's desire to be reelected. Politicians must be politically correct at all times, unable to afford alienating any group or generating any negative publicity that could cost them needed votes. Prevented from speaking their mind, they are trapped in the biggest political catch-22 of all. A politician cannot offend his party, fail those who fund him, or offend any person or group. Imagine a politician who does not support the party line or refuses to support a subsidy for a farming business or legislation for a lobbyist that funded his campaign. Imagine a politician who takes a position against welfare, Social Security, immigration, or any other issue that will alienate some segment of society. His chances for reelection decrease significantly. Do you see the conflict? The results we get are consistently consistent.

Political catch-22s snag every member of the two-party system, every politician who accepts a million dollars, and every incumbent who seeks reelection. Every two years we elect twenty or thirty new politicians, but they immediately get caught in the same trap. The results are the same year after year: rising deficits, declining hope, more government, fewer freedoms, and a country that is three clicks worse than it was two years ago. We need a new way.

Recall Einstein's definition of insanity: "Doing the same thing over and over again and expecting different results." Every two years, we follow the exact same process, and we get the exact same results. We are told we have choice in America, but the choice is always between two clones the parties have selected. We are told that anyone can run and everyone will be considered. Do you believe it? Call "your" party and tell them you want to run for office. Try to run on your own. One of the two hand-selected candidates wins over 99 percent of the time, and we are never happy with either. Yossarian would tell us it is time to either do something differently or to admit that we are insane, though if we are insane we would not be sane enough to realize we are insane—or something like that.

The system is fundamentally flawed. We must do something differently.

THREE GROUPS

We've now covered the broader issues leading to the decline of our country. These are all issues that can only be dealt with by true representatives, which is the main objective of GOOOH. Representatives will be positioned to address all of these issues; politicians cannot. If we can assume we have representatives leading us who are not associated with a party and not indebted to special interest groups, then we know they can act as they believe, not as they are commanded. If we can further assume they are not consumed with getting reelected, political correctness will become irrelevant, and each of the catch-22s will have been solved. Further, these representatives will be positioned to address each of the foundational problems and do the right thing, not the politically correct one.

Representatives can restore our republic, putting an end to a simple majority getting whatever it desires. They can do this by strengthening our guiding principles to match the desires of the predominant majority of our nation. They can clean up the legal system by creating a "Law of Common Sense." They can reestablish that we are a nation with equal rights for all, not special rights for every faction of society. These principles can only be solidified if we have a predominant majority of the population supporting the clarifications, without the political baggage. The changes are possible. Electing true representatives of the people is the most significant thing we can do to save our country. Once we make this commitment, the only challenge will be determining who the best representatives are. The chapter titled "The Plan" will explain how we will determine who is best.

This section of the book focuses on the three groups of people most responsible for our problems: politicians, lawyers, and extremists. There are of course problems with stereotyping, but for these three groups, I trust you are not going to disagree strongly unless you belong to one of them. Each of the groups is described briefly in the next few pages.

POLITICIANS

Milton Friedman warned us about politicians. He predicted, "Even though the men who wield this power initially will be of good will, and even though they may not be corrupted by the power they exercise, the power will both attract and form men of a different stamp." The men of a different stamp have indeed arrived and have succeeded in taking over our government.

My original chapter on politicians was lengthy, and I was tempted to include the entire text; seeing it all in print demonstrates how sorely we need GOOOH to work. But, I think we all get the point. Many of these guys are disgusting. The list of corrupt, power-seeking, special-interest pandering politicians is endless: DeLay, Foley, Ney, Reid, Cunningham, Rostenkowski, Traficant, and dozens of others. If you ask any American to provide an adjective to describe our politicians, almost every response will be negative. The responses in my surveys were 95 percent unfavorable. Here are the words I received, the words used to describe the people running our country:

abusive	arrogant	big-talkers
cheaters	controlling	corrupt
crooked	cunning	dealmakers
deceitful	*dishonest	egotistical

fake	finger-pointers	*greedy
hopeless	hypocritical	idiots
ignorant	immoral	incompetent
inconsistent	ineffective	inept
influenced (easily)	isolated	lazy
*liars	manipulative	me-first
misguided	money-hungry	narcissistic
out-of-touch	partisan	people-pleaser
political	power-hungry	prima-donnas
reelection-focused	salesman	*self-centered
selfish	*self-serving	shallow
slick	smooth	spineless
swayable	two-faced	unethical
unreasonable	untrustworthy	weak
wishy-washy		

* Most common responses

Beyond the adjectives, most politicians share at least two of three traits: above-average wealth; family connections; a law degree. Very few are true representatives of the common man. Roughly 95 percent of all politicians seeking reelection win; we have less change in the House than the Soviet Union had in its Politburo, and the change we do have is often forced by the parties through gerrymandering or Liebermanning (my term for what the Democrats did to Joe Liebermann). Even John F. Kennedy acknowledged the situation and admitted who a politician's true masters are: "Finally, the Senator who follows the independent course of conscience is likely to discover the he has earned the disdain not only of his colleagues in the Senate and his associates in his party, but also that of the all-important contributors to his campaign fund."[33] So much for representing the common man.

Technically speaking, any person in America is allowed to run for office, but it will cost in excess of a million dollars to compete, and they have little chance of winning. "So fed up with the system Americans are, the United States is 139th out of 172 nations in voter turn-out."[34] "In 2002, a non-presidential election year, only 37 percent of adults came to the polls."[35] Term limits would be an easy solution to many of our problems, but even the politicians who get elected on the promise of supporting term limits change their mind. When over a hundred representatives were elected in 1994 promising to support, among other things, term limits, over half failed to keep their promise.[36] In states where term limits have passed, a member of the exiting representative's family assumes the vacated office a large percentage of the time.

Congressional pay is a sweet deal, and the retirement package is out of this world. Representatives make over $168,000 per year and have voted themselves raises of more than $3,100 a year in each of at least the last five years.[37] In one of the most outrageous retirement packages, former Senator Bill Bradley and his wife will reportedly draw $7,900,000 if each lives to their life expectancy. Several Internet sites claim this number to be inaccurate, but then fail to offer what the actual number is. Why? Who are they protecting?[38]

Where are the modern-day equivalents of our Founding Fathers? The men who are pure of heart, loaded with integrity, filled with virtue, and interested in the country we will leave behind for our posterity? Where are the leaders who understand we are a republic, who are willing to support our guiding principles, who believe in equality, and who are not socialists? I am confident they are out there, waiting to step out of their office, factory, church, school, or corn field. People like you must come forward. It is time for the Madison's, Franklin's, and Jefferson's of our day to stand up and be heard. Thomas Jefferson said, "I know of no safe depository of the ultimate powers of society but the people themselves." It is time to take the power from the parties and the politicians and put it back where it belongs—in the hands of everyday people.

Question: Will you vote for term limits of four years (two terms) or less for seats in the U.S. House of Representatives?

LAWYERS

My slam of lawyers is not completely fair. Ninety percent or more of them are perfectly legitimate businessmen operating exactly as the system is designed. I love the joke that 99 percent of lawyers give the other one percent a bad name, but it is just a joke. However, there is a fundamental problem with a small number of lawyers that is a having a profoundly negative effect on our country. This system intends to exclude all lawyers from the process because I can think of no way to sort out the bad ones. I will not be surprised if the system has to give on this point, but for now we're going to exclude lawyers. Let me explain why.

First, the judiciary branch of government consists entirely of lawyers. There is a blatant and obvious conflict of interest in having a lawyer write a law as a legislator and then benefit from that law as a litigator or counsel. This is particularly true with high stakes litigation where class-action lawsuits and boardroom maneuvers are involved.

The second conflict has to do with the pervasiveness of lawyers. We've all heard it said that you can hardly go to the bathroom without a lawyer's permission, and the statement rings true. We cannot start a business without the involvement of lawyers, and they must be consulted on almost every transaction. They insist we sign documents we don't understand before we buy or sell anything of substance, use software on our computers, or accept the job that will feed our family. Lawyers are recommended to draft prenuptial agreements before we get married and then are required to protect your half of the estate if you get divorced. We have ambulance-chasing lawyers who will find someone to extract money from if we happen to get hurt and class-action lawyers who will extend the warranty on our Honda for 3,000 miles while they make enough money to buy an entire fleet of BMWs. We need lawyers to prepare our estate before we die, and our family needs them to divide it after we are gone.

The Democrats least favorite Republican in his time, Newt Gingrich, wrote that he does "virtually nothing without the advice and involvement" of his attorney.[39] And he would like to become our president and lead the effort to reform our legal system. Can you visualize a big, fat, smiling fox standing in front of a hen house?

Forty-five percent of our legislators are lawyers. Do you think if the number were zero we would have less need for litigation in our lives? Would we focus more on clarifying guiding principles and less on establishing pervasive laws? Do you believe that emphasizing common sense and equality would serve us better than litigating ambiguous legislation and debating obtuse technicalities? Removing lawyers from the House of Representatives would allow our nation to operate as our Founding Fathers intended.

The final reason I believe lawyers are contributing to the demise of our country and why I suggest we eliminate them from the GOOOH system is the ACLU, an organization dominated by lawyers. If the legal profession cannot find a way to control a group that argues for the "rights" of NAMBLA members, the KKK, Madelyn Murray O'Hare, and murderers, I want to try.

There are over 750,000 lawyers in America.[40] We have one lawyer for every two Elementary school teachers. We have more lawyers than we do doctors or policemen. We have one lawyer for every one and a half truck drivers. Take notice of how many eighteen wheelers are on the road the next time you drive down the highway.[41] The United States has 70 percent of the world's lawyers but only 5 percent of the world's population.[42] We have three times as many lawyers per capita as England and twenty times as many as Japan.[43] Not surprisingly, with twenty times more lawyers, we have thirty times more lawsuits than Japan, one of our primary trade partners.[44]

Alexis de Tocqueville warned us about lawyers in 1815:

> The government of democracy is favorable to the political power of lawyers; for when the wealthy, the noble, and the prince are excluded from the government, the lawyers take possession of it…The lawyers do not, indeed, wish to overthrow the institutions of democracy, but they constantly endeavor to turn it away from its real direction by means which are foreign to its nature.…If I were asked where I place the American aristocracy, I should reply, without hesitation, that it is not among the rich, who are united by no common tie, but that it occupies the judicial bench and the bar.[45]

The institutions of democracy have been turned away from the intended direction. Some of the wealthiest men in America have secured their riches by litigating: Peter G. Angelos, who used proceeds of asbestos litigation to buy the Baltimore Orioles; Dickie Scruggs, the inventor (if that's the right word) of tobacco litigation; and Bill Lerach, king of shareholder lawsuits against Silicon Valley firms. Lawyers lie to free child murderers (Feldman and Boyce defending David Westerfield[46]), deceive to gain public attention (Mike Nifong and the Duke Lacrosse team[47]), and behave reprehensibly to win settlements (see *Robertson v. Flatley*[48]). These are not exceptions.[49] If we wish to restore any sense of reasonableness to our nation, we must find a way to minimize the pervasiveness and influence of lawyers. Removing them from our House of Representatives is a sensible approach.

> **Question:** Will you vote to amend the Constitution to exclude people with a law degree from serving in the House of Representatives?

EXTREMISTS

The third group of people negatively impacting our country, the group that has trampled the concept of equal rights and walked all over the predominant majority, is made up of the hellish minorities I call extremists. Bill O'Reilly calls them "witch-hunters," Rush Limbaugh "wacko's," Mona Charen "do-gooders," and the ACLU affectionately refers to them as their best friends. Whatever you call them, extremists are manipulating the words of the Constitution against the will of the people and using legal technicalities to suit their often perverse, amoral agendas. They have taken the words of a document, which once were as sweet as honey, and soured them so they now have the acidic taste of a stale wine. Our country is a republic, intended to operate upon the guiding principles established in our Constitution. Two hundred years later, time and ambiguity have left us in urgent need of a few clarifications. It is time to restate a few of the important principles which should be directing our country and our courts. The voice of the predominant majority should be heard, not silenced by morally incorrect "wackos." We need to put an end to their subversive attacks on our Constitution and our nation.

There are several groups that I consider extremists. These groups include the KKK, NAMBLA, the American Civil Liberties Union (ACLU), and lobbyists. Each manipulates the words of our Constitution and the technicalities of our legal system to advance their single-issue agendas. Each is playing a major role in the demise of our nation. Without sacrificing our freedoms, there is a straightforward way to control this outlandish behavior and restore equal rights for all instead of special rights for a few.

I will not attempt to cover each of the groups in detail here, but will take a minute to warn you about the worst of the bunch: the ACLU. The mission of the ACLU was well defined by its founder, Roger Baldwin, who said the following when forming the group, "I am for socialism, disarmament, and ultimately for abolishing the state itself as an instrument of violence and compulsion. I seek social ownership of property, the abolition of the propertied class...Communism is the goal."[50]

Current members of the ACLU may try to argue communism is no longer the goal, but their actions contradict their words. In 1958, former FBI agent Cleon Skoussen wrote *The Naked Communist*. In it, he outlined the forty-five goals of the Communist Party, which included:

16. Use technical decisions of the courts to weaken basic American institutions by claiming their activities violate civil rights.
24. Eliminate all laws governing obscenity by calling them "censorship" and a violation of free speech and free press.
26. Present homosexuality, degeneracy, and promiscuity as "normal, natural, and healthy."
29. Discredit the American Constitution by calling it inadequate, old-fashioned, out of step with modern needs, and a hindrance to cooperation between nations on a worldwide basis.
30. Discredit the American Founding Fathers. Present them as selfish aristocrats who had no concern for the "common man."

33. Eliminate all laws or procedures which interfere with the op-
    eration of the Communist apparatus.

I can find no difference in that original goal and the group's current practices. An example of what these guys represent: The North
America Man-Boy Love Association (NAMBLA), a group that is
arguing not only for the right for adult males to have sex with young
boys, but also for the right to display what 99 percent of Americans
would call outrageous filth. They were trying to display the following
article on their Internet site: "Recommendations for how to seduce
and rape young boys." Guess who defended them?[51] That is correct,
the ACLU.

When the KKK needs legal help, where do they turn? That's
right, the ACLU. Who was the lawyer of Madalyn O'Hare, who was
able to get God expelled from our schools? You got it, the ACLU. If
a seventy-five-year-old convicted serial killer, on death row for over
twenty years, begins suffering from a heart ailment and needs a trans-
plant to continue living, who do you think files a lawsuit and argues
in the courts that not providing the needed medical assistance is cruel
and unusual punishment?

The ACLU is recognized as an extremist group by anyone who is
not affiliated with it. FOX News host Bill O'Reilly said, "Hitler would
be a card-carrying ACLU member. So would Stalin. Castro probably
is. And so would Mao Zedong." What they are doing is legal, technically, but seldom passes the common sense sniff test. Their actions would
never be supported by the predominant majority of the population.
Here are a few more examples of what the ACLU has fought for:

- They threatened to sue Los Angeles County unless it removed
  a tiny cross from its official seal. The ACLU Southern California chapter said Monday the "Latin cross" on the nearly
  fifty-year-old seal is a religious symbol and represents a gov-
  ernment-sponsored endorsement of Christianity. Check out
  the outrageous symbol on the Web at http://newcovenant.
  blogspot.com/2004/05/aclu-lunacy.html.

- They threatened to sue McKinley High School in Honolulu, forcing them to cease reciting a poem that had been read on ceremonial occasions since 1927 because one of the lines mentions a love for God.[52]
- They are for free speech when NAMBLA is trying to seduce teenagers, but against free speech when it comes to the celebration of Christmas. They may claim they are not, but they fail to remember the following:[53]
  - They sued the Bossier Parish (Louisiana) public school system for displaying a Nativity scene and holding a teacher-led prayer group.
  - They threatened to sue Balch Elementary School (Massachusetts) to prevent it from displaying a Nativity scene.
  - Bowing to the ACLU's complaint that using the word in its calendar was "an endorsement of a particular religion," the Newton County (Georgia) school board removed "Christmas" from its calendars.
  - They represented a family of atheists who complained the Gowanda (New York) public schools allowed religious songs at school events. Two of the songs to which the family objected were "White Christmas" and "God Bless America." Earlier, the schools had tried accommodating the family by changing Christmas break to winter break.
  - They sued the Cherry Hill School District (New Jersey) for permitting the display of a Christmas tree, a Chanukah menorah, and a Kwanzaa candelabra. The policy "blatantly disregards the guarantee of separation of church and state," according to the ACLU.
- They support gay marriage and polygamy.
- They support Internet pornography, including guaranteed access from public schools and libraries, on the grounds of free speech.
- They are fighting a Katrina memorial built on private land with private funds because it contains a cross.

- They are fighting to remove chaplains from the military and all prisons.
- They are fighting to ensure International law takes precedence over our Constitution.

Would you be surprised to read some day that the advancement of the ACLU was the foreshadowing of Abbadon's rise from the abyss? They continue to bring forth manipulative litigation from a seemingly bottomless pit. The ACLU throws souls under the altar with no care for our children or our society. It is impossible to understand their devilish intentions or their revolting efforts, but it is within our power to stop them, if we will just organize our effort and hold fast to our convictions.

I believe we should quit doing business with any lawyer or law firm that affiliates with an ACLU member. A simple rule of thumb is that whatever they are for, we are against, and whatever they are against, we are for. They support the most unbelievable factions of our society, including those who abuse children. If you want more information, take a look at *The ACLU vs. America*, written by Sears and Osten. Next time you need a lawyer, first ask them if they support the ACLU. If they do, run.

Have you ever wondered who in the heck is funding these guys? How do they get enough money to pay all of these high-brow lawyers, and who are the lawyers who work for this creepy organization? Further, what companies would hire the lawyers when they aren't doing work for the ACLU? According to guidestar.org, which tracks financial information on nonprofit organizations, the ACLU Foundation had net assets of $175,909,869 as of May 31, 2004. They received an $8 million gift in 2003 from member Peter B. Lewis, who is also chairman of Progressive Insurance, the largest individual donation ever received by the ACLU. The Ford Foundation provided a seven million dollar grant in 1999 (though the ACLU and the Ford Foundation have more recently disagreed over grant terms), which Lewis matched with another seven million to bring the total to fourteen million.[54]

If you want to make your voice heard, let's show Ford and Progressive Insurance what we think of their support. I actually own a Ford truck, but I swear I will never again buy a vehicle from that company, nor will I ever look to Progressive to insure my vehicle. I'd rather see the gecko do a few more commercials and let the leaders of Progressive find someone else to buy their product than support NAMBLA.

I certainly agree not all ACLU cases are destructive or wrong, but too many of them are. Members of the ACLU have vastly different views on what America should be, and as lawyers, they are manipulating the legal system to get their way. It is time to put them out of business. If there is a reason that the lawyers of the ACLU, who are surely intelligent enough to comprehend the radical, disruptive nature of their organization, can justify their actions, I have never seen it articulated. The only conclusion I can draw is that they are radical extremists.

There are many other extremist groups, but I deem the ACLU the most destructive to our nation. But not everyone agrees. A few believe that it is more important to argue for absolute rights, even if it means protecting child molesters, serial killers, or proud racists. What do you think?

Question: Would you support a nationwide boycott of the ACLU and its lawyers?

UNDERMINING ISSUES

We have reviewed the people destroying our nation. Now it is time to look at individual issues that are leading to our country's demise. The undermining of religion, which most would consider another one of the forgotten foundation principles, must be preempted. Nobody is arguing for mandatory church attendance or the adoption of a national religion, but we have allowed the extremists to push their agenda too far.

The prevalence of drugs in our society has reached epidemic proportions and is triggering failure in a dozen different ways. The number of children born to unwed mothers is a crisis and the failure of schools deplorable. Our dependence on foreign oil is comparable to an addiction to crack and every bit as bad. The air and water around every large city has become difficult to breath and dangerous to drink. The media promotes morons and throws gasoline on any fire they can find in order to improve ratings, while the morals in our country continue to decay. Perhaps worst of all, the reach of our government increases day after day. We are amassing a debt that we ourselves will not pay, instead deferring it so that our children will be forced to bear the burden, and accelerating our conversion to socialism under the guise of compassion.

We'll now look briefly at each of the causes leading to our decline. I include one question at the end of the review of each of the causes to provide an example of the questions that will be asked. The complete list of questions is included in the chapter titled "Candidate Questionnaire."

RELIGION

Recall the quote from James Madison, primary author of the Constitution: "We have staked the future of all our political institutions upon the capacity of mankind for self-government, upon the capacity of each and all of us to govern ourselves according to the Ten Commandments of God."

As a society, we have misplaced the importance of religion, allowing it be pushed into the basement of our lives. We have lost sight of the importance of God. The 92 percent of us who believe in God must insist on bringing Him back into the mainstream of our country. I don't mean to impose religion on any individual, but to ensure religion is mixed into the cement that forms our foundation, grown in the lumber used to frame our homes, and sprinkled in the asphalt shingles that shelter us from the rain.

As of the mid-1990s, America is home to an estimated five hundred thousand churches, temples, and mosques, over two thousand religious denominations, and an unknown number of independent churches.[55] Harvard economist Richard B. Freeman found, "Church attendance is a better predictor of who escapes poverty, drug addiction, and crime than family income, family structure, and other variables."[56]

The 5 percent of Americans who are atheists need to take a step back and ask if they are winning the battle, yet losing the war. George Washington said, "Let not that man claim the title of Patriot who labors to undermine our country's fundamental pillars of Religion and Morality." Are the atheists and ACLU lawyers listening? What harm is caused by allowing a prayer at a football game or hanging the Ten Commandments on the wall? Why do they insist on denigrating something that is so important to so many others? More importantly, why do we allow them to progress their agenda?

The Jefferson Memorial proudly displays one of Mr. Jefferson's favorite quotes: "God who gave us life gave us liberty. Can the liberties of a nation be secure when we have removed a conviction that these liberties are the gift of God?" There have been many other leaders who have also expressed the importance of God in our country. William Penn, the first great hero of American liberty said, "If we will not be governed by God, we will be ruled by tyrants." Dwight Eisenhower said, "Our form of government has no sense unless it is founded in a deeply religious faith, and I don't care what it is."

"The smartest people in history have believed in a higher power. Socrates. Plato. Aristotle. Augustine. Maimonides. Aquinas. Da Vinci. Copernicus. Newton. Jefferson. Einstein. What unites them is not faith in the Judeo-Christian God, or even in a personal god, but rather in a divine presence whose existence somehow sustains the natural world."[57] If we asked candidates the following question, how would you like them to answer?

> **Question:** Will you vote to amend the Constitution to specifically affirm that we are a nation under God, that God is welcome in all that we do, but no man can be forced to participate in worship at any time or in any way?

Drugs

Children are exposed to drugs far too early in life, at an age where they clearly are not yet mature enough to fully understand the long-term impact of the decision they are forced to make, and in a situation where the peer pressure may be greater than their inner strength. For many, that exposure vectors them on a misguided path from which they never recover. We must eliminate drugs from schools and the hands of minors. The vast majority of children who have major problems at school or get in trouble with the law are experimenting with drugs. Mensch and Kandel demonstrated in 1988 that the longer drug use is delayed, the greater the probability a student will graduate. I have yet to find a sane, reasonable person who questions the correlation. Whether drugs are the cause of problems for 60 percent, 80 percent, or 100 percent of our kids is irrelevant. The number should be approaching zero.

Drugs lead to failure in school and, for many, a life of crime. Once people become criminals, they tend to stay criminals, as evidenced by the ghastly two-thirds recidivism rate. We have far too many criminals in our society, and worse, our prison system is not an adequate rehabilitator. We face complex, multi-faceted problems in society, but there are several core issues, most notably drugs, that if truly addressed, would go a long way in correcting them.

The National Institute on Drug Abuse reported, "In 2005, 50.4 percent of 12th graders had used an illicit drug, 38.2 percent of 10th graders, and 21.4 percent of 8th graders. For alcohol, the numbers are 75.1 percent, 63.2 percent, and 41 percent, respectively."[58] I believe the reported numbers are low. "High school students who use alcohol or other substances frequently are up to five times more likely than other students to drop out of school."[59] The Swedes have a zero tolerance policy on the use of drugs. "According to the ESPAD (European School Survey Project on Alcohol and Other Drugs) research, only 7 percent of Swedish schoolchildren aged 15–16 (our 10th graders) have used cannabis at any time."[60]

To take drugs out of the hands of impressionable minors, America will have to show a level of fortitude that we have not demonstrated in the last fifty years. We will have to make an example of the bad guys, the dealers who sell drugs to minors. Why we are so "forgiving" when it comes to punishing drug dealers is mind-boggling to me. We need to take a position that is a thousand times firmer than what we take today. Are you willing to take a rock-solid stand and put an end to the decline of our country? How would you like your representative to answer this question?

> **Question:** Will you vote to impose a penalty of life in prison or death for anyone convicted of selling drugs to a minor, excepting only to reduce the sentence to twenty years if information is provided that leads to the conviction of their supplier?

UNWED MOTHERS

Unwed motherhood invites failure into the home. Single-parent families promise poverty to almost 30% of those who choose this lifestyle.[61] They are distantly behind two-parent families when it comes to childhood accomplishment and consistently unable to provide the environment that children need to achieve success in life. There are exceptions, but they are rare.

For black[62] women under the age of twenty-five, almost nine out of ten newborns will live in a house without their father. The number is ugly, though not as bad, for whites and browns[63] as well, with numbers of 25 percent and 35 percent, respectively.[64] We might as well hand each of those kids the keys to a 500 horsepower race car the day they turn thirteen, give them a fifth of Jack Daniels, and turn them lose on the highway to hell. Why do you think we have so many young men in prison?

The chance of these children living a successful life is dismal, and the numbers are getting worse generation after generation. The issue of unwed motherhood must be addressed; our welfare system, as currently designed, is not the solution. The number of children born to a single mom is an appalling statement about the state of our society.

There are several things we could do to immediately address this problem, but political incorrectness prevents most of them. Imagine if we completely eliminated drugs from school and the hands of minors; made birth control more accessible; separated young boys and girls during high school; ensured our youth had less idle time; and better educated young girls on the realities of single motherhood. The ostrich approach is not working, and teaching abstinence is having little effect. We must get beyond political correctness and take action, or soon half of all children will be guaranteed an excellent opportunity to fail miserably in life. Imagine if your representative had to answer the following question. Would a candidate be run out of town if he dared to answer affirmatively?

Question: Will you vote to make birth control pills available for free to every girl under the age of twenty-one?

FAILING EDUCATION SYSTEM

The public education system works reasonably well for those who take advantage, but the problem is with the 50 percent who don't. Thirty percent fail to graduate, and I suspect another 20 percent are given a diploma because it is easier for administrators to do so than deal with the problem. The high school graduation rate today is almost exactly what it was when the Department of Education was founded: 71.4 percent in 1980 and 72.2 percent in 2006.[65] National graduation statistics for the class of 1998 (the last year for which I found this data) are as follows:[66]

- 78 percent of "white" students graduated.
- 56 percent of "black" students graduated.
- 54 percent of "brown" students graduated.
- Georgia had the lowest overall graduation rate in the nation with only 54 percent of students graduating. In 2000, Florida fell to last place with a 55 percent graduation rate.
- Less than 50 percent of black students graduated in seven different states.
- Less than 50 percent of brown students graduated in eight states.
- The city of Cleveland had a graduation rate of 28 percent, with Memphis, Milwaukee, and Columbus close behind.

We spend more on education than any country in the world, but money is not the solution. "According to the National Center for Education Statistics, Washington, D.C., spends $15,000 per pupil, the most in the nation, but students there come in dead last on the Nation's Report Card. In 2003, 90 percent of fourth- and eighth-graders in D.C. failed reading proficiency."[67] We have significantly increased the number of administrators in our systems and have 257 active government programs intended to make the situation better,[68] but there has been no improvement whatsoever.

Teaching is one of the most important but least respected professions in America. We protect the rights of students and treat teachers and administrators who attempt to maintain discipline in our schools like criminals. Unions ignore students and protect inept teachers, ensuring the worst teachers receive the same horrendous salary as the best. While we are fortunate many educators choose to follow their passion, we know, but choose not to admit, that the system discourages our finest students from becoming teachers. The problems are blatantly obvious, but nobody dares to confront them.

If a student cannot graduate from high school, what are the odds he will become a productive member of our society? Roughly half of those who fail to graduate obtain a GED, but imagine the challenges these young adults will face trying to get ahead in life. Thirty-seven million Americans live in poverty,[69] and over 15 percent of the population receives some kind of welfare.[70] "Nearly two-thirds of all state prisoners in 1991 had less than a high school education. One-third of all prisoners were unemployed at the time of their arrests."[71] How do we allow this to continue?

Do you deny the correlation between single moms, poverty, welfare, drug use, and failing to graduate? If we want to improve our country, we must become significantly better at educating all of our children, but to do so, there are other important issues that must be addressed in parallel. Lyndon Johnson said, "The answer for all our national problems comes down to a single word and that word is education."[72] Since he made that statement we have not improved by even one percent. We can improve, but it will take some politically incorrect actions.

Our current legislators do not have the fortitude to take the steps needed to correct our system. They fear the unions and the teachers and dare not risk alienating them. It is time to take politics out of the equation. How would you want your representative to answer the following question?

> **Question:** Would you support a federal law that requires the removal of the bottom 3 percent of teachers in each school district each year, and a graduated pay scale that includes paying the top 25 percent of teachers double what the bottom 25 percent earn?

CRIME

By 1991, the crime rate was 313 percent higher than the 1960 crime rate.[73] That is shocking growth, but what has been the impact since we started getting tough on crime in the eighties? "The homicide rate (today) is at its lowest level since 1965. Overall the national crime rate was 3,982 crimes per 100,000 residents, down 17.6 percent from 4,852 crimes per 100,000 residents thirty years earlier in 1974.... The homicide rate decreased continuously between 1991 and 2000 from 9.8 homicides per 100,000 persons to 5.5 per 100,000, it has remained level through 2005... The year 2005 was overall the safest year in over twenty years. Violent crime overall, however, is still at the same level as in 1974, despite having decreased steadily since 1991."[74] Incarceration has gone way up and costs are sky high, but at least crime in every major category peaked somewhere between 1991 and 1994. In actual numbers:

- violent crime fell from 1,932,270 incidents in 1992 to 1,390,695 incidents in 2005;
- property crime fell from 12,961,100 to 10,166,159;
- murders fell from 24,530 to 16,692;
- forcible rape fell from 109,060 to 93,934;

The same trend holds for robbery, aggravated assault, burglary, theft, and vehicle theft.[75]

When you hear people complain about the unfairness of tougher drug laws and longer sentences, refer them to these numbers. Incarceration costs are a concern, but the eight thousand fewer murders each year is a nice return on the investment. "According to the Department of Justice, the tripling of prison inmates between 1975 and 1989 prevented 390,000 murders, rapes, robberies, and assaults in just the year 1989."[76]

Still, we have a long way to go. "Each day in California there are six more murders, 27 rapes, 38 arsons, 180 robberies, and 360 instances of assault."[77] "Approximately thirteen million people (almost 5 percent of the U.S. population) are victims of crime each year, and one and a half million are victims of violent crime."[78] There are still over sixteen thousand murders per year. While we are doing a lot to put away the bad guys, we also "release 1,600 inmates per day, often with no training or preparation for the real world."[79] Data indicates that the criminals who are released come out more hardened and more likely to commit further crimes. Recidivism rates that hover around 67 percent strongly support this position.

At the end of 2005 the United States incarcerated 2,320,359 people.[80] That same year, the total federal, state, and local adult correctional population—incarcerated or in the community—grew by 60,700 to over 7 million. About 3.2 percent of the (male) U.S. adult population, one of every thirty-two adults, was incarcerated on probation or on parole. Of this total, 4,162,536 were on probation, 784,408 were on parole, 747,529 were in jails, and 1,446,269 were in state and federal prisons; roughly 1 in every 136 was behind bars.[81] Additionally, there were slightly less than a hundred thousand juveniles in prison in 2005. The incarceration rate in the United States is four times the world average.[82]

We have the highest numerical prison population, 714 per 100,000, of any nation that keeps statistics. The rate in America is generally five to eight times that of the Western European nations and Canada The rate in England and Wales, for example, is 142 persons imprisoned per 100,000 residents while in Norway it is 59 per 100,000.[83] The incarceration rates in Sweden, Japan, and India were 82, 61, and 30 per 100,000. These numbers are one-tenth to one-twentieth what they are in the United States![84] Assuming recent inceration rates remain unchanged, an estimated one of every twenty Americans (5 percent) can be expected to serve time in prison during their lifetime.[85]

It is estimated that about 2,250,000 children have incarcerated parents on any day of the year.[86] Youths with a parent in prison are seven times more likely to be involved in the criminal court system and spend time in jail or prison themselves.[87] In 2005, there were 1,278,948 juveniles arrested.[88]

Some of the most alarming statistics involve repeat juvenile offenders. Among juveniles with no prior referrals, four in ten returned to juvenile court. Among juveniles fourteen or younger with at least one prior referral, three-quarters returned to juvenile court. Most interesting is that they show the percent of juveniles who return to court more than *seven* times.[89] If you have been to court seven times, and you are twelve-years-old or younger, 96 percent of the time you will be back again. Is anyone in the world surprised by that statistic? If a child continues to get in trouble after a second or third trip before a judge, is there any hope for rehabilitation without doing something drastically different? Do you think the system we have is working?

Are we too soft on crime, or too hard? Where would you want your representative to stand on this question?

> **Question:** Will you vote to remove juveniles from their parent(s) after their third arrest, sending them to live in a "boot camp" that focuses on education and discipline?

Oil Dependence

In 1972, the United States imported 28 percent of its oil. Today we import 55 percent and projections show that twenty-five years from now the number will be 70 percent. We will import 50 percent of our oil from the Middle East by 2025.[90] Overall, the United States consumes 25 percent of the oil produced in the world each year.[91] Our dependency on oil is growing and our dependency on the radical Middle East is nearing epidemic proportions. Competition for oil with China, India, Russia, and other developing parts of the world will drive prices much higher than they are today. Investors like George Soros and Bill Browder have predicted prices as high as $262 a barrel, four to five times higher than where it was in 2006.[92] Of course nobody really knows, but few expect it to remain at today's levels.

Some predict we are running out of oil, but those predictions continue to prove false. Our problem has never been the lack of oil; it is always the politics of oil. It is possible and likely that there will be another major increase in price when Iran goes to war, or there is a coup in Venezuela or a major accident at one of our refineries, but it will be temporary. It will be painful, but not permanent. "Every major U.S. recession of the past three decades has been preceded by an increase in the price of oil."[93] If we want to control the stability of our economy and improve our environment, we need to either have more control over those who provide oil to us or less dependence on it.

While part of me wishes we were running out of oil and that we had to change, we are not. Our problem is not availability. The problems we have are (1) our dependence on unstable and unpredictable parts of the world, and (2) the impact oil is having on our environment and our health. There are several alternatives to oil, but our politicians will never support any of them in earnest.

The Democrats claim they are environmentally friendly but have not done anything more significant to reduce our dependence on oil than the Republicans. They say they will if they are elected, but their track record proves their words are nothing more than idle promises. They accept money from the oil and energy companies during their campaigns in the same way the Republicans do. And just as bad, they have failed to offer any significant ideas on how to end our dependence on the Middle East. Hillary Clinton, leading Democratic nominee for president in 2008, recently had this to say, "I want to *take* those profits (from oil companies), and I want to put them into a strategic energy fund that will begin to fund alternative, smart energy."[94] Wow! She wants to *take* their profits. Not tax them or take away the billion dollar tax breaks that she approved, but take them. That sounds like communism, and the scary part is, that's not a surprising statement from Hillary. She and her friends throw a lot of rocks, but have you ever seen or heard either party suggest a viable alternative?

Viable alternatives exist. The time has come to think big and be bold. An incremental solution, such as methanol, is like pouring a glass of hot water in a cold bath to try to make it hotter; the impact is insignificant.

When we think of what we should do the choice seems pretty simple: we need to find an alternative to oil. Oil affects the air we breathe, pollutes our water, and creates a dangerous dependence on a radical part of the world. To enable such a shift, we need to cut all ties between the government and "Big Oil." Rather than debating the separation of church and state, it may be more productive to debate the separation of government and oil companies.

Question: Will you vote to reduce our dependence on foreign oil by at least 5 percent year over year each year you are in office?

ENVIRONMENT

The environment is an interesting, controversial, and emotional topic that is worthy of extensive discussion. Air in our cities is filled with smog, rivers and lakes near our towns are polluted, and toxic waste is everywhere, evidenced by the Superfund list. Businesses continue to damage the environment, and our air, water, and land is no longer as pristine as it once was. Our government refuses to work toward a solution on any environmental issue of significance.

Democrats blame the Republicans, claiming they only care about profits, and Republicans blame the Democrats, claiming they do not care about property rights or the economy, while most of us wish they would both shut up so we can find a sensible middle ground. The issue has become emotional and political, and nobody in office is doing anything other than talking. The issue has become so divisive that it cannot be debated reasonably. Endangered species have become pawns manipulated by extreme environmentalists to get their way, and in so doing, they have destroyed the environmental movement's credibility.

Global warming has become such a controversial debate that it cannot be discussed rationally. The Kyoto protocol has become a political wedge. Bureaucracy has taken common sense out of the equation, and economics have become either irrelevant or the only thing that matters, depending on who you listen to. Businessmen point to lunatics chaining themselves to trees and lawyers using insects the size of peanuts to prevent development as proof of how insane the environmentalists have become. Environmentalists counter that such actions are the only way they can prevent the abuse sponsored by the Republicans. Nobody is happy, and the situation continues to decline.

There are many important questions to ask, but the two I find most interesting are listed here.

> **Question:** Will you vote to only apply the Endangered Species Act to animals that are larger in mass than a golf ball (i.e., eliminate protection for species such as salamanders, crickets, and spiders) unless a vital ecological role can be proven?

> **Question:** Will you vote to require annual reductions in total "greenhouse" emissions by 5 percent year over year?

MEDIA

The media cannot be trusted as an accurate source of information. They only tell us what they want us to hear, in a biased way that supports their agenda and in a seductive manner calculated to influence our decision to stay tuned to their show. If we support their position that is fine, but they are most interested in ensuring we are watching their station. They are not here to educate us or to help us understand the facts so that we can make informed decisions; they exist to make money, and to do that they need ratings. They are blatantly biased to both the left and the right, depending on which demographic their sponsor wants them to attract. They have anchors, reporters, and correspondents who mislead, misquote, and manipulate the information we hear or the images we are exposed to in order to make their point.

When Alexis de Tocqueville visited America he "singled out the independence of the press, the ease with which one might set up his own newspaper, the total absence of a centralized press," as a key mitigator in the mass tyranny he feared. Richard Heffner, commenting on the works of Tocqueville in 1956 had a very different view, articulating that "today the American press is marked by a constantly declining number of independent publications, by the rise of great newspaper chains, and by a generally pervasive emphasis upon the manufacture of public opinion, through the various means of mass communications."[95] That was over fifty years ago. It has become far worse.

If a media outlet desires to tell a story, any story, they can find data to support whatever position they want, and they are superb at presenting it in a manner that makes their view appear valid. The media has mastered the process. We need to recognize the media for what it is. They may call it the news, but 50 percent or more of what they sell is entertainment.

When people complain that the media is biased, I say, "So what?" It is biased both ways. The Republicans dominate talk radio, with Rush Limbaugh leading the charge, and Neil Boortz (a Libertarian, but much closer to Republicans than Democrats), Hugh Hewitt, and a hundred or more others spreading their gospel. The liberals control print media. The *New York Times*, *LA Times*, and most newspapers lean strongly to the left, as do all of the major TV outlets, including ABC, CBS, NBC, and CNN. FOX News, clearly friendly to the conservatives, is the one exception. It's hard to make a case that one party has more media power than the other. I guess it depends on where you go for your news.

The key point in all of this is that the media should not be a contributor to our decline, and it will not be if we will accept it for what it is: entertainment. Here's a question for our candidates. I hope this is an easy one.

> **Question:** Will you vow to support a completely free press at all times?

MORALS

John Quincy Adams said, "Our Constitution was made only for moral and religious people. It is wholly inadequate for the government of any other." When you hear people express frustration with America, recognize how often it is because of the actions of amoral members of our society, most notably politicians, lawyers, and extremists.

There will always be amoral, dishonorable people—a sad but uncontested fact. Should the government tell us what behavior is acceptable, defining what our values or morals should be? Should we censure those who consistently do things that the predominant majority consider amoral, restricting what they can do, where they can go, or what they can say? Should they be fined or boycotted? What role, if any, should our government have in such matters?

Moral bankruptcy was personified by Bill Clinton. Not only did he have sex with a girl half his age in the most prestigious, practically sacrosanct, office in the world, he abused his position of power to do so, and then lied to the entire nation about his behavior. The only saving grace was that we had come to expect such behavior from the man. When it comes to setting a poor example, Madonna is like a virgin compared to Clinton. He rehearsed his response so that he could look us in our TV camera eyes and be convincing when he lied.

The morals of our society have eroded so far that New York six-year-olds were actually read to in class from an explicit lesbian advocacy text titled *Heather Has Two Mommies*.[96] As Jerry Seinfeld said, "Not that there's anything wrong with it," but why would grade-school administrators try to force their lifestyle choices on a six-year-old child? Do you think the school's administrators have an agenda? Aldous Huxley in *Confessions of a Professional Free Thinker* wrote, "We were opposed to morality because it interfered with our sexual freedom."[97]

In the case of Danielle Van Damme, defense lawyers tried to incriminate her parents for the murder when they knew without any doubt that their client, David Westerfield, was guilty. He had led officials to the body. Yet the lawyers were determined to get the best deal they could for their client. I think they should have argued the case on its merits and then sent the b*****d to rot somewhere warm. "Winning at all costs" is a great motivational phrase, but it cannot be taken literally. Nevertheless, it has somehow moved to the top of America's

Ten Commandments. Is it too much to ask for honesty in our legal system? Shouldn't we insist on enforcing some kind of a penalty on those who knowingly misrepresent the truth or intentionally fail to share it?

I do not believe we should attempt to legislate morality; the efforts would surely be in vain. However, we should insist that our leaders live to a higher standard, our legal system permits only the truth, and our educators follow an appropriately pointed moral compass.

The lack of clear, guiding principles has led to a precipitous weakening in the moral fabric of our country, allowing morals that seemed clear when our nation was founded to decay to a point almost beyond recognition. The morals supporting our country today are nothing more than pillars of plastic. Actions like those of our former president, while reprehensible, are not legislatable in my opinion. Guidance, however, can and should be provided. What do you think? How would you want your representative to answer this question?

Question: Will you vote for laws that legislate amoral behavior?

GOVERNMENT

The final undermining issue contributing to the decline of our country, and it is a big one, is our government. Our nation was formed with the crystal-clear intention of ensuring that government remained limited. It was expected to do a few basic things, and be limited unless the people gave it specific power via constitutional amendment. The concept has been completely lost on those ruining our country.

Generation after generation, as those in power have insisted on increasing their control, our government has expanded its reach with each administration. Like a wild vine that has been allowed to grow untrimmed for decades, it now fully engulfs the structure it was initially intended to accent. As government efforts are considered individually, most can be viewed as well-intentioned. Nobody argues with concepts like treating the ill, educating our children, caring for the elderly, or taking care of the poor. But there is a fine line between a republic and socialism, and it seems we have reached the point in

America's life where we must decide which type of government we wish to have. The two cannot coexist.

Whether we are discussing the causes of our nation's decline or reviewing our failing systems and the issues we have failed to address, the common thread throughout is government: big government programs that never end, inefficient government bureaucracies that wander aimlessly, spending that is out of control, and issues the government will not resolve.

Thomas Paine warned us, "Government, even in its best state, is but a necessary evil; in its worst state, an intolerable one." George Washington expressed the same sentiment when he said, "Government is not reason, it is not eloquence, it is force; like fire, a troublesome servant and a fearful master. Never for a moment should it be left to irresponsible action." James Madison understood the problem as well, declaring, "The essence of Government is power; and power, lodged as it must be in human hands, will ever be liable to abuse." It is impossible to find a founder who favored big government. Milton Friedman said it best when he argued, "The scope of government must be limited, and the power dispersed." The difference in the men quoted above and those in power today is that the former favored a republic. A socialist nation was never their intention. Today's politicians are nothing more than socialists unwilling to admit the truth.

Can you recall a politician who has sincerely argued for a smaller, less intrusive government, and then taken action? I cannot. If we wish to prevent the demise of our republic, we will need to radically constrain our government, returning the ground it has claimed over the last two hundred years. The only way to do so is to return the government to the people, and the only way to make that happen is to evict the politicians who have taken over our House. November 4, 2008, is coming.

VIII Failure

This chapter discusses, at a high level, the problems with big government and out-of-control spending. It provides a quick look at our failing health, education, legal, welfare, prison, Social Security, and tax systems, and discusses how politicians are using the critically important issues of our day (environment, immigration, abortion, gun control, Internet, military, energy, homelessness, globalization, and terrorism) to divide our country. The parties refuse to work together to address the issues, consistently proving how poorly our government is functioning.

BIG GOVERNMENT

Alexis de Tocqueville wrote in 1830, "Nothing is more striking to a European traveler in the United States than the absence of what we term...government,"[98] but Thomas Jefferson warned, "The natural progress of things is for government to gain ground and for liberty to yield." Two hundred years have lapsed and our government has grown like a Texas grapevine. Do you think anyone touring America today would report what Tocqueville reported—the absence of government? How have we allowed our nation to drift so far off course?

Our government controls 43 percent of our national income. It employs over 10 percent of our people. It collects, and then spends, on average, $13,568 per man, woman, and child.[99] The United States spends at least 50 percent more per person for medical care than the next most expensive country (Switzerland), and 140 percent more than the average among European countries, yet the World Health Organization ranks the U.S. 37th in the world for the overall quality of its health care system.[100] "The United States spends nearly as much on defense as all the rest of the countries in the world combined."[101] Federal outlays account for 20 percent of our GDP[102]—effectively meaning the government controls one of every five dollars. "The federal government's net liabilities, unfunded commitments, and other obligations now amount to more than $43 trillion or about $350,000 for every full-time worker."[103] In the words of Apollo 13 astronaut Jim Lovell, "Houston, we have a problem."

Big government in America might as well be called bad government. There are bad laws, bad ideas, bad programs, and programs that never end. We have pork barrel spending, unnecessary farm subsidies, and programs gone wild. There are so many examples, that this topic should be a book all by itself. Let me show you why.

The *Big Dig* construction scandal in Massachusetts is perhaps the biggest taxpayer rip-off in the history of the United States. The following is hard to believe, but it is the gospel truth. The next time you hear about the bridge to nowhere in Alaska, give this story some thought. In 1987, President Reagan vetoed the Surface Transportation and Uniform Relocation Assistance Act. Senators Edward Kennedy and Robert Byrd of West Virginia then threatened to pull a number of agricultural subsidies unless senators like North Carolina's Terry Sanford supported the bill and kept it alive in the Senate. Sanford caved and the bill was signed by President Bush (the elder) after Mr. Reagan left office. Kennedy was thrilled when $2.5 billion of federal money was approved for the Big Dig, which was going to modernize highways and tunnels in the south end of Boston. Initially budgeted by Massachusetts authorities at $2.6 billion, the *Dig* has now cost American taxpayers close to $15 billion, and money is still being spent. Kennedy's hometown newspaper, the *Boston Globe*, did a year-long investigation on the Dig that documented massive fraud and corruption. Kennedy would not talk to them.[104]

Created by the Clinton administration in 1993, the Partnership for a New Generation of Vehicles (PNGV) was a cooperative research and development partnership aimed at creating a prototype "super-efficient" car. The program brings together the Big Three Automakers (DaimlerChrysler, Ford, and General Motors), federal agencies, and several government defense, energy, and weapons laboratories. PNGV was divided into three stages. The final stage, Goal III, had automakers producing a prototype vehicle that would achieve approximately 80 mpg by 2004, although the auto manufacturers would not have to market this vehicle to the public. In 2002, "The National Research Council concluded in a recent PNGV review that the program was not likely to reach its goal. The government PNGV spending amounted to $814 million, while the industry—General Motors, Ford, and DaimlerChrysler—spent over $980 million."[105] The program was cancelled.

But not to worry, "U.S. Secretary of Energy Spencer Abraham and executives of Ford, General Motors, and DaimlerChrysler have announced a new cooperative automotive research partnership between the U.S. Department of Energy (DOE) and the U.S. Council for Automotive Research (USCAR)."[106] The new program, called Freedom CAR, will focus on fuel cell technology. Jekyll: "Look, we've cancelled a program to build fuel efficient cars. We'll save a billion dollars." Hyde: "Really, we've just started a new program to build fuel efficient cars. It will cost $2 billion. No worry, we'll tell the people we are cutting and saving and then leak the story about the new program during the next election cycle when we are campaigning in Detroit." I'm personally a big fan of fuel cell technology and think there is a way to make it succeed, but I'm not sure I'd place another bet on the same guys who blew the last billion. When do you guess we will see these new cars rolling off the line?

Fannie Mae and Freddie Mac were created by Congress to pump money into the home mortgage market to keep interest rates low and make home ownership affordable for low- and moderate-income people. On December 7, 2006, the Associated Press reported, "Fannie Mae erased $6.3 billion in profit in a long-awaited restatement Wednesday capping the accounting scandal that stunned financial markets," and "Freddie Mac...had its own accounting scandal that came to light in June 2003. The company misstated earnings by some $5 billion."[107]

There are so many others. Here are a few more examples of really bad government:

- Bad laws: Smoot-Hawley Tariff Act of 1930, The Banking Act of 1933, National Industry Recovery Act, Agriculture Adjustment Act.
- Bad ideas: S&L bailout, corporate loans such as the one to Chrysler.
- Bad programs: Federal Emergency Management Agency (FEMA), Tennessee Valley Authority (TVA), the Department of Education.
- Programs that never end: "In the last 40 years, every type of federal spending has grown in real dollars, excepting only foreign aid and veterans programs."[108]
- Pork barrel spending: we wasted $27.3 billion in 2005 according to Citizens against Government Waste.
- Farm subsidies: we spend over twenty billion dollars in farm subsidies each year.[109]
- Programs gone wild: The Americans with Disabilities Act, Defense Department.

"The Pentagon's inspector general conceded that the Defense Department cannot account for 25 percent of the funds it spends. It was reported at a Senate hearing that $13 billion handed out to weapons contractors between 1985 and 1995 was lost."[110] Buried on page 126 in the Department of the Treasury's 2003 Financial Report of the United States Government is a short section titled "Unreconciled Transactions Affecting the Change in Net Position," which explains that these unreconciled transactions totaled $24.5 billion in 2003. We lose $13 billion here. We can't figure out where $24.5 billion went there. Billion, with a capital *B*. Do you sense the magnitude of the problem?

Let me put the size of a billion in perspective. I mention it because I fear many Americans have become numb to how *really big* a billion is. If I gave you a thousand dollars a day, seven days a week, it would take you over 2,700 years to collect one billion dollars—2,737 years, 10 months, and 7 days to be exact! If you laid one billion one dollar bills end to end they would circle the earth almost four times. If you stacked them atop one another they would reach over forty-seven miles high. There are about 300 people in America who have accumulated that much wealth and only 681 in the world as of 2005 according to Forbes and Kahsoon.com.[111] When you hear about a program that wastes three billion dollars or has a budget of sixty-four billion dollars, understand that is an *enormous* amount of money. We hear the government throw around such big numbers so frequently that I fear many no longer understand the magnitude of the numbers. I fear that people have lost perspective that if you made one millions dollars a year it would take you a thousand years to accumulate one billion.

Look at these facts about our *limited* government departments:

- Department of Agriculture: 101,000 employees ($89 billion annual budget).
- Department of Commerce: 36,000 employees with plans to add 15 percent more next year alone ($6.3 billion budget).
- Department of the Interior: manages 507 million acres, more than three times the size of Texas ($10.7 billion budget).
- Housing and Urban Development: provides rental subsidies for 4.8 million homes ($33.6 billion budget).
- Department of Education: has spent over a trillion dollars, and the high school graduation rate has remained exactly the same since the Department's inception ($71 billion budget).
- Internal Revenue Service: 110,000 employees. Former IRS Commissioner Fred Goldberg said, "The IRS has become a

symbol of the most intrusive, oppressive and non-democratic institution in our democratic society,"[112] (will collect almost $1.1 trillion in 2007).

Have you stopped to consider the impact government programs have on society, why government programs fail, and what type of government we truly want? There are only a few legitimate choices: communism, socialism, simple democracy, or a republic. I think our country has lost sight of the significant difference between the last two choices. Do we still want to be a republic, or is a simple democracy, despite all the inherent problems that come with it, what we have become? Or, is our country ready to acknowledge our transition to socialism? What should the purpose of government be?

- To solve our problems?
- To protect us from our vanity?
- To redistribute wealth?
- To centralize control?
- To determine what we can and cannot do?
- To build stadiums for billionaires?
- To invent the Next Big Thing?

I believe we must restate the tenets on which our country intends to operate. Here are my recommendations:

- Reestablish that we are a Republic (not a socialist nation) that operates upon guiding principles and whose government protects our unalienable and equal rights.
- Return power to the states, recommitting to state rights over federal rights.
- Put an end to wealth redistribution (socialism) except in dire situations.
- Once again limit the powers of government.
- Privatize existing government programs wherever possible.

One of the greatest things about our country is our compassion and the willingness of every American to help others in time of need. The outpouring of support after every 9/11 or Hurricane Katrina type event is something we should be proud of. But even in the worst of circumstances, when the country is lined up to offer its full support, the government consistently mismanages the effort. If we can't manage a program when the country is rallying to help, we have no chance when individuals are determined to defraud or steal.

Government agencies and programs have never worked as efficiently as American companies. The fact that they are not trying to make a profit is a big part of the problem, but as programs and agencies increase in size, efficiency decreases, fraud increases, and malaise spreads. Big government programs create organizations that fail to execute. They grow incessantly, like weeds, until they are completely out of control.

There are ways that the government can assist and times when it should be involved, but we must look to the people and count on the market to develop solutions. They will always be more effective than any government institution. Government programs, from the moment they are conceived, become blossoming bureaucracies that never go away, with costs that rocket out of control and results that crash to the ground. They create complex, convoluted, and dysfunctional systems (think tax code) that encourage gamesmanship, cheating, and dishonesty. They are doomed to fail.

In their efforts to solve our problems, politicians create bigger ones. Their answer to every problem is a half-baked bureaucracy that is questionable to begin with, worsens with time, and costs more than we can afford. Politicians want the government to heal every wound that is worthy of a headline or the six o'clock news. Instead, they infect it. Education, welfare, and Social Security are glaring examples of failure, and the health, prison, and legal systems are suffering as well.

Big government programs seldom, if ever, work and certainly not for any extended period of time. It is difficult, perhaps impossible, to create massive "one-size-fits-all" solutions. The people in charge are not bad people; it is just that the concept of a massive bureaucratic solution is fundamentally flawed. Instead of turning to politicians and the government, we must count on the will of the people, competition, and free enterprise to work out whatever problems arise. The government can funnel money toward a problem, but it cannot successfully execute a solution.

We should recognize government programs for what they are—failures—and put them out of business. Problems should be left to each state. If dealt with nationally, they should be addressed in an entirely different way than they are today. If we allow state governments to do what is best for their people, using the divide-and-conquer approach, and then applying the best practices of others, we will evolve, finding what works best and terminating what does not work. The states should go a step further, dividing by region, city, or school district. Centralization does not work. Does anyone other than a politician believe the government can create a fifty billion dollar bureaucracy that will solve the biggest, most difficult problems our country has? It never has. It is time to try a different way.

The Declaration of Independence declared that our government was instituted to secure the rights of all men, each of which has been equally created and endowed by their Creator with certain unalienable rights, among these, Life, Liberty, and the pursuit of Happiness. Our government was intended to protect these rights, and little more. It was not created to grant special rights or usurp power, and the intent was never for the government to try to solve our problems. Government in the United States has expanded well beyond the protection of our unalienable rights. Do we wish to allow it to expand further, to watch our systems continue to fail, and to watch as our nation falls apart? Or do we wish to return power to the people and begin the process of mending our torn and weathered flag? Big government guarantees failure. Are we accepting our demise?

Question: Will you vote to reduce total expenditures on government programs by at least 5 percent each year you are in office, reducing the budget accordingly?

SPENDING

George Washington told James Madison in 1789, "No generation has a right to contract debts greater than can be paid off during the course of its own existence." Thomas Paine in one of the most on-target documents of all time, *Common Sense*, said, "But to expend millions…is unworthy the charge, and is using posterity with the utmost cruelty; because it is leaving them the great work to do, and a debt upon their backs from which they derive no advantage. Such a thought is unworthy a man of honor, and is the true characteristic of a narrow heart and a peddling politician."[113] He is so right.

If anyone claims not to understand how wrong it is to allow the continued accumulation of such a massive debt, that our children will ultimately be required to pay if somehow they possibly can, while our generation reaps the benefits, they are lying. Not only is he a man of dishonor, he is a liar and a despicable thief by every interpretation of the phrase.

We have the largest national debt ($8.7 trillion), the largest trade deficit each year ($250 to $750 billion—depending on how you keep score), and the largest federal foreign debt ($2.4 trillion) of all countries in the world.[114] The $8.7 trillion debt does not include future obligations, such as Social Security payments for those who have paid into the system and have already retired or will retire some day in the future. If you count committed obligations we owe over $43 trillion. Government officials exclude the Social Security money they have collected but not yet spent, claiming it is not a true debt, merely a current obligation that could be cancelled tomorrow if they so choose.

Either way, the problem is getting worse. In 1994, Stephen Moore predicted the national debt would exceed $2.5 trillion by 2010 and $4 trillion by 2020. Here we sit in 2007, and we've already more than doubled the 2020 projection.[115] What will the deficit be twelve years from now? Does $30 trillion sound alarming? How about $40 trillion? Combined spending on Social Security and Medicare will shoot from 7 percent of U.S. economic output today to almost 13 percent by 2030 according to Federal Reserve Chairman Paul Bernanke.[116]

Every man, woman, and child in the United States owes, on average, over $29,000. A family of four, again on average, owes $112,000. At over $8.7 trillion, household debt in our country now exceeds disposable household income.[117] Think about this. Every person in America, on average, owes more than they can afford. On paper, and on average, we are all already bankrupt.

The problem is there is no such thing as "average" debt. The bottom half of all income earners do not or barely pay income taxes, so they do not owe anything. Our tax system is progressive. The more you make, the more you owe, and the bigger the problem becomes. Let me give a crude example. Those in the top 10 percent of wage earners, collectively, pay 61 percent of the taxes, or six times more than you would pay if taxes were proportional. In very rough numbers this translates to a debt of $672,000 per family for those in the upper 10 percent (those making over $75,000 per year).[118]

If you are in debt, personally, what options do you have to get out? You can pay it off if you have spare cash sitting around. If you don't have the cash, you can always work to make more and use the surplus to repay what you owe. You can hope that inflation kicks in and doubles your salary making the amount you owe a smaller portion of your income, but of course if inflation kicks in the cost of everything else will go up accordingly. Or, finally, you could declare bankruptcy, give away everything you have, and start from scratch. The options are the same for politicians.

The bankruptcy of the United States government has been talked about for years by independent observers. The book *Empire of Debt* paints a bleak picture of where the United States is headed financially. "At Oxford they now talk about 'the late period of American democracy.'"[119] But most people have no idea about the ultimate financial consequences of decades of borrowing and spending by Washington, and they remain irrationally convinced that the status quo will remain intact through eternity. No one in any position of power, meaning no politician, has yet admitted that the U.S. government is indeed going bankrupt. But those on the fringes are screaming. You need to listen.

A remarkable paper posted by the Federal Reserve of St. Louis, authored by Boston University Professor Laurence Kotlikoff, reveals in blunt, powerful language that, "The era of borrowing and spending without consequence may soon come to a close." Kotlikoff goes on to explain that "unless the United States moves quickly to fundamentally change and restrain its fiscal behavior, its bankruptcy will become a foregone conclusion."[120]

Today, we run a deficit of over $1.5 billion each *day*. Federal Reserve Chairman Ben Bernanke said, "The United States faces a 'vicious cycle' of rising federal deficits and interest rates unless Congress quickly figures out how to pay for promised Social Security and Medicare benefits...We are experiencing what seems likely to be the calm before the storm when roughly 78 million baby boomers begin retiring next year (2008)".[121] Thomas Jefferson said to William Plumer in 1816, "I place economy among the first and most important of republic virtues, and public debt as the greatest of the dangers to be feared." If we are not wise enough to recognize the danger, may God help us all. Why is nobody worried?

> **Question:** Will you vote for a balanced budget amendment, with exceptions only for periods of declared war or a declining annual GDP?

FAILING SYSTEMS

I contend that we have seven *major* systems in America, and all are failing: tax, health, education, legal, welfare, prison, and Social Security. I consider immigration an issue, as opposed to a system, and will cover it in the next section.

TAX SYSTEM

When the income tax was first proposed in 1909, the suggestion to cap the maximum rate at 10 percent was rejected because Congress feared the rate would immediately increase to that number. "The initial income tax rate, in 1913, was one percent, and this was levied on incomes greater than $300,000 in today's dollars. A maximum rate of seven percent applied to incomes over $7.5 million."[122] They overlooked the possibility that without a specific cap the maximum rate would be 100 percent, and we have at times approached that limit. In 1944, the tax rate climbed as high as 91 percent.

Today, the top one percent of income earners, those who make more than $269,000 in a year, pays 34 percent of all taxes. "To be in the top 10 percent of wage earners, you need to make $75,000 per year, and those 10 percent of the taxpayers pay 62.4 percent of all taxes."[123] "The top 52 percent of all income earners paid almost 100 percent of all personal income taxes collected by the Internal Revenue Service (IRS). We are just a few years away from the point where the majority of American wage earners will have no federal income tax liability at all."[124]

The concept of equality seems to have been lost in our country. Our politicians have forgotten that we are a republic, and under the guidance of our two parties, we now operate as a simple democracy, which Franklin, Madison, Tocqueville, and others specifically warned us about. Tocqueville said, "A democracy cannot exist as a permanent form of government. It can only exist until the voters discover they can vote themselves largess out of the public treasury." Do you think there is a correlation between our deficits and the fact that almost half the country is not paying any taxes?

T. Coleman Andrews, former IRS Commissioner said, "The income tax is fulfilling the Marxist philosophy that the surest way to destroy a capitalistic society is by 'steeply graduated' taxes on income and heavy levies upon the estates of people when they die." This is a guy who ran the IRS. He saw the impact.

Andrews is not the only former IRS Commissioner who saw problems with our tax system and the IRS. Shirley D. Peterson said, "When it comes to the workings of our tax system, I have just about seen it all, and that experience has led me to the conclusion that we should repeal the Internal Revenue Code and start over. Eight decades…have produced an impenetrable maze. I favor replacing the system."[125] The politicians ignore the advice of the people running the system because it would remove their ability to buy votes, and most likely tax wealth (something they already have). There is no other valid reason for them to support the current system.

An income tax encourages dishonest men to lie, cheat, and steal, and honest men to finagle, hedge, and forget. Our system encourages activities that are difficult to track and immune to an income tax, including activities such as dealing drugs, gambling, pornography and sex, and hiring illegal alien workers. "There is some agreement that between $1 trillion and $1.5 trillion in the underground economy goes untaxed."[126] Corporations are encouraged to move offshore where tax rates are lower. The tax code has become exceedingly complex; it now contains over 7,500[127] forms and more than 65,000[128] pages of rules.

Consider the hypothetical case of Wade and Wanda, an executive and a teacher. The tax code is so out of whack, the couple would be financially better off if they were to get a divorce, let Wade marry an illegal immigrant, separate, and then shack up together.[129] Honest men are encouraged to find ways around the system. Taxation has become slavery of the twenty-first century, where we are forced to give away the money we earn with no direct say as to how much gets taken or how it will be used. If you don't believe it, refuse to support any government program by withholding a portion of your taxes. You do not have any say in where or how your money is spent.

We have several choices when it comes to taxation: income, consumption, and wealth are the most likely alternatives. Today, we use all three methods, but with such a heavy emphasis on income that we have created a massive underground economy that benefits those who have figured out, dishonestly, how to transact off the books. I personally favor transitioning to a consumption tax.

The FairTax, as proposed by Boortz and Linder, makes the most sense to me. Let me give you my view of the highlights, but I do most heartily recommend you buy a copy and read the entire text, or at least go to their Web site at www.fairtax.org. The solution is not perfect and would necessitate a 25 percent tax at point of purchase (remember your income would not be taxed; they say 23 percent), but it is so much better than our current system that we should implement it the day after we replace the politicians with our representatives.

The FairTax has the following characteristics:

- a consumption based tax system;
- a simplified tax system;
- progressive taxation—the "rich" pay modestly more than the poor;
- a way to cut the IRS by 75 percent or more—they say eliminate it;
- a way to eliminate tax loopholes;
- a way to eliminate vote-buying;
- a system that encourages savings;
- a system that eliminates overhead;
- a system that allows businesses to make decisions without tax considerations;
- a system that taxes those who thrive in the underground economy as well as the wealthy who no longer have to work (when they make purchases).

Politicians hate this idea because it taxes the wealthy (like them), not those working to make a living, and completely eliminates their ability to buy votes with favorable tax legislation.

Many of you already pay more than 50 percent of your income to taxes of one kind or another, and with our massive debt continuing to increase, the rate is certain to climb even higher, particularly with the pendulum of our current politicians swinging back to the tax-increase party. Paul Krugman said, "If taxes stay 'as low' as they are now, government as we know it cannot be maintained. In particular, Social Security will have to become far less generous; Medicare will no longer be able to guarantee comprehensive medical care to older Americans; Medicaid will no longer provide basic medical care to the poor."[130] Taxes are going to rise! Rabi Lapin pointed out, "Ancient Israel, the Roman Empire, and the British Empire are among dozens of examples of great cultures weakened by undisciplined politicians whose governments gorged on ever-increasing taxation of the populace."[131]

If you do not know who John Galt is or why *Atlas Shrugged*, you should take some time and read the cliff notes. As our debt continues to increase and tax rates begin their steady, inevitable climb upward, ask yourself what would happen if the top one percent of all wage earners, those making over $267,000 per year, decided to take their money and move to Costa Rica, Belize, or New Zealand? Would the country go bankrupt? Would the country collapse? The answers are trouble, yes, and yes.

Question: Will you vote to replace the current tax system with the FairTax as proposed by Linder and Boortz?

HEALTH SYSTEM

George Annas, chairman of the Department of Health Law, Bioethics, and Human Rights at Boston University School of Public Health, said, "Even in the face of galloping health care costs, Americans resist the idea of rationing health care." We spend without limits, "especially in a crisis, and then figure out how to pay for it later." The case of Sonia Fierros and Federico Salinas, Mexican nationals, who came to the United States on a fifteen day tourist visa in 2005 raises multiple issues, including how much should we pay for extreme medical situations and should we pay for the medical expenses of children born to those in the country illegally? Sonia went to the hospital for a urinary tract infection and learned that she was carrying conjoined twins. She was allowed to stay, and when the children were born in Southern California the twins automatically became U.S. citizens (by law).

Published accounts indicated that the cost of a 2004 operation to separate twins conjoined between the breastbone and navel was $750,000 to $1 million. Three years ago, an estimate of the cost of dividing two Guatemalan twins who were conjoined at the head was two million dollars. Your tax dollars paid for these operations and will likely pay for every medical complication and expense these children incur for the rest of their lives.[132]

Our refusal to intelligently discuss and address issues like these is a fundamental reason our system is out of control. Stephen Post, a bioethics professor at Case Western Reserve University School of Medicine in Cleveland sums up the problem well. "As soon as you get to an individual case, human emotions take over. Rationality takes a back seat. If it is your child (and the cost of care is astronomical), you don't care, because it's your child. In the end, people advocate passionately and effectively for their nearest and dearest." But as a country facing out-of-control health care costs and a massive national debt, the time has come to openly debate how much we can afford to pay.

We have an excellent health care system, one of the finest in the world, and most of the complaints about it are unjustified. But, there are some problems that must be addressed. Prices are escalating, coverage is lacking, and our wonderfully generous politicians are once again anxious to jump in and solve the problem. Are we really going to allow politicians to create a national health care system?

The Democratic presidential nominees for 2008 have already made it a part of their platform, and the Republicans are likely to follow suit just as Nixon did in 1972 when he expected Ted Kennedy to make the offer. Both parties need your vote, and just as the Republicans did last election cycle with the $534 billion prescription drug care plan, they will do what they must to win. The parties know national health care will fail miserably, just as it is doing in Germany, the UK, France, and Canada, but they also know it is the natural progression of our conversion to socialism and an important component in securing their absolute power. Our track record with large national "programs" is so far from stellar that it scares me to think there are people in our country who would intentionally agree to turn over one of the most important systems we have to a government that has proven so inept so repeatedly. Do you disagree?

Our nation is not healthy. Poverty, smoking, drugs, obesity, lack of exercise, and a dozen other lifestyle decisions have caused our life expectancy to lag the rest of the world, but we are still living longer than we ever have, and with the aging baby boomers, one of every five adults will soon be dependent on Medicare. We cannot afford it. The tax system already takes one-half of what we make and the health system one-sixth.[133] Two-thirds of our income is spoken for. With the cost of both certain to rise, the problem should be obvious to all.

There are several factors that assure us health care costs will continue to rise: our inability to limit care, administrative overhead, litigation, too few doctors, smoking, drugs, and even the bureaucratic blundering of the Food and Drug Administration (FDA). There are problems we allow to fester. Why don't doctors show their prices before we buy? Who should make the decision when a young child needs medical care, but the parents refuse? Should a terminal patient be allowed to euthanize? Politicians will not address any of these problems; they only allow them to become worse.

If we do nationalize the system, where will we draw the line on how much medical assistance a person can receive and how to prioritize who gets care when? Will care be unlimited and given on a first-come, first-serve basis? Is cosmetic surgery covered, including belly shrinking and lip fattening? Would breast implants be paid for on the grounds that such a procedure can improve the mental health of the recipient or their significant other? Will abortions be paid for? If a person refuses to exercise, swallows two Big Macs, a super-sized order of fries, and a forty-four-ounce Dr. Pepper every day, and then balloons to triple his "expected" weight, will he jump to the front of the line for an emergency bypass surgery ahead of someone who needs the same treatment who has never drank or smoked and worked out for an hour every day but is not considered "critical"?

Will "big-boned" people be given elliptical trainers, liposuction, and stomach reduction surgery? Will it be mandatory? Will people with a bad back be given a free hot tub? If a person drinks a fifth of alcohol every day and destroys his liver, will he be placed in the same queue for a new liver as people diagnosed with liver cancer or meningitis? Will smokers be given lung transplants after they destroy their own? Will a person who is considered fully paralyzed and brain dead, with no hope for recovery, be kept alive by machines and required to "live" for fifty or a hundred years as lawyers litigate to protect their right to life? Will the family or the government determine when to turn machines off? Has a single politician considered any of these questions?

There are many issues that we need to address, but if we do not do something quickly, politicians will present us with the only answer they know: a large national program that costs more than we can afford and will deliver results significantly worse than what the free market will. The government controls 40 percent of all health care costs. Is that why the system is already out of control? We must find a way to control costs, and we need a solution for the uninsured. To do so, representatives must consider what is important, not what will secure the most votes.

Question: Will you vote for a government-controlled National Health Care System that offers "free" health care to all?

EDUCATION SYSTEM

Many think that our education system is working well, at least for those who take advantage of it. Some say we should not expect any better. But if you compare the results of our system to the tiny Caribbean island of Barbados, which is exceptionally poor, black, and fatherless, you may want to think again. Journalist David Beard, writing for the *Sun-Sentinel* of South Florida noted that a Barbadian Scholastic Aptitude Test (SAT) score of 1345 was "about average for the students of...secondary school in this Caribbean nation." The United States average is 1030. The teachers in Barbados earn less money than their U.S. counterparts. Over 50 percent of the students come from single-parent households. Yet, said former Boston University chancellor John Silber, "They defy all of the expectations and all of the clichés passed off as excuses for the poor quality of primary and secondary education in the United States."

"The parents expect the kids to do well," said Beverly Holder, a guidance counselor for Harrison College. Barbados parents have declared that education is the number one objective in their country and they are committed to ensuring that it is. One parent had this to say: "As Barbadians, we don't have many resources. We're just a small, flat country. Our agriculture is declining. Education is the only way we can pull ourselves out of poverty."[134] With commitment, schools can succeed. Without it, they cannot.

Contrast the situation in Barbados with the opening of one of President Bush's recent speeches. Bush said,

Today, nearly 70 percent of inner city fourth graders are unable to read at a basic level on national reading tests. Our high school seniors trail students in Cyprus and South Africa on international math tests. And nearly a third of our college freshmen find they must take a remedial course before they are able to even begin regular college level courses...**Since 1965, when the federal government embarked on its first major elementary-secondary education initiative, federal policy has strongly influenced America's schools.** Over the years Congress has created hundreds of programs intended to address problems in education without asking whether or not the programs produce results or knowing their impact on local needs. This 'program for every problem' solution has begun to add up—so much so that there are hundreds of education programs spread across 39 federal agencies at a cost of $120 billion a year. Yet, after spending billions of dollars on education, we have fallen short in meeting our goals for educational excellence.[135]

Bush's solution, consistent with all politicians, is more government involvement and spending.

Are you satisfied with our education system? Since the Department of Education (ED) was formed twenty-eight years ago, we have given the federal government over one trillion dollars to improve education, yet neither graduation rates nor SAT scores have budged. No change whatsoever! As I discussed earlier, almost one-third of our students fail to graduate from high school, the same as when ED was created. ED now has over 4,400 employees and a $71 billion budget, and look at the results: 72.2 percent of students graduated from the twelfth grade in 2006.[136] The data provided earlier showed us that in 1998 only 56 percent of black and 54 percent of brown students graduated. In Georgia, the state with the lowest overall graduation rate, only 54 percent of students graduated. In the city of Cleveland the graduation rate was 28 percent. What do you think happens to kids who fail to graduate?

Our government spends plenty of money on education, more than any other country in the world, but even the Web sites seem confused on how much. In one place they claim to spend $450 billion[137] and in another $900 billion.[138] Which source do you believe? The fact that the numbers are so far apart should not be surprising. Regardless, spending is not the problem.

Massive overhead wastes money with minimal documented improvements. They create program after program with little to show for their effort. The ED Web site lists 257 education programs that are in flight.[139] Scanning the list you find things like We the People, U.S.-Brazil Higher Education Consortia Program, Statewide Longitudinal Data System Grants, Ready to Learn Television, Randolph Sheppard Vending Facility Program, and the National Coordinator Program. You have to look at the entire list to get a true feel for the magnitude of what ED is doing, but the list is daunting, and the examples of what money is being spent on is unbelievable.

Unions have commandeered the teaching profession, bureaucracy has made the job unbearable, and we fail to support our teachers and administrators. As a result, teachers are treated like dirt, receive lackluster pay, and are given every reason in the world not to teach. High school kids see this and wisely, for them, veer away from the profession.

The value of an education is undeniable, but we are failing at least a third, and more honestly half, of our children by not ensuring they receive a proper education. We do not need every child to go to college, but we do need them all to graduate from high school. To do so, we need to recruit and retain the best possible teachers, and that means paying the good ones more and firing the bad ones. The tenured union system is failing our children.

We need parents that are more involved, and we need to create alternative learning tracks, including the development of better vocational programs that enhance the education experience for those who are not bound for college. We need to get the drugs completely out of our schools, and we need to take a much firmer stand with those that misbehave. There are many things we can do to improve our schools, including providing more discipline, rethinking the concept of student "rights," and demanding attendance. We should experiment with student pay, insist on English immersion, and eliminate educational pollution. Should we go even further?

"The public schools have so deteriorated that four in ten public school teachers send their own children to private schools."[140] Most of our politicians do the same. The system is messed up, but perhaps the solution is simple. Should we seriously consider privatizing the entire education system? Private universities do exceptionally well. We could start by taking the federal government completely out of the process and returning control to the states. Then, we could encourage the states to return control to the districts and the districts to privatize. Before you dismiss the idea, ask yourself what makes you believe the federal government will be any more successful than it has been in the last forty years?

Every president has talked about the importance of education, but our government has yet to do anything that produces better results. There has been no measurable improvement, despite the money spent and the programs created, in over forty years. Could it be that politicians and the government are simply not the right people to solve the problem?

> **Question:** Will you vote to eliminate the federal Department of Education and vote for a plan to return all authority to the states over a period of four years or less?

Legal System

There is an attorney in California, whose name I will not write here for obvious reasons, who has a Web site that brags proudly about his following "wins." If you ever find yourself in a bind and need to get away with murder, you may want to contact this guy. He claims he has successfully used legal technicalities and suppressed police evidence to have charges dismissed. That includes having murder charges dropped against a guilty client facing two counts. He has "persuaded the court to show mercy in one of the most punishing counties on the three strike issue," enabling his client to avoid a life sentence and "look forward to a day when the prison gates would open to his freedom."

He has successfully defended a client, saving his driver's license, despite a blood alcohol level of over .30. One of his clients was charged with killing a neighbor in cold blood in front of many witnesses, yet he was able to convince a jury that the client was not guilty of murder but of the lesser charge of voluntary manslaughter, thus avoiding a life sentence and allowing him to one day be set free. Another of his clients was charged with burglarizing a house. The owner of the house came home in the course of the burglary, and even though he was able to identify the client, the lawyer convinced the jury his client was not guilty, "whereupon the client walked out of the courtroom into the loving arms of his mother."[141]

How nice. This manipulation of our legal system is unfortunately not atypical of American lawyers, whose guiding principle has become "Just win, baby!"

Generally speaking, our legal system functions well; the system reaches a reasonable conclusion most of the time. But as soon as we get away from simple and obvious cases, the process begins to break down. It disintegrates when we get to fringe cases, when lawsuits are filed, malpractice is accused, or a technicality is identified. With no check in place, the system has tilted out of balance. The intent of the system is good, but the execution is failing.

Thomas Jefferson said, "The germ of dissolution of our federal government is in the constitution of the federal judiciary, an irresponsible body, working like gravity by night and day, gaining a little today and a little tomorrow, and advancing its noiseless step like a thief, over the field of jurisdiction, until all shall be usurped from the States, and the government of all be consolidated into one."

Has the thief stolen our government as Jefferson predicted? Has the federal judiciary usurped the power exactly as was feared? Not only has it taken the power it was never intended to have, it has spread its control, driving society to a point where we are ruled by laws instead of principles and semantics instead of sense.

The mantra in America has become, "When in doubt, sue!" Young brothers were severely burned in a fire they started with a lighter their parents had left inside the family van. They settled a lawsuit with the New York Lighter Co. Inc., whose lawyer, David Chamberlain, said, "We didn't think we were at fault, but if the jury had sided with the plaintiffs…it would have been $25 million to $30 million."[142] International Harvester was sued when a man fell into a machine. His company had specifically ordered the removal of a safety device that may have prevented the accident. The wife of a soldier killed in action sued the government because it did not have a Wiccan symbol to put on his tombstone. Discrimination claims were up by 2,200 percent from 1969 to 1990.[143] Class-action lawsuits have become money presses for lawyers. Alita Ditkowsky was part of a class-action suit against a company that made faulty televisions. When the case was settled in Madison County, Illinois, Alita's lawyer took home twenty-two million while she got a fifty dollar rebate on another TV, built by the same company that had ruined the first one.[144] You and I are about to pay eight billion dollars to settle a case between the Interior Department and American Indians. The EEOC manages over 75,000 charges annually.[145] How have we allowed this to get so out of hand?

Judges and the legal system have somehow become protectors of the guilty, the very people the system is set up to prosecute. In New York, Judge Baer ruled in favor of a driver who had fled from police with seventy-five pounds of drugs in her car. He called the arrest "illegitimate" and said, "The subject's right to flee was justified because police in the area were viewed as corrupt, abusive, and violent."[146]

"When a democratically elected tenants union sought to bring order to the Robert Taylor Homes public housing unit by proposing metal detectors, photo Ids, and a policy that would permit guards and police to perform emergency searches without warrants in response to gunfire, the ACLU objected. The fact that the people living in the housing project had agreed to the rules in an effort to cut back on the crime and murders was irrelevant."[147]

"New York's Legal Aid Society, along with other liberal groups, kept up a decades' long fight against measures that would make it possible to evict drug dealers from public housing. This amounted, they said, to denying the 'rights' of accused drug dealers."[148]

"In San Francisco, a multiple murderer was let off with a lenient sentence because of speculation that his eating 'Twinkies' might have made him more excitable."[149]

"Medical authorities in the United States...were legally prohibited from warning anyone about a homosexual airline steward who, as of 1982, had been linked to at least 40 of the first 248 homosexual men found to have AIDS. He...would have sex in the dim lights of a gay bathhouse and then turn up the lights to show his partner the lesion on his skin and say: 'I've got gay cancer. I'm going to die and so are you.'"[150]

"A jail inmate with AIDS who was kept separated from other prisoners (to prevent the spread of the disease) was awarded $155,000 in damages."[151]

"Convicted burglar Kurt Prochaska is proceeding with his lawsuit against the doctor who shot him after he broke into the doctor's house....Prochaska claims Rainiero (the doctor) used excessive force and caused him permanent pain and injury. Prochaska's lawsuit admits he was an intruder in Rainiero's home."[152] Who are we protecting?

Lawyers use the insanity defense to free their clients, and go as far as lying to try to shift the blame from the guilty. Recall David Westerfield, who attorneys knew had murdered a seven-year-old girl yet still insinuated the parents were the murderers in their effort to free their client.[153] The total cost of America's tort system has grown to more than $240 billion a year, largely because of junk lawsuits.[154] Cases drag on forever; the Exxon Valdez case went on for over twenty years. Out-of-work claimants died waiting for settlement of the case while the litigating lawyers became millionaires.

The very threat of litigation affects everything we do. The cost of malpractice insurance has gone through the roof, jumping 20 to 25 percent in 2002 alone.[155] "Regardless of one's view about the merits of the (smoking) suits, the mega-fees from the 1998 tobacco settlement were nothing but egregious. Some 300 lawyers from 86 firms will pocket as much as $30 billion over the next 25 years even though, for many of them, the suits posed minimal risk and demanded little effort."[156] Remember the O.J. Simpson trial? When are we going to say "enough"? The system is completely out of control.

We have special rights for so many different groups—including blacks, browns, women, minorities, gays, lesbians, seniors, students, minors, bugs, animals, height-challenged, poor, obese, disabled, prisoners, Jews, Muslims, Indians, immigrants, the insane, sex offenders, Wiccans, terrorists, and even people with accents—that 80 percent to 85 percent of society is now "protected." "Even the most dedicated fighters of discrimination acknowledge that it is possible to create a discrimination claim out of almost any workplace dispute."[157]

"A state Supreme Court jury in Manhattan awarded $14.1 million to a woman who walked into a train tunnel, laid down on the tracks, and was hit by a train. Police concluded the woman had been trying to commit suicide."[158] Personal responsibility has become an oxymoron.

The legal system is in shambles. Lawyers are working the system to make a dollar, and judges are abusing it to forward their political agenda. They have begun to go as far as referencing international law where it is convenient. Supreme Court Justice Ruth Ginsburg gives her account of why referring to foreign law makes sense, and has wondered aloud if we should be our own country or what the rest of the world wants us to be? I always thought we were our own country, but we have a Supreme Court Justice saying we should be what the rest of the world wants us to be. Is that what France or Canada want, or what Korea or Iran feels is appropriate? Have some of our judges lost their minds? The 9th Circuit Court of Appeals and the California Supreme Court would suggest they have.

"In more than 60 consecutive death penalty cases—*every* such case to reach the California Supreme Court during her tenure—Chief Justice Rose Bird voted to overturn the penalty, on grounds that the defendant had not had a fair trial as required by the Constitution."[159]

In 2002, "The 9th Circuit accounted for…30 percent of the reversals (18 of 59) that the Supreme Court decided by full written opinions. In addition, the 9th Circuit was responsible for more than a third (35 percent, or 8 of 23) of the High Court's *unanimous* reversals that were issued by published opinions."[160] In 2006, the Ninth Circuit had 18 cases reviewed by the Supreme Court and 15 were reversed, including the case of Fernando Belmontes, whom the 9th Circuit had ruled did not deserve the death penalty. "In order, as he (Belmontes) explained to one of his accomplices, to 'take out a witness,' Belmontes used perhaps 20 blows with a metal dumbbell bar to bludgeon to death Stacy McConnell, whose home he had entered for a burglary. He emerged drenched with her blood and carrying her stereo that he sold for $100. She was 19. Belmontes killed her 25 years ago."[161]

We need to have judges who will practice restraint, not activism. We need judges who behave like referees, whose purpose is to ensure that the rules, as written, are enforced equally, not that the team they favor wins. We do not need judges who rule based on personal preferences.

Our juries do not help the situation, largely because lawyers are able to handpick those most likely to be sympathetic to their cause. The number of outrageous examples is again extensive, but here is one of the worst. When a drunk driver, going seventy miles per hour, plowed into a car waiting at a red light, who do you think the jury found at fault? The mental pause you just went through, the "no way" thought, is what is indicative of everything wrong with the legal system. But first, a little more information: the six victims sitting at the red light in the 1979 Chevy Malibu survived, but they suffered severe burns because the immense force of the crash had burst the Malibu's gas tank.

"Although the National Highway Traffic Safety Administration did not (and does not) deem the Malibu's gas tank defective in placement, design, construction, or any other way, lawyers for Anderson (one of the victims sitting in the car) disagreed and proceeded to sue General Motors, saying the fire might have been averted had the company located the tank somewhere other than toward the rear of the Malibu."[162] The jury in *Anderson v. G.M.* initially awarded the plaintiffs $4.9 billion, though the amount was later reduced to a mere $1.2 billion.

"L.A. County Superior Judge Ernest Williams had agreed to exclude from evidence various matters that G.M. wanted to introduce, including federal government statistics from twenty years of real-world highway experience showing the Malibu among the safest cars of its time."[163] GM was ordered to pay $1.2 billion dollars for selling a car with a gas tank that ignited when hit from behind at fifty or seventy miles per hour. How can a business survive when decisions that ignore all common sense are reached time after time? It is so wrong, and sympathetic juries and activist judges make it all possible. We need change.

It costs over a million dollars to prosecute a death penalty case, that may at times extend over a period of more than twenty-five years, so instead we allow convicted murderers to sit in a cell for fifty or sixty years at a cost of thirty thousand dollars per year. Criminals are set free on technicalities or because the judge doesn't like the arresting officer. Convicts have more rights than the person they are assaulting, even in one's own home. The legal system protects the criminals as much or more than the innocent.

"In the decades since World War II, we have constructed a system of regulatory law that basically outlaws common sense. Modern law, in an effort to be 'self-executing,' has shut out our humanity."[164] Is it time to amend the Constitution with a "Law of Common Sense"? We must get back to equal, not special, rights. We need to remove the law-making ability that judges have discreetly stolen by cleaning up the language of the Fourteenth Amendment. We need to clean up our legal system, but as long as we have lawyers writing the laws, do you think it will ever happen?

> **Question:** Will you vote to amend the Constitution with a "Law of Common Sense" that requires judges to hold individuals accountable for their actions, particularly when the predominant majority of society would have known better?

Welfare System

The nation spends more than $16 billion annually on the child welfare system. Yet horror stories abound. Monica Wheeler was beaten and strangled by her mother's boyfriend Michael Tubman three years after her two-year-old brother, Andre, had mysteriously drowned. Brianna Blackmond was taken away from loving foster parents hoping to adopt her and returned to her mentally retarded mother, who had an IQ of fifty-eight and eight other children. The two-year-old died twelve days later. Joseph Wallace was returned to his mother on three separate occasions before being hung by an electrical cord at the age of three. Bruce Jackson and his three brothers were starved their entire lives by their foster parents. At age nineteen, Bruce weighed forty-five pounds and was found by police, scrounging through a dumpster for food after having escaped from his house. The Jackson's had been receiving $28,000 a year to care for the children. Catrina was finally taken away from her mom for good (she had been returned nine times) when the two-year-old was found with forty-eight cigarette burns on her head. One month old Kendra was beaten to death.[165]

The stories are terribly disturbing until you read them in their entirety, and then you recognize they are absolutely horrifying. The common threads in almost all of these stories are unwed mothers, drugs, welfare, poverty, and lack of a good education.

Welfare destroys people. The exceptionally liberal Robert Kennedy, a member of "The Family," once said, in what must have been a moment of weakness, "In our generosity we have created a system of hand-outs, a second-rate set of social services, which damages and demeans its recipients, and destroys any semblance of human dignity that they have managed to retain through their adversity. In the long run, welfare payments solve nothing, for the giver or the receiver; free Americans deserve the chance to be fully self-supporting."[166] Most on the right would go even further. But look at what our politicians have done.

"In the Great Depression year of 1936, 147,000 families, about 1 percent of the population, received welfare. In 1994, a strong year economically and a world away from the Depression, 15 percent of the population was on welfare."[167] The U.S. Census Bureaus said, "37 million people were living in poverty (12.6 percent) in 2005…and 7.7 million families."[168] "Welfare for the poor works out to a national average of $12,000 to $13,000 a year per recipient."[169] "By 1995, the

Nation had over 300 social programs, and federal and state spending on the poor had jumped from around $40 billion to about $360 billion."[170] "In 2005, the number is projected to be $573 billion."[171] The situation is not getting better. It becomes significantly worse each year. Why?

The problem begins with education, or lack thereof. Remember the 30 percent of kids who do not complete the twelfth grade? It gets worse when teenage girls have babies. I've already shared the shocking data that over a third of children are born to unwed mothers; almost 90 percent of black women under the age of twenty-five who have a child are single. Drugs compound the problem. Finally, those who are not mentally healthy are often preyed upon by young men and then left with a child they are not capable of caring for. We ignore the problems. The one thing that has proven to make the situation better, God, is the one thing that certain members of our society insist on excluding. Why?

There are many problems with welfare, the biggest of which is welfare itself. The system undermines the work ethic. Philip Howard says, "It is difficult to imagine a system that more perfectly combines the evils of inhumanity and ineffectiveness."[172] Yet our solution is to continue to extend the welfare state, increasing the number that receives assistance year after year. The system is abused, as Robert Rector reported in the *Wall Street Journal* over sixteen years ago: "Well over $150 billion in government benefits for lower-income people go uncounted for…more than $11,000 per poor household."[173]

Our government created housing projects like Cabrini-Green, Robert Taylor, Dearborn Homes, Pruitt-Igoe, and Schuylkill Falls that were so bad Congress had to outlaw future development, but only after hundreds of thousands of the poor had been shuttled into the unbarred prisons. Government is not capable of providing for the masses. Why do we allow them to try?

We need to do something drastically different. Should we start by ensuring kids can get the education they need? For that to happen, we must take drugs entirely out of the equation. The earlier segment on drugs discusses how I would suggest we make that happen. We need to put an end to teenage pregnancy. Teaching abstinence should certainly be continued, but it is not enough. We need to ensure that the need for birth control is understood and that birth control "solutions" are readily available. Again, that does not mean we should not teach abstinence, but until we can show that the message is getting through, birth control is a necessity.

We should experiment with ideas like paying those who do not get pregnant and those who pass drug tests. Just as importantly, if not more so, we need to give all children earlier and more exposure to God. Not government-controlled or government-mandated religion, but more readily available access. I know there are a few of you who are going to throw the "separation of church and state" flag, but the 92 percent of us who believe need to take a stronger stand.

Our welfare system is broken. I personally believe we need to invest more than what we currently spend in order to appropriately address the problems, but we should not look to the federal government to run the system. I have a proposal for what I would do, and I am sure there are probably a thousand other ideas floating around. We need to experiment with many of them, with the government providing the funding but churches and charities responsible for the implementation. What we should not do is continue the existing government-run welfare state. It is destroying the people it is intending to help, as well as our country.

> **Question:** Will you vote to terminate all current federal welfare programs but spend at least 10 percent more on programs run by individual states, churches, or charities, holding them accountable for results in order to receive funding?

Prison System

The federally funded Alternatives to Incarceration program in San Jose California program was a bad idea from the start. The program sent selected imprisoned criminals to colleges to complete their sentences, instead of keeping them behind bars. After a series of rapes at San Jose State University, the city's police chief discovered imprisoned rapists had been released to that institution. When the police chief voiced his concerns about the program to the director of the project, and they later became public, he was censured by the students and faculty and advised by his superiors in city hall to go easy. A few months later the tragic denouement occurred when the police arrested an "honor" student in the Alternatives program for brutally torturing, raping, and murdering two women near the university. He had been an "articulate" person, and the project often used him to show how wonderful it was that bright people could get a college education instead of languishing in prison. During the entire decade of this program, not one client actually graduated from the university, but a number were arrested for crimes against women.[174]

Two hundred years ago, Adam Smith said, "Mercy to the guilty is cruelty to the innocent." Often, it is much worse.

At the end of 2005, the United States incarcerated 2,320,359 people.[175] The incarceration rate in the United States is four times the world average.[176] Of the (male) U.S. adult population, 3.2 percent—one of every thirty-two adults—is incarcerated, on probation, or on parole.[177] A disproportionate number of blacks are in prison. While blacks make up only 13 percent of the U.S. population, 68 percent of all inmates are black, 22 percent brown, and 9 percent white.[178]

Jamie Fellner of the Human Rights Watch has concluded the reason is racial, choosing to ignore the factors discussed earlier: unwed mothers, failure to graduate high school, drug use, or living in poverty. The U.S. Department of Justice reports that per capita expenditure for the prison system has increased to $638 in 2003. Multiplied by three hundred million Americans, we are spending almost two hundred billion dollars a year on the various components of our incarceration program. "The average cost to house a criminal for a year in 2004 was $23,183.69."[179] And the costs are about to go up. Medical care has become not just a nice perk for inmates, but an unalienable right.

We have forty million people in America who do not have health care, but our politicians have decided that we should spend more on criminals serving time behind bars than average Americans spend on themselves. The skyrocketing costs of providing health care to an aging population of inmates who are afflicted with serious, expensive diseases is about to break the bank. Twenty-eight percent of the inmates arriving in state prisons from county jails test positive for Hepatitis C, and many receive drug treatments that can cost ten thousand dollars or more a year.[180] And of course we have cases like seventy-five-year-old death row inmate Clarence Ray Allen and the lawsuit his attorney filed because he hasn't received adequate medical care for his ailing heart.[181] The situation will only worsen if we don't step in.

As we have cracked down on criminals and imprisoned them longer, we have a new problem brewing: recidivism. Criminals are not being rehabilitated; they are being hardened. A June 2006 U.S. prison study by the bipartisan Commission on Safety and Abuse in America's Prisons reported, "Within three years of their release, 67 percent of former prisoners are rearrested and 52 percent are re-incarcerated."[182] For juveniles, the rate is even worse. The root causes are the same: drugs, missing father, lack of education, absence of God, and a new one that is developing—no fear of the system. The practical absence of the death penalty does not enhance the situation.

Prisoner "rights" have become another outlet for lawyers to litigate. *Ruiz v. Estelle* was one of the longest running prisoner class-action lawsuits in U.S. history. Ronald Banks, formerly an inmate in the Pennsylvania Department of Corrections, filed a class-action lawsuit after he was prohibited from receiving a particular newspaper. We allow prisoners to sue over what reading material we provide?

"The American Civil Liberties Union (ACLU) and Human Rights First announced…they had filed a lawsuit in Illinois against U.S. Defense Secretary Donald Rumsfeld and several other U.S. military officials on behalf of eight Iraqi prisoners who claim they were tortured and abused by U.S. personnel in Iraq and Afghanistan."[183] Prisoners of war can now file class-action lawsuits in America?

"The ACLU of Rhode Island announced today that it has filed an appeal in federal court on behalf of a Christian prisoner who was barred from preaching during religious services at the state prison."[184] Yes, this is the same ACLU that files lawsuits for outrageous abuses like saying the Pledge of Allegiance or offering a prayer before a football game.

The impact of incarceration has been dramatic. Crime rates, while still higher than the rest of the world, have fallen, but an already bad problem has become worse: children being raised with a parent, most often their father, in jail. Is it any surprise that the vast majority of youths in the juvenile system have at least one incarcerated parent?

One of the most encouraging stories I came across when tracking down information on the prison system was the story of Sheriff Joe Arpaio of Arizona County. He runs prisons the way they should be run. Inmates live in tents in the hundred-plus degree heat of the desert, wear pink clothing, work in old-fashioned chain gangs, and are served meals that cost less than forty cents per helping. Since federal law says they must be allowed access to the cable channels on TV, he complied by filtering all but the Disney and Weather channels. For the mandatory movie fix, he permits only G-rated movies.[185] Should we be sending more of our convicted felons to Joe? Should we model more facilities after Arizona County? The rate of recidivism of inmates who served time in Joe's prisons is reportedly one-fourth of the national average. Why have we not copied this model a hundred times? Are "prisoner rights" getting in the way?

There are many, many things we can do to improve the situation, but all will require we show a little less compassion to those who violate the law. The current system is not working. We can become softer on the criminals, or harder. Which way do you want to go?

> **Question:** Will you vote to declare that a person who commits a crime, and is subsequently found guilty of said crime, has forfeited all but his most basic rights from the moment his crime was committed until the moment he is released?

RETIREMENT SYSTEM

In 1920, Charles Ponzi and his Boston-based postal coupon enterprise promised to double your money in ninety days. They had collected $9.5 million from ten thousand investors before his bubble burst—and all those who entered late lost their investment. Circuit Judge Anderson later explained, "His scheme was simply the old fraud of paying the earlier comers out of the contributions of the later comers."[186] Because these systems are not sustainable, they are illegal.[187] Individuals and businesses that set up Ponzi schemes are prosecuted aggressively, as they should be. Enron and Pinnacle Development Partners LLC were blatant abusers. California and Florida have recently shut down schemes that had bilked investors out of $117 million and $68 million, respectively.[188]

When Social Security was created in 1935, forty-two workers supported each retiree. In 2005 the ratio was three to one, and by 2030 it will be two to one. When Social Security was launched in 1936, there were approximately seven million Americans over the age of sixty-five. Last year there were over 35 million, they are living five years longer, and the cost to care for the elderly is more than ten times as expensive as it was in 1935. "If the entire working-age population of Mexico were to move to the United States in 2025, there still would not be enough people to restore the old-age dependency ratio that existed in 2000."[189]

To get back to the same ratio we had in 1936 we would need to move the entire working age population of the world, twice, to the United States. "The Congressional Budget Office (CBO) projects that spending for Social Security, adjusted for inflation, will rise from $483 billion in 2003 to $2.5 trillion in 2075."[190] Not only is the present system illegal, collapse is inevitable. Every Ponzi implementation known to man has ultimately failed, and Social Security in its current form has no chance of being the first exception. An ostrich on the beach could not ignore this problem, but politicians do.

The reason politicians ignore the problem is that they know doing the right thing will cost them their job and their party its power. The political catch-22 has them trapped. The Cato Institute's Doug Bandow, discussing the 2003 prescription drug plan that Bush signed, derided the legislation as "the largest expansion of the welfare state in 40 years...Republicans are merely Democrats-lite when it comes to using taxpayer monies to buy votes."[191] Neither Democrats nor Republicans can afford to lose the votes of seniors, so they have little choice but to continue to give more.

Part of the problem—and there are many parts—is that seniors get to vote and those who are going to have to pay the bill do not. Do you believe that the voting age should be eighteen? I do not. I believe every person should have an equal say in our government from the moment they are born. Children under the age of eighteen should be represented equally, particularly given the dishonorable manner in which politicians pander to retirees while amassing debt their grandchildren will have to pay. I believe mothers should receive an extra vote for their daughters, and men for their sons, in order to restore a modicum of sanity to our government. If we evict all 435 politicians from our House this change may not be as critical, but it would still be the right thing to do. Our government has shown it cannot be trusted.

There are many other things that could or should be done. We need to completely overhaul the retirement system for government employees, which for some ridiculous reason is better than what everyone else in America receives. The retirement plan for congressmen is so outrageous it should be outlawed. The retirement age must change, and every person in America who is not already retired will have to concede this fact. The change need not be drastic, but we can no longer afford to allow people to collect retirement pay at sixty-five or even sixty-seven. Every person in America understands we are living longer and able to work longer, and many are already choosing to do so. The time has come to sacrifice a little of our comfort so that we do not bankrupt the nation for those who will follow. We should give serious consideration to privatizing the system; in a republic, private is always better than government controlled.

Surveys have shown that more Americans believe in the existence of unidentified flying objects than in the promise that they'll ever get back what they've put into the Social Security system.[192] Our retirement plan is not sustainable, and we all know it. The White House reported in 2005, "If we do not act to fix Social Security now, the only options will be dramatically higher taxes, massive new borrowing or sudden and severe cuts in Social Security benefits or other government programs."[193] The chairman of our Federal Reserve has warned us that action must be taken. Explain the situation to a sixth grader and watch how quickly he grasps the problem. If we want America to remain the greatest country in the world, we must take action now.

Question: Will you vote to change the retirement age to sixty-nine immediately, and index the retirement age for those under the age of fifty to "life expectancy" minus five years?[194]

Question: Will you vote to grant parents an extra vote for each child who is not yet of voting age (men get an extra vote for each male child, women for each female)?

Issues We Have Failed to Address
Environment

On July 10, 2001, four Forest Service firefighters were killed while fighting the thirty-mile fire in the Chewuch River Canyon in the state of Washington. Representative Scott Mcinnis of Colorado claimed in an interview on CNN, "Frankly, the Forest Service was recklessly cautious about the Endangered Species Act, did not allow field authority to take place and as a result water drops that could have saved the firefighters were delayed. It was reported that fire helicopters were not deployed while waiting for bureaucrats to get clearance to scoop water from a nearby stream which was under the political hammer of the Endangered Species Act...Forest Service policy in the northwest requires that special permission be obtained before fire helicopters can dip into certain restricted rivers, lakes, and streams."

If ever there was an issue that personifies all that is wrong with our two-party system, it is the environment. For too many years, businesses and business owners have abused their workers and the environment for their personal gain. Unions developed to combat bad bosses and "environmentalists" emerged to keep abusive companies in check, but their methods have become unreasonable, and the system has gone haywire. Unions have lost sight of what is important, and some of the environmentalists, in their efforts to "save" the environment, have lost their minds. A few have become so extreme that neither party could represent their views in the 2000 election; they ran their own candidate for president, knowing with certainty they had no chance of winning.

In response, the Democrats have shifted even further to the left in their attempt to bring the environmentalists back into their camp. To appease the new members they now label anyone who supports the Republicans as an environmental abuser, using the occasional corporate disaster as proof of how out of control big business is. The red party, in response, has moved further right, labeling anyone who supports the blue party as an extreme environmentalist, using their absurd chain-me-to-a-tree tactics as proof of how out of line the entire party has become.

We need to address issues like the environment apolitically. While I tend to lean to the right on the majority of issues, one reason, and there are several, that I can never get myself to say "I am a Republican" is they do not do enough to protect the environment. I do not blame the party in the way the Democrats do, but it is true that Republicans could and should do a lot more. We need to protect the environment and the truly endangered animals. We need to protect it at a cost that is reasonable and without trampling the rights of human beings under the "foot" of a bug. When idiots can chain themselves to trees on private property, claiming they are worried about a spotted owl, or use an insect the size of your thumbnail to prevent a road from being built or a city from expanding, the system is out of whack.

The focus should be on our environment, not our bugs. Our air is not clean. "The combined long-term effect of studies in several large cities predicts 60,000 deaths each year.... Some research has estimated that people living in the most polluted U.S. cities could lose between 1.8 and 3.1 years because of exposure to chronic air pollution."[195] "Air pollution claims 70,000 lives annually. U.S. air pollution deaths are equal to deaths from breast cancer and prostate cancer combined."[196] We can and need to do more.

The Environmental Working Group provides a list of the most polluted waters in the United States. It includes sixty-three rivers, harbors, and bays, each receiving more than a million pounds of toxins a year.[197] "Most freshwater fish in New York and Connecticut are now under consumption advisories due to mercury poisoning."[198] The Division of Environmental Health for the state of Washington "cautions anglers against the consumption of fish or shellfish from any of the industrialized urban embayments of Puget Sound."[199]

"The (New York) state toxicologist says 30 percent of the wells tested near hog farms are already contaminated....115 farms were caught illegally dumping hog waste into waterways...At one farm there was a massive spill when the walls of an eight-acre lagoon collapsed, spewing out 25 million gallons of liquid manure into rivers, farms, and highways."[200] "One in four people in America, including 10 million children, live within four miles of a Superfund toxic waste site. There are 600,000 known or suspected hazardous waste sites scattered across the nation...the worst sites have been identified by the federal government as serious threats to human health and are listed as Superfund sites."[201]

Global warming has become the biggest environmental issue of the day. Yes, the climate is warming, slightly, but nobody will discuss the situation intelligently. Data is being manipulated, scientists are taking sides, and emotions are high. I do not find people disputing the fact that temperatures have risen, but I also haven't heard anyone explain why it was warmer in the nineteenth century than it is today or what caused the nineteen prior glacial declines.

It seems clear that our planet warms and cools in cycles, but the Democrats insist on sweeping changes when their own scientists say, "Climatically, Kyoto would do nothing."[202] Others add, "No matter how much civilization slows or reduces its greenhouse gas emissions, global warming and sea-level rise will continue for centuries. This is just not something you can stop. We're just going to have to live with it."[203] The Republicans, on the other hand, regardless of what you believe about global warming, refuse to admit that burning oil is destroying our air and polluting our waterways, and thus take no action. The two parties refuse to consider a middle ground. Sensibility has been dismissed. While the politicians politic, our environment worsens.

The bureaucracy that has built up around the environmental movement is a big part of the problem. Rather than focusing on issues of importance, we have created a nightmare of rules and regulations that lead to actions that make no sense. "The EPA alone has over 10,000 pages of regulations…Federal statutes and formal rules now total about 100 million words."[204] The results are usually the opposite of what was intended. The Occupational Safety and Health Administration (OSHA) estimated that "80 percent of workplaces are not in compliance with the law."[205] In a 1993 survey of corporate general counsels, National Law Journal found, "Only 30 percent of the attorneys believed that full compliance with the matrix of U.S. and State environmental laws was possible."[206] When politicians cannot agree, they create bureaucracies, who create regulations, which do nothing but create overhead.

The Endangered Species Act, as an example, has led to 1,869 species being listed as endangered, but has removed only one since 1970, the gray whale.[207] It seems there are a couple of others that have come off the list, but critics contend the few that have been delisted never should have been on the list to begin with.[208] For the most part, instead of protecting legitimate animals, the Act has become a way to prevent land development. Frogs, flies, rats, and hundreds of tiny insects have been used, manipulatively, to prevent or delay the construction of roads, hospitals, factories, and a thousand other legitimate developments, and to burden every project with unnecessary and exorbitant construction costs. There are so many examples of abuse (dryopid beetle, Peck's cave amphipod, riffle beetle, cave shrimp, fairy shrimp, etc.) they merit a chapter of their own. If we wish to make progress in America, we need to sensibly approach the protection of our environment and endangered species while allowing our nation to continue to progress. Politicians have turned the Endangered Species Act into a tool to manipulate our emotions and divide the nation.

Question: Will you vote to support the Kyoto Protocol (as written)?

IMMIGRATION

There are two kinds of immigration: good and bad. The following two stories from WorldNetDaily and Predatory Aliens are indicative of the trend that is accompanying bad immigration. There are thousands of similar stories. These are not one-off anecdotes.

Juan Leonardo Quintero had been deported to Mexico in 1999 after having been charged with molesting a twelve-year-old girl. He was pulled over after a routine traffic stop in 2006 by Officer Rodney Johnson, a married, twelve-year veteran with five children. Quintero was arrested, handcuffed and put in back of the police car. "But Johnson missed the gun in Quintero's waistband. The prisoner pulled it out and fired four times at Johnson at close range. When Johnson was laid to rest this week after his execution-style murder he joined a growing list of law enforcers gunned down by foreign criminals."[209] Predatory Aliens provides summaries of cases involving illegal aliens. Following are excerpts from their Web site. They report a case involving Manuel Cantu, twenty-eight, an illegal alien from Mexico who had plead guilty to raping and sodomizing an autistic eighteen-year-old girl just months after having been arrested on rape charges elsewhere. They report that Daniel Jose Ventura, twenty-nine, an illegal alien from Mexico, was wanted for lewd sexual battery on a minor. A third report claims that Juan Chavez-Diaz, thirty-two, an illegal alien from Mexico, was arrested after the Integrated Automated Fingerprint Identification System (IAFIS) identified him while trying to enter the country. He is a convicted and registered sex offender with an outstanding warrant for "Continuous Sexual Abuse of a Child." They report that Santo Gustavo Valle-Sosa, forty-three, an illegal alien from Honduras, was found living in Florida after having been arrested in 1997 for raping his four-year-old stepdaughter. Eligio Hernandez-Zepeda, forty, an illegal alien from El Salvador, was deported after having been convicted for raping and impregnating a twelve-year-old girl. The list goes on.[210]

Deborah Schurman-Kauflin of the Violent Crimes Institute reports, "There are approximately 240,000 illegal immigrant sex offenders in the United States."[211] Year after year, politicians have been unable to do anything that will control illegal immigration, particularly immigrants that we do not want.

Over the years, I have worked with a hundred or more of the most intelligent, hardest working computer scientists and business-men you will ever meet. They come from all over the world, most of them schooled in our universities, and all of them striving to build a successful life for their family. Our country is a thousand times stronger because of the contributions of immigrants like Albert Einstein, John Kenneth Galbraith, Andy Grove, and a million others. However politicians have consistently made it more difficult for those wishing to immigrate to our country legally to do so, often turning away the very immigrants we need.

When addressing immigration, we must be careful that we distinguish between the educated who follow our immigration processes, the laborers who provide valuable contributions to our businesses, and the criminals who enter the country illegally. Our country benefits immensely from immigrants, but we need to control how many enter, who enters, and what we do when they violate our laws. Our current system, like so many others, is completely out of control. We need to address immigration, not by granting amnesty to every person that has illegally entered our country, but in a controlled manner that allows us to choose who can come and who must go.

"Between 12 million and 20 million illegal aliens are living in the United States. But as that range suggests, no one—not the Border Patrol, not Immigration and Customs Enforcement, not the FBI or the Department of Homeland Security—has any true idea how many illegal aliens are here."[212] The American Resistance group says, "In agreement with Senator McCain, our counters are calibrated to reflect an increase of 10,000 total additional illegal aliens added to the United States population each day... There are an estimated 4 million illegal immigrants entering our country per year."[213] That is enough to fill a city the size of Houston, but don't worry, the government is working the problem. "By 2002 the Immigration and Naturalization Services (INS) estimated that more than 7,500,000 illegal aliens lived in the United States, and it fined all 13 of their employers."[214]

Illegal immigrants are providing valuable low-cost labor, a fact we cannot deny, but there is a cost that comes with that labor. Steve King, a member of the House from Iowa wrote an article titled "Biting the Hand that Feeds You."[215] In it he reported that less than 7,000 Americans have died on or after 9/11 due to terrorism, including those who died fighting terrorists in Iraq and Afghanistan. During the same time period, over 19,000 Americans have died a violent death at the hands of murderous illegal aliens (twelve a day). He claims that over 20,000 people have died at the hands of uninsured drunk driving illegal aliens since 9/11 (thirteen a day). He reports that over 13,000 American children have been the victim of a sex crime at the hands of an illegal alien since 9/11 (eight a day).[216] We have 250,000 illegal immigrant sex offenders in our country! Are we fighting the right war?

We are spending billions of dollars trying to guard our borders and keep drugs and illegal aliens from entering our country, but we have stopped neither. The number of illegal immigrants has now doubled, and Congressman Ted Poe projects the cost to the American taxpayer is over $60 billion per year.[217] The *New York Times* much more conservatively says, "We spend an estimated $7.3 billion annually just to secure our borders, an increase of 58 percent since the terror attacks of 9/11; $20 million per day, and yet Governors of New Mexico and Arizona tell us that the international borders of their states are as porous as sieves."[218]

I believe there are three steps we need to take to solve the immigration program:

1. Control the border; put an end to the unabated influx.
2. Establish a Guest Worker Program; allow business owners to employ temporary workers in a controlled manner.
3. Ensure proper deterrents are in place for those who violate the rules; force those who enter illegally to work on the "Great Wall of Mexico" for 365 days without pay.

There are probably a thousand other ideas on how we should address this problem, but it is clear that politicians will never bring a systematic solution forward. If they take any action, it is almost certain they will grant amnesty to those who are here illegally, and demand that they pay a twenty-five dollar registration fee, recite the pledge, and swear to vote for them in the next election. In 1994, Congressman Dick Armey said that while immigration is the issue of the day in California, "The mood will pass." It has not, and will not. It is up to us to take action.

Question: Will you vote to grant amnesty to those in our country illegally?

ABORTION

Abortion is one of the most difficult and emotional issues in America today. Many have tired of the discussion, but it needs to be put to rest. It is certain that our existing bi-polar political system will never craft a solution the entire country can live with, and the fact that many Americans take such a hard stand based upon personal beliefs does not help the situation. Given where we are, it is important we find a middle ground and end this divisive debate, at least for our generation.

As far back as the year 406 A.D., when the Hippocratic Oath was written, the issue of abortion was addressed with the line, "I will not give a woman a destructive pessary (a stone to induce abortion)."[219] Most doctors around the world still adhere to an updated variation of the Hippocratic Oath, though it has evolved. The abortion comment is no longer included in the United States version of the oath. Abortion was debated at the time our Constitution was written, but like slavery, was selectively not addressed.

Abortion was illegal in the United States until *Roe v. Wade* in 1973. Estimates of the annual number of illegal abortions in the 1950s and 1960s ranged from 200,000 to 1.2 million.[220] Levitt and Dubner report, "There are 1.6 million (clinical) abortions a year, one for every 2.25 births."[221] Since 1973, there have been an estimated 42 million (clinical) abortions.[222] "Today, 98.6 percent of all abortions are performed within the first 20 weeks of pregnancy, 88 percent within the first 12 weeks, and 59 percent within the first eight weeks. Only 1.4 percent occurs after 20 weeks."[223] Those numbers only account for clinical abortions. A declaration has been signed by 217 pro-life physicians asserting that "the pill and similar birth control products act, part of the time, by design, to prevent implantation of an already created human being" and "these products clearly cause an early abortion."[224] The Pill is used by about fourteen million American women each year.[225]

The answer must obviously and ultimately lie somewhere between the papal view that birth control is abortion and should never be allowed, and the extreme view of the pro-choice that until the baby has exited the womb, only the mother has a say on what is permissible. Leaving the issue unresolved prevents us from addressing other issues of importance. It throws an unnecessary emotional wrench into election after election, each already loaded with unproductive hostility. It makes the selection of judges political. It is our duty to put this issue, and others like it, to rest. The predominant majority should establish the principles on which we shall govern our country, not whoever yells the loudest. We need to formalize where we want to draw the line, and then amend the Constitution accordingly so that the issue is put to rest.

Allowing the debate to continue serves no purpose other than dividing our nation and making judicial appointments a political game. Our position on abortion should not be determined by the personal opinion of five Supreme Court Justices. The issue has been clearly known and passionately debated since the Constitution was written. Our founders left the issue unresolved, as they did slavery, because a consensus could not be reached. It took a civil war to settle the slavery issue. It is our duty to settle the abortion issue. Let us determine precisely where the line should be drawn and then amend the Constitution accordingly. We have left this issue unresolved for far too long.

> **Question:** Will you vote to amend the Constitution to make an abortion legal for only the first three months after conception excluding cases of rape, incest, or serious risk to the mother's life?

Gun Control

In 1991 at a Luby's in Killeen, Texas, Dr. Suzanne Gratia Hupp survived, but her parents and twenty-three others did not. Handgun laws in the state at the time prevented licensed carriers from bringing weapons into most public places, such as restaurants, so, following the law, she left her gun in her car in the parking lot. When Benjamin Nathaniel Smith drove his pickup truck into the restaurant, took out two pistols, and began to slowly and methodically kill twenty-three diners, the patrons were all helpless.

If any one of them had had a gun they almost certainly could have saved lives. Dr. Hupp was not the only person inside Luby's that day that had dutifully left her gun in the car.[226]

Thomas Jefferson wrote, "Laws that forbid the carrying of arms… disarm only those who are neither inclined nor determined to commit crimes…Such laws make things worse for the assaulted and better for the assailants; they serve rather to encourage than to prevent homicides, for an unarmed man may be attacked with greater confidence than an armed man."[227] Are we protecting the right people with our gun control laws?

Thomas Jefferson also wrote, "The Constitutions of most of our states assert that all power is inherent in the people; that…it is their right and duty to be at all times armed…" In a letter to George Washington, he said, "No free man shall be debarred the use of arms in his own lands."[228] George Washington said, "The very atmosphere of firearms anywhere and everywhere restrains evil interference—they deserve a place of honor with all that's good." Alexander Hamilton, in The Federalist Papers, said, "The best we can hope for concerning the people at large is that they be properly armed." Richard Henry Lee said, "Arms discourage and keep the invader and plunderer in awe, and preserve order in the world as well as property….Horrid mischief would ensue were (the law-abiding) deprived the use of them." Thomas Paine said, "To preserve liberty it is essential that the whole body of the people always possess arms and be taught alike, especially when young, how to use them."

The debate that a few anti-gun zealots are waging today, that the Constitution was never intended to give individuals the right to bear arms for anything other than military purposes, is without question the weakest argument I have ever heard. Our Founding Fathers were clear that Americans should be armed.

The argument should also be irrelevant. If a predominant majority of society does not want the citizens of this country to possess firearms they should amend the Constitution and make that the law of the land. I suspect that will not happen in my lifetime, but I wish the no-gun crowd would stop trying to find an activist judge who will manipulate words written over two hundred years ago to say what they want them to say. I have found, personally, that the people supporting this tactic and making this argument are about as trustworthy as snakes, and come to think of it, most of them have a temperament to match.

"There are more guns in the United Status than there are adults."[229] *Gunsafe* estimates "there are 235 million guns in the United States and that 42 percent of all households possess a gun."[230] "The overwhelming predominance of data we have examined shows that between 25 and 70 lives may be saved by a gun, for every life lost to a gun."[231] A gun control study done for the Cato Institute showed, "When a robbery victim does not defend himself, the robber succeeds 88 percent of the time, and the victim is injured 25 percent of the time. When a victim resists with a gun, the robbery success rate falls to 30 percent and the victim injury rate to 17 percent."[232]

On July 6, 2001, an unnamed man fatally shot seventeen-year-old Jacob W. Walton during a road rage altercation in Spokane, Washington. Walton was a passenger in a car and got into an altercation with the shooter. According to police, the shooter had a concealed-weapons permit.[233] This is a truly sad story reported on the *Brady Campaign* Web site, and I can understand where opponents would be outraged by the shooting. But what do you think caused the incident? Did Walton and the vehicle he was in threaten the shooter? Was Walton waving a gun at the shooter? Did the shooter have a really bad day? Without more information it is impossible to form an opinion, but that is all that was known almost six years ago when the story was initially posted.

The rest of the story was published just two months after the incident. The Brady Campaign didn't share this part:

A man who admits he shot and killed a teenager won't be charged with any crime. Investigators now say Walton and several friends actually started the fight that led to Walton's death. As a result, no charges will be filed...Investigators say the 17-year-old and several friends had thrown at least one beer can at the unidentified man's car. He stopped to call police but was followed to a north Spokane parking lot where Walton got out and hit him in the face. Prosecutors say the 28-year-old warned Walton and his friends to stay back...He drew his weapon, told the person don't make me shoot, the person kept coming.[234]

Tragic, I agree, but should this man have been forced to allow someone to pound his face or worse? The story is sad, but even sadder is the way it is still being exploited by those opposed to possessing firearms. The Brady Campaign site only has the initial story about a road rage maniac killing a teenager in cold blood. Why do you think they never told the rest of the story?

Gun control has failed miserably in the U.K., Australia, and most cities where it has been tried, including New York City and Milwaukee. Those who are against the right to bear arms consistently misrepresent data and misuse examples like the one above to try to make their point, but their efforts are disingenuous at best and usually disgustingly dishonest. The National Rifle Association (NRA), at times, goes too far the other way, and politicians use the issue to stir their constituents. It is time to close the book on this issue, though I am not really sure why it is open, and move on.

Question: Will you vote to support the right of citizens to bear arms?

INTERNET

The Internet is one of the most wonderful creations of the last fifty years. Is the Internet global property or can the United States control what goes on within our borders? Should we allow it to operate without restraint or should we control specific areas? Should we permit pornography as freedom of speech and make it available to all, or should we partition questionable content to restricted domains that we can control, keeping the "art" away from the eyes of children? Should spammers and hackers be tolerated as wildcat businessmen or punished like hardened criminals? Should we continue to ignore gambling or regulate and tax it? Has the government addressed any of these issues to your satisfaction, or should it address them at all?

> The FBI announced that more than 89 persons in over 20 states have been charged in the first phase of a nationwide crackdown on the proliferation of child pornography via the Internet....Known as 'Operation Candyman,'...To date, 27 persons have been arrested and admitted to the prior molestation of over 36 children....Individuals identified as subjects in Operation Candyman include Little League coaches, a teacher's aide, a guidance counselor, a school bus driver, a foster care parent, and professionals in the medical, educational, military, and law enforcement fields.[235]

That was just the start. Days later the FBI said, "It expects to arrest at least 50 more people by week's end as it busts up an Internet child-pornography ring that allegedly included two Catholic priests, six other members of the clergy, a (second) school bus driver, and at least one police officer."[236] By now you know how this goes. "The FBI arrested 65 people for using peer-to-peer networks to exchange child pornography on Friday (May 14, 2004)."[237] We see the same thing story after story.

"Internet porn makes up $2.5 billion of the $57 billion pornography industry. Twenty-five percent (25 percent) of all search engine requests are porn-related, 12 percent of total Web sites are pornographic, and the largest consumer of Internet pornography is the twelve-to-seventeen-years-old age group, according to the Web site Healthyminds.com."[238] Did you catch the part about the teenage use? Should we allow this temptation to remain so accessible to our children? I believe we should demand the use of an .xxx extension for all sites containing X-rated material and impose stiff fines and jail time for those who do not cooperate. What do you think?

Internet gambling is also a fast-growing industry with estimated 2003 revenues of more than $4 billion.[239] Should we establish a specific domain for gambling and ensure that transactions are appropriately taxed and minors are kept away in a manner similar to the .xxx pornography domain I propose?

The *New York Times* reported that spam has doubled in the past year and now accounts for 90 percent of all e-mail messages.[240] The Radicati Group estimated that spam cost businesses $20.5 billion in 2003.[241] They say that an organization with 10,000 employees spends an estimated $71.91 per mailbox per year because of spam.[242] Should we more seriously consider spamming the spammers? I hate spam, and believe we could and should do more to those who abuse the system. I think the 90 percent number above is high, but it may be that my provider is doing a good job of filtering messages. The solution seems pretty clear: harsher penalties for those who send spam on multiple occasions. Supreme Court Justice Potter Stewart said he couldn't define pornography, "But I know it when I see it." The same is true for junk e-mail. We need not allow hucksters to abuse the system.

> **Question:** Will you vote to establish an .xxx Internet domain (e.g., www.notforkids.xxx), to impose steep fines, and to demand jail time for all sites that provide access to pornographic material outside of this domain?

MILITARY

It is unfortunate, but even in today's world tyrants and dictators do exist and must be tolerated. Parts of the world are not ready for our form of government and some countries may never be. We are far from perfect and are in no position to dictate our lifestyle or type of government to others. As long as human rights are not violently being abused, I do not believe we have any right to intervene in the business of other nations. Issues of foreign sovereignty and international politics are well beyond the scope of this book. They are, however, mentioned here to ensure our representatives have declared their position on the most obvious issues.

We have the strongest military in the world and are generally safe from the military threats of other nations. That does not mean we can relax, that we will never be attacked, or that terrorists will not continue to plot the next 9/11, but generally speaking, we can sleep well. Building and maintaining a strong military will always be critical if we wish to remain the leader of the free world, but it can also be a burden.

Paul Kennedy, in *The Rise and Fall of the Great Powers*, asserts that the great powers of history have floundered as they overextended themselves militarily. If a nation spends too much of its productive income on an unproductive military apparatus, its vitality will be sapped. He warns that the United States is on this path, and unless it cuts back on its military apparatus forthwith, it will soon be a former great power.[243] James Madison warned us, "Of all the enemies to public liberty war is, perhaps, the most to be dreaded because it comprises and develops the germ of every other. War is the parent of armies; from these proceed debt and taxes...known instruments for bringing the many under the domination of the few....No nation can preserve its freedom in the midst of continual warfare."[244]

The defense budget requested $647 billion for national defense in 2007.[245] Twenty percent of our $2.65 trillion budget is spent on the military. If you factor in all related costs that organizations such as The Friends Committee on National Legislation report, "41 percent of our taxes are going toward war."[246] As of mid-November 2006, there were approximately 152,000 U.S. troops deployed in Iraq.[247] We have over 70,000 troops deployed in Germany, 47,000 in Japan, 32,000 in South Korea, 12,000 in the UK, and 11,000 in Italy.[248] Since 1950, fifty-four countries have hosted at least 1,000 American troops.[249] The war in Iraq has now lasted longer than United States involvement in World War II.

Have we lost sight of what the purpose of our military should be? Have the bureaucratic tendencies of government infected the mission of our Defense Department, redefining its goal so that, like so many of our other government bureaucracies, it is as focused on expansion and justification as it is on security and strength? There are few who question the importance of maintaining a military stronger than our potential enemies, but how strong must we be? Can we afford to spend 4 percent of our GDP and 25 percent or more of our budget on soldiers, ships, tanks, planes, missiles, and guns? "The United States spends nearly as much on defense as all the rest of the countries in the world combined."[250] Power is one thing, but excess leads to demise.

I believe we need to tighten the reins on military deployments and spending, and focus more energy on securing our borders. If we cannot protect an invasion of our own soil, I see little benefit in policing the rest of the world. Can we afford to spend such a large percentage of our budget on the military when we are not truly at war? The war on terrorism is not a war in the classic sense; it is now a way of life, a never-ending battle. We must combat terrorism in the same way a runner approaches a marathon; it is a battle that requires we pace ourselves, one that calls for patience and perseverance, skill and intelligence. With terrorism, the battle will continue for decades. We cannot spend at our current pace any more than the marathoner can run an entire race at full speed. The fury of war cannot be sustained for extended periods; the passion, focus, funds, and energy will wane with time. We must stay ahead of the enemy, but understand they will always be present.

> **Question:** Will you vote to limit total military spending to 3 percent of GDP, excluding periods when our nation is imminently at risk of war with another country or a recognized military unit (i.e., claiming we are at war with terrorists is not the same as being at war with another country)?

ENERGY

Our dependence on oil and the problems with energy in our country are topics that also require significant discussion, but once again I'll try to be brief. Our national transportation system works very well. We have multi-lane highways that cross the country, reasonably priced gasoline available at every street corner, and automobiles of every shape, size, and style that are affordable and comfortable for anyone who is willing to work a steady job. But our economy and our transportation system are at the mercy of radical countries and dictators who could create havoc in a heartbeat.

Do you believe we should continue to utilize the system as it is, incrementally improving vehicle efficiency, or is it time for the government to initiate another "moon landing" that creates an entirely new way to get from place to place? Should we be investing in affordable and efficient mass transportation or continuing the development of new highways and toll roads for multi-person vehicles that have a single occupant 75 percent to 95 percent of the time? Should we provide incentive for the development and purchase of vehicles that can only carry one or two passengers, get a hundred miles per gallon, and discourage or more severely tax vehicles that are made for four, six, or eight? Should we more strongly provide incentive for the purchase and use of fuel-efficient vehicles? Should we continue to base our transportation system on Middle Eastern oil, develop new oil fields of our own, or mandate a transition to a cleaner, more efficient fuel that comes from within our borders? Is the government providing the direction that we need?

There are alternatives within our reach that will benefit the environment and lessen our dependence on the radical oilmen of the world, but we need to accelerate their maturation and make a commitment to breaking our habit. There is a place for nuclear power, one of the cleanest and most efficient energy sources. Sailors transitioned from sail to steam, and our forefathers from horseback to automobile. The time to put oil derricks in our rearview mirror has come. Just as we established a goal of putting a man on the moon, and then delivered, the time has come to change the way we travel from place to place.

We do not want or need the government to "invent" the solution; we just need them to create an environment where scientists and entrepreneurs can do their thing. One of the few things government can do well is build infrastructure and facilitate research, and that is what we need to develop an alternative solution. It is up to us to tell the government how we want them to help, not the other way around.

Question: Will you vote for the establishment of a government program to facilitate the design of an alternative Transportation System, developed by private companies that can propose solutions which utilize cleaner, more efficient fuels (such as fuel cells), are not dependent on a foreign energy source, and can begin deployment within five years?

HOMELESSNESS

Larry Hogue, addicted to crack and insane by the account of most, is known as the "Wild Man on 96th Street." "He has been in and out of mental hospitals since 1972, but he has never been hospitalized for longer than six months. Usually the hospital releases him within 24 hours after the police bring him in. The city's psychiatric emergency rooms are intimately familiar with him. On one occasion the police were turned away from six emergency rooms with Hogue restrained in the back seat."[251] What should we do with Larry?

We have at least "sixteen different programs, costing $1.7 billion in 2001, targeted for the homeless. The homeless were also eligible for another thirty-four federal programs, including housing, health care, job training, and transportation. Twenty-six programs administered by six agencies offer food and nutrition services."[252] There are wide variations on the estimated number of homeless, but most estimates come in at over two million, about the same number as we house in our prisons. Is there not a better solution?

We have exasperated the problem by eliminating the development and even existence of low-cost housing. Building regulations, urban sprawl, inadequate mass transportation, and a dozen other factors have driven people to the streets. We will never make this problem go away entirely, but having almost one percent of the population living on the streets feels like failure to me. Can we do better? I think we should try.

Question: Will you commit to lowering the number of homeless by 5 percent each year?

GLOBALIZATION

America is the cornerstone of the global economy. There are those who believe we should not be and who favor varying degrees of isolation and protection, but that mindset has flaws. Today our country depends on the rest of the world, and much of the rest of the world depends on us. Going back to a day when countries were self-contained and self-sufficient is an option, but not a serious one. However, there are those who believe limited interaction with the rest of the world would solve many of our problems. Regardless of anyone's beliefs, our role in the world should be reconsidered on a periodic basis. The global economy is shifting constantly, and our role must be reevaluated continuously.

Should we give up on the concept of the United Nations and withdraw our support? Should we pronounce the United Nations ineffective, as we did the League of Nations, and begin anew? Should we try to find a more moderate position, somewhere between the corrupt doormat known as France and the bludgeoning bully, which is how much of the world views the United States? Should we adjust our military strategy, our policing efforts, and our spending accordingly? Should we work to regain the respect of the countries around the world, working harder to build consensus? Or should we continue just as we are, doing what those in power insist is the right thing, addressing issues on a case-by-case basis, and accepting that there will always be a vocal minority who disagree with whatever our philosophies and actions are? Do we have an obligation to the rest of the world, or have we just allowed our belief that we have an obligation become too consuming?

According to Joseph Farah, Communist and militant Islam regimes continue to persecute Christians in eleven different countries: China, Pakistan, Laos, North Korea, Vietnam, Cuba, Saudi Arabia, Sudan, Egypt, Nigerian, and Uzbekistan.[253] The United Nations has taken no action, nor have they done anything in Rwanda or Darfur. They have time to complain about the cleanliness of rivers in the United States, but remain silent when genocide is evident or when terrorists cry for jihad. Should we continue to support such an organization?

Are we providing an appropriate amount of foreign aid to the right number of countries? Author Doug Bandow says, "Since World War II, the Unites States alone has provided $1 trillion (in current dollars) in foreign aid to countries around the world."[254] "In 2004, the United States is providing some form of foreign assistance to about 150 countries. After hitting an all-time low in the mid 1990s, total foreign assistance (excluding Iraq reconstruction in 2004)...has been larger than any two-year period since the mid-1980s."[255] "In 2004 dollars, we have spent an average of $19 billion per year for the last 3 years, excluding the $20 billion plus being spent on Iraq, on aid to foreign countries."[256] The top recipients of foreign aid in 2004 were:[257]

1. Iraq ($18.4 billion);
2. Israel ($2.6 billion);
3. Egypt ($1.9 billion);
4. Afghanistan ($1.8 billion);
5. Columbia ($570 million);
6. Jordan ($560 million);
7. Pakistan, Liberia, Peru, Ethiopia, Bolivia, Turkey, Uganda, Sudan, Indonesia, and Kenya (each receiving over $100 million).

Can we continue to give away so much money when we are in so much debt? Some complain we are not giving nearly enough. "The United States is the largest international economic aid donor in dollar terms but is the smallest contributor among the (22) major donor governments when calculated as a percent of gross national income. The United States contribution is 0.2 percent of GNP."[258] Should we give more?

> **Question:** Will you vote to limit the total dollar amount of foreign aid given or loaned to any individual country in any single year to 5,000 times the median income in the United States (approximately $230 million today), and to limit contributions to any country to a maximum of three years out of ten?

TERRORISM

Do you feel safe from terrorists? Should the government have more leeway to locate and monitor suspected terrorists, or should it be forced to follow the laws of the land as rigorously as if it were pursuing one of our citizens? Should we prosecute terrorists as U.S. citizens within our judiciary or should they be prosecuted by the military? Should we protect the free speech of terrorists, or should we adopt a more aggressive position that limits threatening speech? Do you believe this is a real problem or are politicians fanning the flames to enhance their political position? Are we encouraging terrorism with our military engagements overseas or are we keeping ourselves safe by taking the war away from our homeland?

Brandenburg v. Ohio established that yelling "fire" in a crowded theatre is not protected because it is "speech brigaded with action." *Schenck v. United States* ruled that free speech is limited during time of war. Should we more aggressively go after those who suggest "jihad" publicly, calling such a statement an act of treason or a call to action? Do you believe doing so would violate our freedom of speech, or is it a necessary protection that our citizens deserve? Should we be more specific in defining what treason is, or is it adequately understood? If someone is promoting imminent lawless action or suggesting inhumane treatment of our citizens, should they be afforded the same rights as our countrymen?

"There are 15,000 facilities across the United States that produce or store deadly chemicals—chemicals that terrorists could use against us as weapons of mass destruction."[259] Should we be doing more to protect chemical facilities and ports, or are there so many targets that protection is not possible? If a person suggests in a public speech that the plants should all be blown up to punish America for our transgressions, should we (a) ignore the comment as free speech, (b) arrest and detain him for a few weeks, (c) lock him up for years, or (d) lock him up in a military prison for the rest of his life. How would you vote?

In my opinion, terrorism is a significant problem that will only get worse. There is a large contingent of radicals who truly believe that taking their own lives and the lives of those who do not share their views is acceptable and, in fact, rewarded. I consider calls to take someone's life a crime, not free speech, and do not believe we should tolerate people who make such statements. I expect the ACLU will argue with me on this one. After all, free speech is free speech, even if it comes from a terrorist who is not a citizen of our country and who fails to abide by the most basic laws of humanity. I believe there are limits, even to free speech, and the Supreme Court has already ruled that it agrees with me. What about you?

Question: Will you vote to support free speech, regardless of what is said and regardless of whether or not the speaker is an American citizen?

IX Economy

Our economy is an amazingly resilient, magnificently awesome engine. It took a while, but we have fully recovered from the bursting of the Internet bubble and the attacks of 9/11. The unemployment rate in 2006 was 4.6 percent, a number lower than all but three years (1998, 1999, and 2000) since 1970.[260] Despite the negative publicity over tax cuts for the rich, the declining middle class, and jobs moving overseas, our economy has had its best eight-year run since the late 1960s, and that is with the bubble and 9/11 catastrophes smack in the middle of the run. While most Americans, including me, are unhappy with politicians, government, and a dozen other things, it is impossible to be unhappy about the economy. The economy is the one thing in our society that the government does not have dominant control of and it is, surprise, doing exceptionally well.

You may hear some politicians talk about the declining middle class, but they are merely trying get to you mad at "the rich." "It's true that the middle class is shrinking—but that's because more families are better off. The share of prime-age (25–59) adults in households with real incomes above $100,000 rose by 13.1 percentage points from 1979 to 2004. The share of households making less than $75,000 dropped by 14 percent. Fully 41 percent of prime-age American adults are in households with incomes above 75,000."[261]

The fine print in this quote is the age boundaries and the term "prime-age." As the baby boomers begin to retire, what do you suppose happens to their income? It goes down, of course. What do you suppose that does to the number of people in the middle class? The lowest segment is a little more deceiving, with both good and bad news. More people are going to college, delaying the time until they make more money. That is a good "problem." The downside is that we have a growing problem with those not graduating from high school, those being raised in poverty, and those in jail or with a parent in jail. Combined, the negatives will impact the middle class in the long run. But the bigger point in this chapter is that you must watch how politicians present information. They can find numbers to support whatever case they want to make. Statistics can be skewed and misrepresented to support any opinion. Always scrutinize numbers—even mine.

Bankruptcy is another problem and one that will get worse. As our debt increases, tax rates rise, and the cost of health care goes up, so will the number of bankruptcies. The solution is to get the debt under control, lower taxes, and keep the economy growing. If we do not, bankruptcies could begin a chain reaction that would lead to a recession, which, in turn, could lead to other, more serious problems.

Rather than bother with important issues like bankruptcy, politicians are more likely to tackle emotional issues such as the minimum wage which, in the grand scheme of things, is a non-issue. Increasing the minimum wage does nothing but lead to unnecessary inflation that ultimately hurts senior citizens and everyone else living on a fixed income. More generally, we would all be better off if the government would not get involved in establishing prices or wages of any kind.

Mario Palmieri, in *The Philosophy of Fascism* (1936) wrote,

> Economic initiative cannot be left to the arbitrary decisions of private, individual interests. Open competition, if not wisely directed and restricted, actually destroys wealth instead of creating it....The proper function of the state...is

that of supervising, regulating, and arbitrating the relation-
ships of capital and labor, employers and employees, individuals and associations, private interests and national interests....More important than the production of wealth is
its right distribution, distribution which must benefit in the
best possible way all the classes of the nation, hence, the nation itself. Private wealth belongs not only to the individual,
but in a symbolic sense, to the state as well.

The U.S.S.R. was a great test case that shows us how well Palmieri's philosophy works. We should make sure our leaders are not
reading from this playbook, and if they try to supervise, regulate, or
arbitrate our economy, we should replace them immediately. Some
argue that the government should be responsible for inventing and
innovating. Watch out for calls for such action; that is not the role of
government.

Our economy is strong. Free enterprise works if we allow it to.
The government needs only to ensure the rules are followed and the
playing field is level. We can listen to scholars tell us about Marshallian
curves or Walrasian analysis, but the solution to economic problems
is not that complex. It is so simple, in fact, that it is known by almost
every common man in America: keep the hands of government off!
But politicians insist on getting involved. They look for opportunities,
claiming they hear the "voice" of the people, or at least the press, as
they complain about the disappearing middle class and the über-rich.
I have never heard that "voice" personally, nor do I know anyone who
has other than an intervening politician or a closet socialist. Both insist on solving nonexistent problems by protecting companies, wages,
and jobs with complicated tax schemes, credits, and breaks.

Intervention is seldom, if ever, needed. In most cases, it is nothing
more than payback or backslapping. If we wish to continue flourish-
ing economically, all we have to do is keep the hands of our government off the free market engine and out of the special interest cookie
jar. The market will do the rest. It will be up to the people to choose
representatives with the right mindset to run the country. Consider

carefully how much governmental intervention you want in the daily operation of our economy. When you vote for your representative, it is critical that you understand what his perspective is.

Question: Will you vote to support free market activity over government intervention in all situations, excluding war, catastrophes caused by nature, industrial accidents, and periods where the GDP is contracting for more than six consecutive months?

X The Candidate Questionnaire

As stated in the introduction, large sections of the original draft of this book have been set aside. Each of the topics discussed earlier had been reviewed in extensive detail and a much lengthier list of questions for candidates to answer was developed. All of the original questions appear here, separated by category. The list of questions is long, and not all will make the final questionnaire, but they are included here so you can get a feel for the complexity of the problem and help decide which questions should ultimately be presented in the final questionnaire. Give some thought to how you would answer each question and how you want your representative to respond. More importantly, engage in the forums on the GOOOH Web site to help us determine if there are better ways to word the questions or other questions that should be asked. Help us determine which questions are most important and if the line should be drawn in a different place. I have built a strong team of American patriots who will moderate the initial forums where the questions will be debated, but we will be looking for others to actively engage. I hope you will join us.

The questionnaire will be finalized six to eight months before the election. Candidates will be required to provide a yes-or-no response to every question on the list. They cannot skip even a single question. "No response" is not an option. More importantly, candidates will be required to sign a binding commitment document that says, if elected, they will vote exactly the way they said they would or they will resign from office immediately. There will be no room for waffling, no flip-flopping, and no vote trading.

An Override Clause is discussed in the next chapter. It allows a candidate to seek approval from the people of his district if he wishes to change his position. He cannot change his mind on his own; he can only switch his vote on the core issues if his district permits him to do so.

A common question that comes up is what does a candidate do if he is committed to voting for one issue, but against another, and both are combined on the same bill? The answer is simple: the candidate cannot vote, for doing so would violate his commitment. Ideally, a quorum will not be obtained, neither issue will pass, and the items will be voted on independently. The objective is to put an end to politicians combining bills, adding riders, and attaching earmarks, things they do to sneak their pet projects through the system. We need each and every issue to be voted on based on its own merits.

As you contemplate this system and the questions being asked, remember that the only relevant issue is how those in your district who are seeking to represent you answer the questions. My opinion is completely irrelevant when you are answering the questions or choosing your representative. Collectively, the members of your district will have to decide which answers are preferred. I suspect most of the participants in San Francisco will answer in a very liberal manner, while those in Dallas will answer in a very conservative manner. The final nominee from San Francisco is likely to lean left and the one in Dallas right. Participants in each district will decide.

I am confident you understand why it is important that we require those seeking to represent us to answer the questions and commit to their responses before they are elected. We have watched politicians break promises for too long. Being bound to the answers will ensure we have representatives, not politicians, serving the people.

CANDIDATE QUESTIONS
POLITICIANS

1. Do you commit to not accept any item valued at more than five hundred dollars from any person from this day until the end of your two-year term?
2. Do you commit that you will not publicly campaign for office, allowing GOOOH to raise all funds and perform all marketing for you?
3. Will you vote for term limits of four years (two terms) or less for seats in the U.S. House of Representatives?
4. Will you vote for a presidential line item veto?
5. Will you vote to set the congressional pay rate to four times the median income, index the rate, and replace the congressional pension with a standard 401k retirement plan?
6. Will you vote to allow each state to continue drawing its congressional districts, in a partisan manner, as is done today?

LAWYERS

7. Will you vote to amend the Constitution to exclude people with a law degree from serving in the House of Representatives?
8. Will you vote to exclude a plaintiff's legal representative from receiving any portion of a punitive award and split the payment between the plaintiff and charity?
9. Will you vote to limit the legal fees a plaintiff's legal representative can receive to one hundred times the amount a plaintiff in the case receives? As an example, if a plaintiff receives $10,000, the combined legal fees could not exceed one million dollars.
10. Will you support the right of lawyers to use whatever means necessary to defend a client, including concealing information

and using "technicalities," as long as they do not violate a written law?

EXTREMISTS

11. Do you support the ACLU, and will you support the organization with government funding?

12. Will you vote to amend the Constitution to re-establish and re-clarify equal rights for all over special rights for a few (e.g., prisoners, seniors, students, gays, minorities, and women)?

13. Will you vote to amend the Constitution to state that the guiding principles of the country should always override technicalities and extremist groups?

14. Will you vote to amend the Constitution with a "law of predominant majority," which says the "rights" of groups can be denied if they have consistently demonstrated behavior that 95 percent of the population considers unacceptable? For example, 95 percent of the population would likely vote that a public KKK rally should *not* be allowed, overriding the "right" of free speech for that particular group.

15. Will you vote to require that campaign contributions must be made anonymously, directed to a specific contest instead of a candidate, and that the funds be split equally among all men on the ballot?

RELIGION

16. Will you vote to amend the Constitution to specifically affirm that we are a nation under God, that God is welcome in all that we do, but no man can be forced to participate in worship at any time or in any way?

17. Will you vote to permit religious activities on local, state, and federal property (such as schools, libraries, and municipal buildings), at the discretion of the members of each site?

18. Will you vote against the teaching of religion in public schools, as an elective?

19. Will you vote to allow established churches to manage federal welfare distribution for recipients who agree to use them instead of a government agency?

20. Will you vote to declare atheism a religion?

Drugs

21. Will you vote to impose a penalty of life in prison or death for anyone convicted of selling drugs to a minor, excepting only to reduce the sentence to twenty years if information is provided that leads to the conviction of their supplier?

22. Will you vote to reward informants whose information leads to the conviction of a person selling drugs to a minor with at least $5,000, excluding those who have been arrested?

23. Will you vote to multiply by ten the prison sentence of those convicted of possessing drugs that are not willing to provide information that leads to the conviction of their supplier?

24. Will you vote to set the legal drinking age to eighteen *and* high school graduation (excluding early graduation and GEDs)?

25. Will you vote to legalize marijuana?

Media

26. Will you vow to support a completely free press at all times?

27. Will you vow to provide honest and timely information to the press on all issues at all times, excluding personal, military, or confidential matters?

Morals

28. Will you vote to define marriage as the union between any two people?

29. Will you vote to allow gay couples to adopt children?

30. Will you vote for laws that attempt to define amoral behavior?

Miscellaneous

31. Will you vote to allow parents to have a vote for each of their

children under the age of eighteen, fathers for their sons and mothers for their daughters?

32. Will you vote to deny the right to vote to those receiving welfare or Social Security payments?

33. Will you vote to elect our president with a popular vote, replacing the Electoral College?

BIG GOVERNMENT — All Questions on government spending and reduction will be waived in periods where the Nation's GDP has been in decline for two consecutive quarters, or our country has been attacked on our soil and we have been or are in a declared state of war with a specific country within the last twenty-four months.

34. Do you believe that our country is a Republic, that the role of government should be limited as defined in the Constitution and the Bill of Rights, and will you generally vote for laws that support this view?

35. Will you vote to support states' rights over federal rights at least 90 percent of the time?

36. Will you vote to reduce total expenditures on government programs by at least 5 percent each year you are in office?

37. Will you vote to reduce the total number of federal employees by at least 5 percent each year you are in office?

38. Will you vote to require that all government programs have a clearly established objective and an end date of no more than ten years from the date of creation?

39. Will you vote to permit the sale of all goods over the Internet?

40. Will you vote to limit the total value of business subsidies (welfare) that are permitted in any single year to no more than one percent of federal tax receipts?

41. Will you vote to limit the total value of personal subsidies (welfare, excluding Social Security and Medicare) that are permitted in any single year to no more than 2 percent of federal tax receipts?

42. Will you vote to reduce farm subsidy allocations by at least 25 percent each year you are in office?
43. Will you vote to limit the imposition of a tariff on any good to a period of two years out of any five, excluding goods that are legitimately subsidized by foreign governments?
44. Will you vote to privatize government initiatives, including at least one of the following: national parks, highways, mail, licensing, or the airwaves?
45. Will you vote to limit the amount of foreign aid provided to any one country to a maximum of 10,000 times the median income ($460 million) and a maximum of two years in any five year period, excepting those nations in a declared war with a foreign enemy or a genocidal situation?
46. Will you vote to limit foreign aid to ten or less countries in any year?
47. Will you vote to eliminate federal government involvement in licensing in at least 50 percent of the industries it is involved in today?
48. Will you vote to eliminate all government price and production controls, including abolishment of the minimum wage?

SPENDING

49. Will you vote for a balanced budget amendment, with exceptions only for periods of declared war or a declining annual GDP?
50. Will you vote against a federal budget that includes any item whose benefit is primarily for a single state (e.g., a bridge in Alaska, or a levee in Louisiana)?

TAXES

51. Will you vote to replace the current tax system with the Fair-Tax as proposed by Linder and Boortz?
52. If we do not change to a consumption tax, will you vote to replace all regressive taxes with progressive taxes?
53. If we do not change to a consumption tax, will you vote to establish an indexed Corporate Minimum Tax (CMT) of 15

percent, similar to the personal Alternative Minimum Tax, requiring profitable corporations to pay at least that amount (as a percent of revenue), independent of expenses, deductions, and overseas activities?

54. Will you vow to not increase income taxes, excepting only during a period of declared war?

55. Will you vote to maintain the current income tax system over all other proposals?

56. Will you vote to limit the amount of money that any person can inherit in their lifetime, including through trusts and other "loopholes," to 250 times the median income ($11.5 million)?

57. Will you vote to prevent the U.S. Government from doing business with any corporation that has more than 33 percent of its assets in accounts outside the United States?

58. Will you vote to eliminate automated payroll deductions for taxes and dues, requiring individuals to submit monthly or quarterly payments (so that citizens feel the pain of paying)?

HEALTH SYSTEM

59. Will you vote for a government controlled National Health Care System that offers "free" health care to all?

60. Will you vote for complete government funded Health Care for all Americans under the age of twenty-five?

61. Will you vote for the government to provide Health Care vouchers to every American citizen that can be used to purchase health insurance from either the government or a private provider, thus ensuring that every American has some coverage?

62. Will you vote to allow citizens who are mentally sound, older than their "life expectancy" and terminally ill, to opt for euthanasia?

63. Will you vote to allow a panel of doctors to overrule the health care decision of a parent for a critically ill minor? For example, if three doctors recommend chemotherapy as the only viable treatment, but the child or parents oppose, should the doctor's decision prevail?

64. Will you vote to cap medical expenditures, paid by the government in any five year period for any one person, to twenty-five times the median income (approximately $1.1 million dollars)?

65. Will you vote to allow the government to mandate medical treatment for its citizens, such as vaccinations, for non-contagious concerns?

66. Will you vote to terminate all medical litigation by creating a separate account, funded by a 2 percent take of all medical procedures, that will be used to compensate patients or their families when the medical system fails?

EDUCATION SYSTEM

67. Will you vote to eliminate the federal Department of Education and vote for a plan to return all authority to the states over a period of four years or less?

68. As long as the federal government remains involved in the education system, will you vote to establish vocational/trade opportunities for those who have completed the ninth grade and are not interested in pursuing a college education?

69. Would you support a law that requires the removal of the bottom 3 percent of teachers in each school district each year?

70. Would you support a law that requires a graduated pay scale that includes paying the top 25 percent of teachers double what the bottom 25 percent earn?

71. Will you support corporal punishment in schools, but allow individuals to opt out by choice?

72. As long as the federal government remains involved in the education system, will you vote to give vouchers to students so that they can attend the school of their choice (including home school)?

73. Will you vow to have your children attend the public school in the district in which you live?

74. Will you vote to require that home schooling be fully supported by the federal government, as long as the government remains involved in the education system?

75. Will you commit to ensuring that spending on any one student is no more than four times the average spent on the others in the same school, and that no more than 5 percent of students will be authorized to receive more than twice the average of all others?

76. Will you vote to use 95 percent or more of federal tax dollars allocated for education on K–12 programs, leaving college education to the private sector?

LEGAL SYSTEM

77. Will you vote to amend the Constitution with a "Law of Common Sense" that requires judges to hold individuals accountable for their actions, particularly when the predominant majority of society would have known better? For example, Exxon would not be held liable if a teenager douses his hair with gasoline and then sets it on fire.

78. Will you vote to eliminate the "by reason of insanity" defense?

79. Will you vote to restrict the use of eminent domain laws, limiting their use to roads, schools, utilities, military needs, or emergency purposes?

80. Will you vote to remove the worst 3 percent of judges each year, determined by the number of decisions overturned by a higher court? This question targets those who are actively adjudicating rather than interpreting the law, and who show a consistent tendency to rule based on political or personal preference rather than written law.

81. Will you vote to force judges to retire from the bench by their retirement age (as defined by the Social Security system)?

82. Will you vote to allow a defendant or claimants personal history be admitted as evidence during a trial so that we focus more on protecting the innocent rather than the "likely" guilty?

83. Will you vote to require that only the Constitution and the laws of the United States be considered when deciding cases or writing opinions, in effect preventing judges from applying the "standards" of international behavior?

84. Will you vote to cap the fees that lawyers can collect in class-action lawsuits to one hundred times what any single defendant receives?

85. Will you vote to prevent lawyers from knowingly misrepresenting the truth to defend their client?

86. Will you vote to support the death penalty in cases of murder?

87. Will you vote to establish a maximum timeline for all criminal cases, ensuring that court proceedings begin within three months, end within one year, that appeals extend no more than two years through the highest court possible, and that both the defense and prosecution must adhere to the timeline with penalty of contempt of court charges and license revocation if they do not—this includes death penalty cases?

WELFARE SYSTEM

88. Will you vote to terminate all current federal welfare programs but spend at least 10 percent more on programs run by individual states, churches, or charities, holding them accountable for results in order to receive funding?

89. Will you vote to amend the Constitution to cap the amount of money spent on all types of welfare payments (excluding Social Security & Medicare) to less than 3 percent of federal tax receipts each year?

90. Will you vote to demand that all welfare recipients participate in course work to complete their high school education, some kind of vocational training, and a personal finance management course?

91. Will you vote to limit the time that any person or family can receive welfare to twenty-four months or less in any five year period?

92. Will you vote to require that birth control pills be made available to all teenage girls?

93. Will you vote to authorize frequent random drug tests for anyone receiving welfare payments?

94. Will you vote to impose lifetime sentences on those found guilty of welfare fraud?

PRISON SYSTEM

95. Will you vote to remove juveniles from their parent(s) after the juvenile's third arrest, sending them to live in a boot camp that focuses on education and discipline?

96. Will you vote to declare that the rights of a person who commits a crime and is subsequently found guilty to have forfeited his rights from the moment his crime was committed until the moment he is released?

97. Will you vote to reduce the cost per inmate, currently estimated at almost $30,000 per year, by 10 percent year over year, until the number is less than the national average spent on public education?

98. Will you vote to allow the movement of prisons and prisoners offshore?

99. Will you vote for programs to provide vocational training for prisoners in their last year of incarceration, in an attempt to rehabilitate them, limiting the expense to 25 percent of the average cost per prisoners (this would be a $7,500 limit with today's $30,000 average)?

100. Will you vote to require prisoners to work while incarcerated to help pay for their incarceration costs, and to mandate that all release decisions be tied to an inmates demonstrated readiness to work once released?

101. Will you vote for a life in prison or death penalty sentence for the first offense of child molestation?

102. Will you vote for the government to offer a job to all prisoners on the day they are released (it is not expected that these are high-paying or highly desirable jobs, but would help each ex-con have a better opportunity to get started)?

103. Will you vote to limit medical care for those serving life sentences or on death row to only comforting medication?

RETIREMENT SYSTEM

104. Will you vote to change the retirement age to sixty-nine, immediately, and index the retirement age for those under the age of fifty to "life expectancy" minus five years?[262]
105. Will you vote to reduce retirement payments to the wealthy, those whose children are wealthy, or those who did not raise children, by at least 50 percent?
106. Will you vote to eliminate government funded retirement (i.e., abolish Social Security)?
107. Will you vote for allowing individuals to invest a percentage of their retirement benefits in an option of their choice, including mutual funds, bond funds, and index funds?
108. Will you allow people who entered the country illegally to receive Social Security or other government benefits?
109. Will you vote to repeal all special retirement benefits for future congressmen, including yourself, requiring each to build his own retirement savings through a 401k (allowing the government to match 4 percent) as most other Americans must?

ENVIRONMENT

110. Will you vote to require annual reductions in total "greenhouse" emissions by 5 percent year over year?
111. Will you vote to support the Kyoto Protocol (as written)?
112. Will you vote to only apply the Endangered Species Act to animals that are larger in mass than a golf ball (i.e., eliminate protection for species such as salamanders, crickets, and spiders) unless a vital ecological role can be proven?
113. Will you vote to repeal the Endangered Species Act, rewriting it to consider the Law of Common Sense and the Rule of the Predominant Majority?

114. Will you vote for a law that says under no circumstances should the life of a man or his home be jeopardized at the expense of any plant or animal, regardless of the situation?

IMMIGRATION

115. Will you vote to formally establish English as the national language, and require its exclusive use in all public institutions and on all public material?

116. Will you vote to require that all students demonstrate mastery of the English language, at their grade level, before being allowed to enter the public school system, and that those who cannot do so be required to successfully complete an English immersion class?

117. Will you vote against amnesty for those who enter the country illegally?

118. Will you vote to grant amnesty to those in our country illegally?

119. Will you vote for a more efficient Guest Worker Program that allows non-U.S. citizens to work in the United States in a controlled fashion?

120. Will you vote to require those who have entered our country illegally to, when caught, work on a government project without pay for one year before being deported? An example of a project could be a wall that separates the United States and Mexico.

121. Will you vote to create a law that limits the number of immigrants who can become citizens in any single year to one percent or less of the population (that would be approximately three million immigrants this year)?

122. Will you vote to only grant citizenship to children born in this country who have at least one parent who is a U.S. citizen?

123. Will you vote for legislation that declares that those in the country illegally do not have any of the rights granted to citizens of our country, other than the right to humane treatment?

124. Will you vote to open the borders and allow any person wishing to enter the country to do so without restriction?

125. Will you vote to fine employers who hire illegal immigrants not approved by a guest worker program 3 percent or more of their gross income?

126. Will you vote to deny federal funding for anything other than life-threatening emergency care to those who are in the country illegally?

127. Will you vote to allow those seeking citizenship an opportunity to serve in the military for six years in exchange for citizenship, but ensure that mercenaries make up no more than 10 percent of military personnel?

ABORTION

128. Will you vote to amend the Constitution to make an abortion, for any reason, and from the moment of conception, illegal? This would include making "the Pill" and the newer "morning-after pill" illegal.

129. Will you vote to amend the Constitution to make abortion illegal at all times, from the moment of conception, except under specific circumstances such as rape, severe birth defects, incest, or threats to the mother's life? This would include making "the Pill" and the newer "morning-after pill" illegal.

130. Will you vote to amend the Constitution to make an abortion legal for only the first three months after conception excluding cases of rape, incest, or serious risk to the mother's life?

131. Will you vote to amend the Constitution to make abortion legal at all times?

132. Will you vote against the funding of abortions with tax dollars?

GUN CONTROL

133. Will you vote to support the right of citizens to bear arms?

134. Will you vote to limit possession of firearms to pistols, rifles, and shotguns, excluding the right to possess high-caliber, rapid-fire weapons?

135. Will you vote to support the right of every citizen to carry a concealed weapon, assuming they can demonstrate basic firearm competence, and excluding those that have been convicted of a felony?

136. Will you vote for lifetime prison terms for those possessing a gun illegally (e.g., ex-cons)?

137. Will you vote for lifetime prison terms for those who possess a gun while committing a felonious act?

INTERNET

138. Will you vote to establish a .xxx Internet domain (e.g., www. notforkids.xxx), to impose steep fines, and to demand jail time for all sites that provide access to pornographic material outside of this domain?

139. Will you vote for harsh penalties and fines for those who send spam e-mail, undesired messages, and other computer clutter as determined by the predominant majority?

140. Will you vote for harsh penalties and fines for those who "hack" into systems, or intentionally create or spread viruses or other items that degrade or limit computer performance?

141. Will you vote for the government to provide free Internet access to all Americans?

142. Will you vote for the government to provide free computers to all minors?

MILITARY

143. Will you vote to use our military to control our borders and prevent illegal immigration?

144. Will you vote to limit deployment to 10,000 troops, for a maximum of three years, in any country which we are not at war with and have not been for any of the last ten?

145. Will you vote to create a sixth branch of the Armed Services whose role is to contract out policing services to other parts of the world, ensuring the branch is financially self-sufficient?

146. Will you vote to limit total military spending to 3 percent of GDP, excluding periods when our nation is imminently at risk of war with another country or a recognized military unit (i.e., claiming we are at war with terrorists is not the same as being at war with another country)?

147. Will you vote to cut spending or force troop withdrawals if you are in disagreement with the president on military issues?

ENERGY

148. Will you vote against all financial backing of the oil industry by the government?

149. Will you vote for the establishment of a government program to facilitate the design of an alternative Transportation System, developed by private companies who can propose solutions that utilize cleaner, more efficient, fuels (such as fuel cells), are not dependent on a foreign energy source, and can begin deployment within ten years?

150. Will you vote to reduce our dependence on foreign oil by at least 5 percent year over year each year you are in office?

151. Will you vote to eliminate all fees and taxes on vehicles that get over twenty-five miles per gallon, increasing the efficiency threshold by at least 5 percent year over year?

152. Will you vote to require a minimum of 10 percent year over year improvements in two-stroke engines?

153. Will you vote to fund nuclear power plants to help address our energy needs?

154. Will you vote to fund the development of fuel cell technology beyond all others?

155. Will you vote to fund the development of solar technology beyond all others?

156. Will you vote to fund the development of wind technology beyond all others?

HOMELESSNESS

157. Will you commit to lowering the number of homeless by 5 percent each year?

158. Will you vote to consolidate all support for the homeless into one government department and then shift funding and responsibility to each state?

159. Will you vote to support the creation of special "towns" for the homeless, piloting the idea in five locations in the first year you are in office?

GLOBALIZATION

160. Will you vote for the United States to withdraw from the U.N.?

161. Will you vote to replace the U.N. with an alternative organization?

162. Will you vote to decrease total foreign aid contributions to match the average contributions of the leading countries in the world in absolute dollars: Britain ($4.9), Germany ($5.3), France ($5.5), China ($0), Russia ($0), Australia ($1.0), Canada ($1.0), and Japan ($9.9), or approximately $3.5 billion per year ($27.6 / 8)?

163. Will you vote to increase the percentage of foreign aid contributions so that we contribute at a rate equal to the average GDP contributions of Britain, Germany, France, China, Russia, Australia, Canada, and Japan (increasing our annual contributions)?

164. In 1996 U.S. soldier Michael New was court-martialed for refusing to wear a U.N. uniform and serve under a foreign commander in Bosnia. Do you support the decision to court-martial him?

165. Do you agree to abide by United Nations recommendations or dictates given to the United States?

TERRORISM

166. Will you vote to declare that any person who commits an act of terror or treason against any citizen or establishment belonging to our country shall be sentenced to life in prison without parole, or death?

167. Will you vote to process all non-U.S. citizens who commit a crime against a U.S. citizen in military tribunals instead of the U.S. legal system? (Effectively declaring they do not have the same rights as our citizens.)

168. Will you vote to support free speech, regardless of what is said and regardless of whether or not the speaker is an American citizen?

169. Will you vote to support legislation that declares the right to life and personal security overrides freedom of speech, and that threats against life will not be tolerated?

ECONOMY

170. Will you vote to support free market activity over government intervention in all situations excluding war, catastrophes caused by nature, industrial accidents, and periods where the GDP is contracting for more than six consecutive months?

171. Will you vote against government assistance of any kind for any company that does not have at least an A- bond rating (S&P)?

172. Will you vote against government-funded job programs and training except in periods immediately following war, catastrophes caused by nature, industrial accidents, and periods where the GDP is contracting for more than six consecutive months?

173. Will you vote to index the minimum wage to inflation, as long as there is a minimum wage?

174. Will you vote to abolish the minimum wage?

175. Will you vote to require that companies with revenues in excess of $200 billion (indexed) be separated into two or more entities?

There are clearly numerous other questions to ask, specific issues of the moment that will likely be added when the time nears, and even additional categories that should be explored. What you will find, as you begin comparing your answers to others, is that you can quickly ascertain whom you would vote for and whom you would not. We will all prioritize these questions in a different way, so the Web site will allow you to sort the questions in the order you deem most appropriate. My answers will be posted on the Web for all to see. Your answers will remain private unless you make it to the final fifty in your district.

XI The Plan to Take Over Our House

The people we must control have been identified and the decline of America documented. Information on our failing systems has been presented and the core issues we need to resolve discussed. The time has come to act. Questions about the people, the decline, the systems, and the issues have all been laid out so that those who wish to represent us can tell us exactly where they stand. The answers each candidate provides will tell us how they will vote on specific issues, as well as how they are likely to vote on issues more generally. This chapter outlines the plan for how we are going to choose the best 435 candidates from across the country to compete against the politicians—the Democrats and Republicans put on the ballot by the two parties. It will lay out a step-by-step timeline leading up to Election Day, November 4, 2008, and give us a chance to break the political death grip choking our country.

A Web site has been created which will serve as the headquarters for our revolution. You can find it at www.goooh.com. The site will include all the information you need to participate in the process, including how to sign up and run for Congress yourself. It is a place where you can interact with other Americans between now and Election Day, and a place where you can learn how to help advance the revolution. Even if you don't personally want to become a U.S. Representative, you should sign up and participate in the process. Use the forums to interact with other interested countrymen and learn how you can help secure the signatures we need to get on the ballot. You will find fundraising information, marketing material, reference material, the Candidate Questionnaire, and everything else related to our effort on the Web site. Make this a priority and help us succeed.

The goal is to remove the politicians and eliminate the influence the two parties and special interest groups have, and to identify the best candidate in your district to replace them. If you wish to be considered as the replacement, or to become a part of the selection process, the steps you will need to take are easy and straightforward. You will need to become a member of the GOOOH system, ensure you are qualified to run in our system by completing a screening test, document your position on the issues, and then commit in writing that if elected you will vote according to your documented position.

One of the biggest problems we have is a candidate's dependence on money from special interest groups and the parties. In order to end this dependency, we will require that every participant donate one hundred dollars to the cause and request that interested backers fund the system, not individual candidates. The funds we raise will be used for the national campaign promoting our 435 nominees and to pay all expenses incurred by the system. The most difficult challenge you will face, as a candidate, will be convincing three to eight groups of ten people that you are the best choice to represent them. The individuals you are trying to convince will also have completed the Questionnaire and many will be offering to serve as a United States Representative, just as you are. If the hundred dollars is more than you can afford, convince a friend or family member to support your entry; raising the money should be easy. The real challenge will be convincing your peers you are the best person to represent them. You will not need a million dollars, or any money beyond the hundred dollar support fee. You will not have to sell your soul to lobbyists or the devil. You will not have to quit your job to run for office. You will not have to print signs with your name on them and put them on every street corner. You will not have to shake 50,000 hands or kiss a hundred babies. All you have to do is convince your peers you are the best person to represent your district.

Please read this next part very carefully. This is not a competition in the classic sense. Your objective should not be to win at all costs. Coming in second or tenth place may be the best outcome possible. The intent is for you to work with the other members in your pool and identify the best person or persons, excluding yourself, to advance. If the others in the pool select you, congratulations, but recognize you cannot vote for yourself. Therefore, you should be focused solely on determining which of the other candidates you want to represent you. This is your chance to handpick your representative. Find the best candidate and support him or her; that is your patriotic duty.

Process Overview

1. Any person interested in participating will complete an online questionnaire. A few categories of people will be screened: Felons, Politicians, Wealthy, Lawyers, Minors, etc.
2. Candidates will be randomly assigned into pools of up to ten participants in their congressional district. There will be as many pools as are needed in each district, likely four to six rounds, but absolutely no more than eight. Pools will meet simultaneously at predetermined locations across the country. If, for example, there are 1,000,000 entrants, there will be 100,000 pools in the initial round, all occurring on the same Saturday morning.

3. Each pool of participants will select two candidates to advance to the next round via the "Selection Session" process. Sessions will last approximately five hours and be held on consecutive Saturdays, beginning at 9:00 a.m. local time.

4. Advancing candidates will be randomly assigned into a new pool in their district that will meet on the following Saturday. Steps two and three will repeat until there are only ten candidates remaining in each district.

5. The final ten candidates in each of the 435 districts will select a single nominee to represent their district. Before the final round, all 4,350 finalists will be asked to participate in a weekend retreat to ensure they fully understand how the final round will work and to confirm they are completely dedicated to representing their district if selected.

6. The 435 nominees will be placed on the November ballot to compete against the Republican and Democratic politicians.

7. The campaign for each of the 435 candidates will be orchestrated by the GOOOH system, which will provide all campaign funding and collateral.

TERMS

Here are a few definitions to ensure everyone understands the basics:

- **Candidate:** Any person who submits answers to the questionnaire, signs the Commitment Agreement and pays the support fee becomes a candidate.

- **Candidate Questionnaire:** The list of questions that all candidates must answer. Candidates will submit their answers to the questionnaire so that other candidates can evaluate them based on their responses. The initial questions are documented in this book. Input will be accepted via the online Web site until thirty to sixty days before the first selection session. Modifications to the final questionnaire will be made and posted by the system moderator twenty to thirty days before the first session.

- **Commitment Agreement:** The legally binding document each candidate will be required to sign that promises they will resign from office if they vote counter to any answer given in their questionnaire.

- **Host:** A member or place that offers to host a selection session.

- **Moderator:** A member who volunteers to facilitate a selection session.

- **Nominee:** The top candidate in each congressional district, selected by the other candidates in a series of selection sessions, who will compete against the Republican and Democratic politicians in the national elections.

- **Pool:** A group of ten or less candidates who will choose from among themselves two candidates to advance to the next round of sessions, or the single nominee to compete against the candidates of the parties.

- **Selection Process:** The steps the candidates will follow during a selection session to select the candidates to advance, or the final nominee.

- **Selection Session:** A one day event where ten candidates meet and together select the top candidate(s) via the selection process.

- **System Moderator:** The creator of GOOOH will initially serve as the system moderator in 2008 and will have final say in all disputes.

THE ELECTION TIMELINE

A current version of the timeline will be maintained on the Web. The initial plan is as follows:

Time to Election Day	Estimated Date	Description of Activities
14 Months	September 4, 2007	• Web site goes live • Fundraising begins • Forums for input on the Candidate Questions go live
13 Months	October, 2007	• Early versions of book available
12 Months	November 4, 2007	• Book is published • Begin collecting signatures to get on the ballot in each state • Formal promotion campaign kicks off
11 Months	December 4, 2007	• Ballot Committees are formed for each state to ensure our "party" is added to the ballot
10 Months	January 4, 2008	• Candidates begin registering
9 Months	February 4, 2008	• Candidates for hosts and moderators begin registering • "Party" added to the ballot of each state
8 Months	March 4, 2008	• Marketing campaign begins
7.5 Months	March 24, 2008	• Input to the questionnaire closes (deadline will be as late as possible)
7 Months	April 4, 2008	• Hosts and meeting locations are selected for each district

6.5 Months	April 15, 2008	• GOOOH Day 1 • March on each state capitol • Candidate deadline
6 Months	May 4, 2008	• Candidate selection begins
4 Months	July 4, 2008	• Final candidate weekend retreat
3.5 Months	July 12, 2008	• Nominee selection (depending on number of candidates, the selection process could take up to eight weeks)
3.25 Months	July 27, 2008	• GOOOH Day 2
3 Months	August 4, 2008	• Nominees are announced and added to all state ballots
2.5 Months	August 20, 2008	• Nominee conference • Nominees meet for weekend retreat
2 Months	September 4, 2008	• Advertising campaign begins
1 Month	October 4, 2008	• Public advertising of individual nominees begins
15 Days	October 20, 2008	• Nominee interviews
1 Day	November 3, 2008	• Election Eve (GOOOH Day 3)
0	**November 4, 2008**	• **Election Day**

ROLES

CANDIDATE

Any person in America is invited to run for the House of Representatives in this system as long as they can answer affirmatively each question in the screening process documented below. There are certain people who are not permitted to run by law, and in order to return control to "the people" we are also considering the exclusion of a few additional groups, groups that are overrepresented today. Any candidate who provides false information during the screening process will be replaced by the next-in-line candidate from the prior round, if timing allows.

We hope to encourage as much participation from the public as possible. Anyone who meets the screening criteria, even if they are not interested in becoming a representative, should follow the same process as the candidates. These candidates will participate in the process, but by declaring they don't want to win will let the others know not to vote for them. They would likely "pass" during the opening comments and not be asked questions by the others during that part of the session. They would not automatically be eliminated, but practically speaking, it is unlikely they will get many votes. A participant can declare their position at any time, but it is recommended that those wishing to participate but not actually win wait until the next-to-last round to make such a declaration. Waiting to declare has the benefit of allowing the participant to remain active in the selection process as long as possible. For the good of the country, any candidate who does not intend to accept the nomination, if chosen, should identify himself prior to the final round.

Candidates will be assigned two unique numbers for each selection session. Each will be assigned a temporary number, one through ten, that will be used throughout a selection session. The other number, the "voting ID," is a unique identifier that should be kept secret from all parties other than the person they vote for in the final vote of their selection session. This voting ID will be used to report results, and ensuring the number is only given to the candidate you vote for in the final round will minimize errors or fraud in the reporting process. Additional details will be provided as the event nears.

Before each session begins, candidates should present their voter registration card and driver's license or passport to the other candidates, and each candidate should ensure they have reviewed the material of the others. Candidates should present a preprinted card to each of the others in their pool with the following information: name, congressional district number, address, high school (which high school would a senior attend if living in your residence), phone number, and e-mail address. The purpose of this exchange is to confirm the candidate lives in the district, and to enable candidates to connect thereafter with others in their district who are interested in our country.

HOST

A host is a volunteer who has offered a facility that can be used for a selection session. The Web site allows individuals or businesses to volunteer to become a host. Hosts will be contacted two weeks prior to the selection session. A person or business volunteering to host will need to provide the following information on the Web site: name of location(s), e-mail contact, address, facility type (church, school, hotel, restaurant, business, home, etc.). Businesses with multiple locations, such as churches, hotels, school districts, or restaurants with a banquet room are highly encouraged to offer to host sessions. The right to host a selection session will be auctioned to the highest bidder, assuming the location is convenient and appropriate. The default locations will be high schools, but any location may bid for the right to host. As an example, a restaurant may offer to host a session in its banquet room so that they could advertise the activity, entice the public to watch the proceedings, and then hopefully stick around for dinner afterward. Funds raised via this process will be used to fund GOOOH.

If the offer to host is accepted, the host will be responsible for ensuring facilities are open and available for the selection session. If the facility is not available for any reason, all candidates should still meet at the assigned location and then determine an alternative meeting location: the parking lot, an alternative spot, or wherever the majority of the candidates agree to meet.

MEMBER

Any person who registers at the GOOOH Web site becomes a member. They will be afforded opportunities that visitors do not have, such as participating in forums, hosting a session, or moderating a session. Note that only registered members will be allowed to become candidates, hosts, or moderators.

MODERATOR

A moderator will facilitate a selection session. A moderator may be one of the candidates participating in the session, but ideally will be an independent volunteer who will lead the session. The following guidelines will apply:

- The moderator must be a member.
- Moderators will be randomly assigned to selection sessions as positions are available. Where possible, two moderators will be assigned, one serving as an assistant.
- If a moderator is not available, the group will select a person from among the candidates to facilitate the session. If there are no volunteers or the group cannot agree, the candidate designated as #1 in the pool will become the moderator.
- Moderators are requested to take notes from the session they moderate and post them on the Web site for historical and educational purposes.
- Moderators should review the driver's license or passport of each candidate before each session.
- Moderators should report final results to the system.
- Moderators will be rated by the candidates.

NOMINEE

Each of the 435 congressional districts will select, via a series of selection sessions, a single nominee to represent their district in the election.

SYSTEM MODERATOR

The system moderator will have final authority on all questions, issues, and disputes until a broader process is established and leaders are selected to run the system. The system moderator role, for future elections, will be established after the 2008 election. It is the intent of GOOOH to delegate future ownership of the questions for each congressional district to the final ten candidates, excluding the nominee, but the plan to do this will be solidified at a later date.[263]

BECOMING A CANDIDATE

REGISTRATION

Any person who has an interest in GOOOH is invited to become a member, and almost all are welcome to participate in the process. You must register at the Web site if you wish to enter the selection process, moderate a session, or serve as a host. Membership details and information are posted on the Web site.

NOMINATE A FRIEND

In an effort to attract the best possible candidates and the broadest possible audience, registered members may send candidate invitations to others via the GOOOH e-mail system. They may even make a donation that will cover the fee if they so choose. If the candidate does not choose to run, the money will be considered a donation to the system. This will allow any person in America to provide incentive for and strongly encourage someone they know to get involved. Imagine receiving an e-mail that says, "A personal acquaintance has requested that you run for Congress. To encourage you to do so, they have made a donation on your behalf that will allow you to enter the system for free. All you have to do is fill in the questionnaire, sign the agreement, and submit your responses. If you choose not to run, the donation will be used to fund GOOOH." The e-mail will include a link for the individual to begin the process. Rather than being forced to vote for a political clone, convince the best people you know to run for office.

SCREENING

Those willing to participate in the process must affirmatively answer each of the following questions:

1. Can you confirm you are a U.S. citizen?
2. Can you confirm that you are a high school graduate (not a GED)?
3. Can you confirm that you are at least twenty-five years of age?
4. Can you confirm that you have never been convicted of a felony?
5. Can you confirm that you are registered to vote in the district in which you are applying?
6. Can you confirm that by November 4, 2008, you will have been an inhabitant of the state and district in which you are applying for the last three years?
7. Can you confirm that you have either a valid driver's license or a passport that establishes residence in the district in which you are applying?
8. Will you commit to telling the truth 100 percent accurately at all times, and will you remove yourself from office if you ever violate this promise?
9. Will you promise not to admit, deny, or discuss anything you did before the age of twenty-five?[264]
10. Can you confirm that you have never had a direct family member (father, mother, son, daughter, brother, or sister) who has held a seat in Congress (House or Senate), who was president, or who has been a governor?
11. Can you confirm that you and your immediate family members (spouse and children) do not have and have never had assets valued at more than 250 times the median income ($11.5 million)?
12. Can you confirm you have never received a law degree?
13. Can you confirm you have never been a member of, or made a donation to, the KKK, NAMBLA, or the ACLU?[265]
14. Will you promise to support our nation as a republic, not a socialistic, communistic, or fascist society?

15. Will you promise not to advertise or campaign publicly for this position, nor have others campaign for you, until sixty days prior to the November election?

16. Will you promise not to discuss other candidates personally or speak of them publicly, and to compete for this position in a professional manner?

17. Will you promise to only use money provided by the GOOOH general campaign fund, and not accept money or use personal wealth, to campaign for this position?

18. Will you promise not to accept money or gifts valued at more than five hundred dollars from any person or company while participating in the selection process?

19. Will you promise not to manipulate the selection system in any way, including intentionally voting against candidates to improve your odds of being selected?

20. Will you commit to publicly support GOOOH and the candidate that emerges in your district, though you are (of course) not required to vote for this person?

21. Will you commit to voting for term limits in the House of Representatives of four years or less?

22. Do you understand that all of your answers must be truthful, and do you agree to remove yourself from the process and make a donation to GOOOH of one thousand dollars within three days if you knowingly provide a false response to any of these qualifying questions?

ANSWERING THE CANDIDATE QUESTIONNAIRE

Every person who registers at our Web site is allowed to submit his answers to the questionnaire. You are guaranteed to make a 100 on the "test," as long as you complete it. Each person taking the exam will be required to respond yes or no to every question. Answers will not be locked until two weeks prior to the initial selection session. Answers will remain private until the week before the initial selection session and then can only be seen by those in your pool. Answers for the final fifty candidates in each district may be made public. If you choose to run for office via this system you will be required to "submit" your answers two weeks prior to the initial session. No personal information (phone, e-mail, etc.) will be made public other than your name. Candidates are not required to complete the questionnaire in one sitting and can change their answers as often as they like before the deadline.

Commitment Agreement

Once a candidate submits his answers, he will be prompted to electronically sign an agreement that legally binds him to his answers. Candidates can still modify their answers after this point, up until the change deadline, but they will be required to re-sign the Commitment Agreement if they make any changes. Once the deadline has passed, and if the candidate is elected, he will be bound to all but three of his answers, which can only be changed if his district approves via the Override Clause defined below. The responses for every answer should be considered locked and the commitment binding for the next two-plus years. Candidates who violate the terms of the Commitment Agreement will be legally bound to resign from office within seventy-two hours. Lawyers will be retained to ensure the agreement is legally binding.

Support Fee

Once a candidate has submitted their answers and signed the Commitment Agreement they will be required to donate one hundred dollars to GOOOH, either online or via snail mail. The fee is required for two reasons: (1) to eliminate those who are not serious candidates, and (2) to seed the fundraising effort. Those paying online must submit payment two weeks prior to the initial selection session. Those paying via the postal service will be required to have their payment postmarked three weeks prior to the initial session. Payments received after the deadline will be considered donations to GOOOH, and the candidate will not be entered in a selection session. There will be no refunds.

Submission

Members who take the test are not considered candidates until they (a) pass the screen, (b) complete the test, (c) sign the online commitment agreement, (d) submit their support fee (online or via mail), and (e) submit their answers. The last task, submitting your entry, is a simple step that locks your responses and confirms your entry.

The Override Clause

It is a fact that none of us are perfect. It is certain that each of us is wrong every now and then. It is guaranteed that our nominees, once elected, will not be perfectly aligned with the desires of their district on a few important issues. Given that each representative will be required to vote as he declared in his questionnaire, he has two options when a vote is requested on a topic where he is not aligned with his constituents. He can abstain from voting or he can implement the Override Clause. Use of the Override Clause will be limited to three changed votes during the two year term. It works as follows.

If a representative wishes to vote counter to the way he responded in his questionnaire, he must seek the approval from the members of his district. The exact mechanism and logistics for the override voting will be defined later, but the intent is to use an Internet survey. At least 20 percent of the district's registered voters must respond and of those, at least 75 percent must approve the change. Let me give an example.

Assume a representative answered no to the question, "Will you vote for a national health care system?" If Congress brings forward a bill that creates a national health care system for every person in America, the representative would be legally committed to vote against this law per his questionnaire response. If he believed his district wanted him to support the law, he could request a vote on a proposition within his district that said, "The people of District N would like our representative to vote for the national health care system." The question would be posted for seven days, and at least 20 percent of the district's registered voters would be required to respond to the

Internet survey (for example, if there were 500,000 registered voters, 100,000 responses would be required). Seventy-five percent of those votes (75,000) would need to respond affirmatively. There is a way for a representative to change his position, but only with the staunch support of his district.

Marketing

The marketing of this system will kick off with publication of this book. The GOOOH Web site will be operational a month or two before the book becomes available. Specific marketing activities will be formalized later, once a Director of Marketing is hired, but here are a few sample ideas. This is not the marketing or promotion plan we will use, but rather a starting point for the effort.

Bleachers

Political parties hold dinners that cost a thousand dollars to attend. GOOOH representatives will hold bleacher "parties" at as many locations as the public desires. The Web site will explain how any interested person in any interested town can organize a bleacher party. We'll invite every person in the surrounding area to join a conversation on GOOOH in the bleachers of a local high school football stadium. Donations will be accepted, and we will order pizza for all who contribute. Who knows, perhaps we can even get the local school to open the concession stand.

Soap Party

Flash-Mob gatherings will be coordinated at city centers around the country on dates announced on the Web site. Our objective is to clean out the House, so similar to the Boston Tea Party, we will ask all GOOOH supporters to add "environmentally friendly" bubbles to public water displays or put bars of soap on the lawn of government buildings nationwide—assuming, of course, it is legal. The Web site will suggest that all supporters meet at 6:30 p.m. at locations to be announced. The crowd will gather for thirty minutes and dump their soap.

TV

A formal promotion plan is being developed, but your calls to TV shows requesting they invite a member of GOOOH to appear will be critical to helping us get the word out. Will Oprah Winfrey, Lou Dobbs, David Letterman, Bill O'Reilly, Greta Van Susteren, or Jay Leno invite me onto their show and give the concept air time? Will CNN, *Meet the Press, 60 minutes, 20/20* or any of the news shows send an invitation? Can we get invitations to chat with the announcers on *Monday Night Football*, the College World Series, or other similar events? Can we get spots on TV shows, perhaps a green GOOOH sign appearing in the background of a scene in *24* or *Grey's Anatomy?*

RADIO

Your calls to talk radio shows to discuss GOOOH with Limbaugh, Boortz, Hewitt, Hannity, Savage, and others will be important in spreading the word. There are over a thousand local talk radio shows. Can we get the local hosts to contact GOOOH to have a member discuss the system? It will take grass root patriots like you to ignite the revolution, but all we need is a few dozen proactive people in each town in America to gain traction.

PRINT MEDIA

Stories or interviews with print media will be important in our effort to spread the word. Will the *Wall Street Journal, USA Today, New York Times, LA Times, Washington Post, Boston Globe* or any of the other prints across the country give this concept front page space?

MERCHANDISE

The Web site will be our outlet for GOOOH merchandise. Green stickers that can be placed on walls and signs will be made available, but please keep it legal.[266] Bumper stickers, buttons, tee-shirts, sweat-shirts, caps, visors, coffee mugs, yard signs, advertising cards in the shape of business cards, and more will all be made available via the Web.

SIGNS

Those wishing to support GOOOH will be asked to organize groups that raise funds, rent billboards across the country, and place our symbol on them. Those who have access to marquees are requested to add "GOOOH!" to the message boards whenever and wherever possible. Yard signs will be made available.

GOOOH PARTIES

Patriots across the country are asked to host GOOOH fundraising parties. The Web site will provide ideas and details for these parties.

GOOOH DAYS

GOOOH Days are designed to spread the word of our revolution. There are three pre-planned events. Mark Twain said, "In the beginning of change, the patriot is a scarce man, and brave, and hated, and scorned. When his cause succeeds, the timid join him..." While the concept may feel a bit odd, it is an easy and free way to get our message out. If you truly want to change the system, to replace the politicians, you must make an effort. Here are a few things you can do to spread the word. Be creative. Come up with ideas of your own.

- Wear a GOOOH sticker.
- Say, "I'm in, are you?" to every person whose path you cross on a GOOOH Day.
- Send an e-mail to every person on your e-mail list saying, "I'm in, are you?"
- Link to our Web site from yours.
- Business owners are asked to send their employees home one hour early so they can check out the Web site and sign up— or let them do so from work.
- It is suggested that employees, if your business owner does not give you the hour off, take it anyway. Take an hour of vacation. Use the time to contact others and tell them about the revolution.

- Drive with your flashers on.
- Call a talk radio show and ask the host what he has to say about the plan.
- Call ten friends and family members and ask, "I'm in, are you?"
- Drop in on your neighbors, and ask, "I'm in, are you?"
- Put pieces of paper that ask, "I'm in, are you?" on your co-workers' desks.
- Those who own billboards, marquees or any kind of advertising medium, are requested to display the GOOOH symbol.
- Write the question, "I'm in, are you?" on your car window, like kids going to a sporting event do.
- Answer your phone by asking, "I'm in, are you?"
- Order "I'm in, are you?" bumper stickers from the Web site.

CAMPAIGN

The campaign for our 435 candidates will be very straightforward. Initially, it will focus on the alternative system for selecting candidates, and ask the populace to engage and consider running. It will encourage citizens of our country to encourage qualified, competent patriots who they personally know to register and run. Once the candidates in each district have selected their nominee, we will begin an advertising campaign enlisting the support of Americans and their consideration of the non-party nominee that candidates in their district have selected. The campaign will not address the politicians against which our nominees are competing. It will not discuss their record, attack their character, or question them in any way, other than to point out they are responsible for the current situation and have abused their positions of power. GOOOH will remain focused on selling the benefits of the "alternative" to the two-party system, the goodness of selecting non-party representatives, and ensuring voters know where they can go to learn more about their nominee, and the need for change. In the last month of the campaign, as funds allow, advertisements for individual nominees may be generated and presented by GOOOH. Nominees will not be allowed to raise their own funds or produce their own ads, nor shall they support or endorse any third party that does so. The intent is to ensure that nominees do not have obligations to any special interest group.

SELECTION SESSIONS

Candidates who apply to compete for a seat in the House will be randomly grouped with other candidates from their congressional district into a "selection pool." Two candidates will advance to the next round from each pool. The final round of selection sessions in each congressional district will name a first, second, and third place candidate, but only one will be named the nominee. GOOOH will work to get the nominee placed on the ballot.

It is important to agree upon what the goals of each session should be for all candidates. Your goal should not be to win, particularly not to win at all costs, but rather to select the best candidate. If that is you, congratulations, but keep in mind we are trying to get rid of vain and aspiring politicians. This should not be about your personal desire to become a representative; it should be about finding the person whose views represent your district and who has the appropriate demeanor and communications skills to serve in this very demanding office. Our intent is to replace the politicians in the House of Representatives with the best representatives the people of each district can identify. If you have a vain and aspiring candidate in your pool, vote to eliminate him. If you are a vain and aspiring politician, please stick with one of the two parties.

SESSION IDENTIFIER

Each selection session will be assigned a unique number, which will be used by candidates and the moderator to report results after the session completes.

PRE-SESSION PREPARATION WORK

Once a candidate has registered, completed the questionnaire, signed the Commitment Agreement, and submitted the fee, they are ready to run, but there are additional things the candidate should do prior to the first session. Each candidate may optionally post a written essay discussing his "platform" and beliefs on the Web site. The paper will be constrained to 750 words and, initially, only available to others in their pool. Each candidate is requested to upload a digital photograph if possible. Candidates have the option of identifying the five categories that are of most importance to them as well as the three that are of the least importance.

Candidates will be randomly assigned into pools of ten (perhaps more or less in the first round), one week prior to a selection session. Each candidate will be randomly assigned a number between one and ten, prior to the event. This number will determine order and possible assignments during the session. Efforts will be made to group candidates by location in the initial sessions, but no guarantees can be made other than somewhere within or near your congressional district.

A meeting location for each selection session will be posted seven days in advance of the session. It is requested that the selected host coordinate all logistical arrangements for session(s) held at their location,[267] but each candidate should bring all needed materials in case the host is not adequately prepared. If the location is not open or available when the candidates arrive, it will be up to the participants in that pool to determine where they will hold the session, which could be in the parking lot of a school in the worst case scenario.

A unique Candidate Scorecard for each candidate will be available online three days prior to the session. It will include the percentage of items that each of the other candidates gave the same answer for. In the sample below, Candidate #5 agreed with Candidate #2 86 percent of the time, while Candidate #9 only agreed 42 percent of the time.

	Candidate Scorecard									
	1	2	3	4	5	6	7	8	9	10
2	62		49	59	86	82	77	52	42	73

A unique Comparison Scorecard will also be available online three days prior to the session. The scorecard will be a sortable list that candidates can use to compare their responses with the other candidates, in the order they deem most important. Candidates will be able to review the responses of others in their pool in advance of the session so that they can determine which candidates are most closely aligned with their views. The scorecards will list the questions, the candidate's response (yes or no), and for each candidate in their pool, whether or not the candidate agreed or disagreed (blank).

#	Question	Ans	1	..	5	..	9	10
1	Would you vote for 4 year term limits for U.S. Representatives?	Yes	agr		agr		agr	agr
2	Would you vote to exclude political family members from GOOOH?	Yes	agr		agr		agr	agr
3	Would you vote for a Presidential line item veto?	Yes			agr		agr	agr
4	Would you vote to eliminate the filibuster in Congress?	No	agr		agr			agr
5	Would you vote to eliminate the Electoral College?	No	agr				agr	agr
6	Would you vote to exclude people with a law degree from the House of Rep?	Yes			agr		agr	agr
7	Would you vote to cap lawyer fees in class action suits?	No	agr		agr		agr	agr
8	Would you vote to prevent lawyers from using "technicalities"?	Yes						
9	Would you amend the constitution to constrain activist judges?	No	agr		agr			agr
10	Would you vote for a balanced budget amendment?	Yes	agr		agr		agr	agr
			62		86		42	73

Each candidate is expected to study these scorecards thoroughly prior to the session. They will be required to record their first vote just sixty minutes into the session, so it is critical they have a feel for which candidates they are most and least interested in before they arrive. The agreement percentage is important, but candidates must take time to ensure they place emphasis on the importance of the issues. In general, you will likely consider only those who agree with you on at least 65 or more percent of the items. Those who disagree more than that are not likely to get your support, and you are not likely to receive theirs.

Each candidate is required to bring twenty 3x5 index cards, a timer, a set of blank name tags, highlighters, pens, blank paper, and any other material they may need during the session. Candidates may not use phones, computers, or any other electronic or communication device during a selection session. Cell phones, pagers, computers, and such must be turned off. Each candidate will be required to print his registration confirmation "ticket" and bring it to the Web site. Those who do not have access to a printer will need to write the information on a piece of paper and bring it with them.

ROUNDS

The initial selection session for every Congressional District will occur on the same day, as will the final selection sessions. All selection sessions will be held on a Saturday morning, beginning at 9:00 a.m., local time. The number of rounds will depend on the number of candidates who register in each district, but will likely be between three and six. Each congressional district represents more than 660,000 people, but we know that not every member of a district will choose, or be qualified, to run for office. For planning purposes, participation within a district will likely be limited to the first 31,250 candidates that apply, which would mean a maximum of six rounds of selection sessions. There is no way to predict how many participants will actually apply, so it is recommended you enter the process before it fills. According to the list below, if, for example, 5,000 candidates in a district registered, there would only be five rounds, beginning with Round 2.

- Round 1: 31,250 (or more) candidates
- Round 2: 6,250
- Round 3: 1,250
- Round 4: 250
- Round 5: 50 candidates—10 advance
- Final Round: 10 candidates compete—a single nominee is selected

In the initial two rounds it is likely that there will be more or less than ten candidates per pool.

VOTING

Focus groups have shown that superb nominees will emerge via this system. The biggest challenge GOOOH will face is getting on the ballot and dealing with the scare tactics expected from the political parties. There will be tremendous emphasis placed on getting out the vote. While every party attempts to do this every election, at least for those likely to support their message, this campaign will focus on every person, regardless of demographics. It will particularly seek the vote of those who have historically not voted. The campaign will focus on getting those who vote against one candidate or the other to support the new system. It will strive to get those supporting the system to encourage others to vote for this new alternative more ambitiously than ever before. It will encourage voters to support the nominee, regardless of their view, based on the thought that a committed non-politician is a better choice than a political partisan. The campaign will remind you that while you will not agree with any nominee on every single issue, at least you know where they stand and how they will vote, things you cannot say for modern-day politicians. The voting process is defined below.

SESSION VOTING—a more detailed explanation will be made available on the Web site prior to the first round of sessions.

- There will be three votes taken during each selection session.
- Candidates are not required (or intended) to show their scorecard until all votes have been taken. Candidates should not attempt to look at others' cards, though they may of course discuss who they like or dislike as they choose, including during their private interview sessions.
- Candidates will identify their preferred candidates in the "For" section of their card. They will vote against candidates in the "Against" section of their card. A sample is shown below.
- A candidate must complete all votes. Failure to do so will eliminate them from the process. None of the votes on an incomplete scorecard will count in the scoring. If there are not enough candidates present to complete a pool, "Against" votes are not required once all attending candidates have been voted "For" (e.g., if there are only seven candidates present, no

more than three candidates must be listed in the "Against" section; if there are only three candidates, no candidate must be listed in the "Against" section)

- Each pool of candidates can vote to eliminate any one of the candidates in their pool at any time during the process. A candidate may request an Elimination Vote that must be seconded by another candidate in the pool. Six votes are required to eliminate a candidate, regardless of the number active participants in the pool. A candidate may only make one proposal for an Elimination Vote in a selection session. No more than two candidates may be eliminated from any pool. This rule is intended to eliminate disruptive or obnoxious candidates. There will be no refund or recourse for an eliminated candidate. "For" votes cannot be made for a candidate after he has been eliminated. Doing so invalidates all votes on the scorecard and disqualifies the candidate voting for the eliminated candidate.
- Scorecards must be completed in ink.
- After each vote, all cards should be placed facedown in front of the owner, positioned so that all other candidates can see the back of the card.
- Once a "round" of voting is complete the votes cannot be changed. If there are any scratch-outs on the card, they must be initialed by two other candidates immediately after a round of voting has been completed. Changes cannot be made once a new round begins. Violators of this rule will be eliminated and votes from his scorecard disallowed.
- A candidate may not vote for himself, at any time. If a candidate does place his own number in the "For" section, he is automatically eliminated and his scorecard is not counted.
- A candidate may not vote against the same person more than one time. Each candidate will be required to vote against exactly 5 candidates, assuming a full pool.
- A candidate can vote against himself—once.
- All candidates have the option of voting for or against any of the other nine candidates present when the session begins, even if a candidate departs during a session.

- A candidate who departs the Host location, for any reason, is not permitted to return.
- A candidate who does not show up or arrives late should be listed in the "Notes" section of the card as eliminated, and cannot be voted for or against.
- A candidate may not formally withdraw from a selection session once it begins, though he can announce that others should not vote for him, that they should vote against him, or that he intends to withdraw from the process before the next round.

VOTING CARDS

Each candidate will record all of their votes on a single 3x5 index card during a selection session. The candidate should record his name, the number of his pool, and his number (1–10) for that session, on the back of the card. The front of the card should have "For" and "Against" sections with slots for Vote 1, 2, and 3 as shown in the following example. The "For" candidates will appear on the left of the card, labeled 1), 2), and 3), listing their number for this session, and initials. The "eliminated" candidates, will appear on the right side of the card, clearly labeled as 10), 9), 8), 7), and 6), with the least favorite candidate listed in the 10) slot, the second least favorite in the 9) slot, and so on. If any candidate is eliminated because of failure to show on time (there is zero tolerance for late arrivals), or elimination vote, or departure, they should be listed in the "Notes" section of the card with the word "eliminate" preceding their number. An example of the voting side of the card follows.

For				Against
Vote 3	Vote 2	Vote 1		
1)	1)	1)		10)
	2)	2)		9)
		3)		8)
				7)
				6)
Notes:				

VOTE 1

Each candidate will record their top three candidates (#7, #6, #5 in the example below) in the "For" section and their bottom three (e.g., #4, #3, and #2), in the "Against" section with points assigned as followed: five points for the top choice (#7), four for the second choice (#6), three for the third(#5), negative one for (#2), -2 (#3), and -3 (bottom slot: #4). The maximum points any candidate could have after Vote 1 is 45 (9 * 5), and the lowest possible total is -30 (10 * -3). The Voter Card would look as follows:

For				Against
Vote 3	Vote 2	Vote 1		
1)	1)	1) #7 - EF		10) #4 - GH
	2)	2) #6 - CD		9) #3 - IJ
		3) #5 - AB		8) #2 - KL
				7)
				6)
Notes:				

VOTE 2

Each candidate will record their top two choices, in order, in the "For" section. They can select any person who was not one of their "Against" choices in Vote 1 or Vote 2—this means they can vote again for any of the seven choices not listed in the "Against" section in Vote 1, including any of their top three choices from Vote 1, in any order. They will also select two additional *and different* candidates to eliminate. They can vote to eliminate a candidate who was listed in the "For" section in the prior vote (#5, #6, #7), or one who was not voted on at all in Vote 1 (#8, #9, #10). Points for first, second, and the two eliminations are 8, 6, -1, and -1, respectively. After the second vote, the card could look like this:

For				Against
Vote 3	Vote 2	Vote 1		
1)	1) #9 - OP	1) #7 - EF		10) #4 - GH
	2) #5 - AB	2) #6 - CD		9) #3 - IJ
		3) #5 - AB		8) #2 - KL
				7) #8 - MN
				6) #7 - EF
Notes: #10 Eliminated (obnoxious)				

VOTE 3

Each candidate will record their top choice. Ten points will be awarded to this candidate, but they cannot vote for any of the five eliminated in Vote 1 or Vote 2.

For				Against
Vote 3	Vote 2	Vote 1		
1) #5 - AB	1) #9 - OP	1) #7 - EF		10) #4 - GH
	2) #5 - AB	2) #6 - CD		9) #3 - IJ
		3) #5 - AB		8) #2 - KL
				7) #8 - MN
				6) #7 - EF
Notes: #10 Eliminated (obnoxious)				

- Assume this is the scorecard for candidate #1. Note that he never voted for or against himself. In this example, candidate #5 would have nineteen points (10+6+3), #9 would have eight points, #6 would have four, #7 would have four (5-1), #4 would have negative three, #3 would have negative two, #2 and #8 would have negative one. Candidate #1 would have zero points. Number 10 was eliminated during the second vote, and none of the points from his card would be tallied.

- Points are not totaled until all three votes have been taken.
- Votes from all rounds are counted toward the final score.
- Votes from eliminated, absent or departed candidates are not counted.

FINALIZING THE VOTE

The top two candidates from each pool are requested to have all candidates sign a brief statement saying, "On Month, Day, Year, Selection Session N has chosen Candidate Number X, John Doe, and Candidate Number Y, Jane Doe, to advance in the GOOOH system in Congressional District No. X." They should also get each participating candidate and the moderator to sign the document, which will be requested if there are any discrepancies in the reported outcome.

When the session is complete, each candidate should make a copy of their personal scorecard to keep for themselves. This card should be saved in case there are any discrepancies reported. The top two candidates should retain the final scorecards of the other eight participants, with the advancing candidate receiving the most points taking possession of the card. The advancing candidates should also obtain the candidate ID (that has been kept secret until that moment) associated with each card they take. They are not required to get the ID of the other advancing candidate unless the other advancer awarded him the most points. The voting cards will be requested if there are any discrepancies in the reported outcome.

Each candidate who participated in the session is requested to visit the Web site after the session and submit the pool number (#1 through #10) of the two candidates selected to advance, in the order they were selected, within twenty-four hours of session completion.[268] If a moderator is present, he should also report the results. Any discrepancies will be settled by the system moderator. All candidates may be eliminated if the system moderator cannot settle a dispute in a timely manner. The system moderator will have the final say in all matters.

The final rules for the selection session will be posted on the GOOOH Web site. The rules outlined in this book are intended to provide a summary of how the process works, but may be modified prior to the beginning of the process. We are attempting to elect honorable representatives for our country, so please, if anyone attempts to abuse, cheat, or game the system or voting process in any way, use the Elimination Vote and get rid of them.

VOTING RECOMMENDATIONS

I have been questioned by many on why candidates are forced to answer yes or no. Some have wondered if that is really a fair way to determine a person's position on a topic. Others are concerned that "locking" our candidates into a position, when they may not have enough information, will not leave them negotiating room once they are in office. The conversation is always the same. Those who don't like the yes-or-no questions will say that many of the questions are more complicated than a simple yes-or-no answer affords. They say they must have an opportunity to explain their position, much as politicians do. Politicians will say that while they may agree with the thought, the issues are too complex, and they simply cannot agree with the exact number that is written. They neglect the fact that all votes require a yes or no vote.

As an example, someone would tell me that they want to reduce the size of government, but are not sure they can commit to a 5 percent reduction. Or they are for term limits, but do not know if four or six or twenty years is the appropriate time that we should allow our representatives to serve. Or they are against abortions, but don't know if drawing the line at three months is the proper point at which they should become illegal.

In researching and writing this book, I have tried very hard to listen to the views of anyone who would express them. I tried to understand each and every perspective. But on this issue I did not find a single reasonable argument against asking a candidate to answer a legitimate yes-or-no question. I agree that there are illegitimate questions that don't avail an answer, but the solution is simply not to ask conundrums, or stupid questions, such as the classic: "Do you still beat your wife?" On every issue, there are two extreme views, endpoints if you will, on the line of possible answers, and then an almost unlimited number of views in the middle. A yes-or-no question will establish a clear dividing line that puts candidates on one side or the other. On every question the line could be drawn in a different place, but that does not prevent a candidate from declaring on which side he stands. It is no longer sufficient for a candidate to say he is for term limits, but later declare only if they are fifty years. Politicians have abused the system for too long. Representatives will not have a problem answering yes or no. Politicians will struggle.

What I inevitably find when I ask these yes-or-no questions are politicians disguised as candidates, wanting to wiggle without committing. If the question asks, "Will you vote for four-year term limits?" there are only a few legitimate options:

- You are for term limits of exactly four years, so you would answer yes.
- You are not for term limits at all, so of course your answer is no.
- You are for term limits of six years or more, in which case you would answer no.
- You are for term limits, but believe they should be two years. In this case, you have two options: (a) vote yes, figuring limits of four years is better than no term limits at all, or (b) vote no, insisting the number must be two.

In any of these cases, an answer of yes or no declares your position, but don't try to convince someone you are in favor of two-year term limits and voted no simply because you believe four is too long. Nobody in their right mind is going to believe you. Further, if you are set on six-year term limits answer the question no and then explain why to all who will listen. Those who attempt to wiggle out of an answer without making a commitment are doing exactly what our existing politicians do today. You should not support candidates who do this, and I recommend you eliminate them as quickly as you can.

Another example of a politician disguised as a candidate can be found when someone, usually in the one-on-one sessions (which will be explained next), declares they agree with the concept but are not sure the number provided is appropriate. In one focus group there was a question asking if the candidates would commit to a 5 percent cut in government spending. At least one candidate told the others he was for smaller government, but 5 percent was too drastic a cut. My view on this, and the reason the "line" is important, is that if someone cannot commit to a 5 percent cut, they are really saying they do not believe that our government is too big. They do not think that government spending is out of control. That is a perfectly valid view, but you should not support someone who says they are for smaller government but will not commit to a 5 percent cut.

My advice to anyone who enters the process is to watch out for those whose response contradicts yours but then attempts to convince you that you are not really that far apart. Watch out for those not wanting to make commitments. I suggest you eliminate them from the process as soon as you can. If you are looking for representatives instead of politicians, the ones who cannot commit are not the kind of people you want.

THE FLAW IN VOTING

There is one basic flaw in this system that all should be aware of. If the candidates in the process all vote against the best candidate in hopes of improving their odds of being selected, then the best candidate will not be chosen. I have no doubt that a few arrogant people, those who care more about themselves than the country or our children, will try to do just this. If it holds true that no more than 10 percent of Americans are liars we should be able to overcome this flaw. If it proves that 30 percent of Americans, or more, are liars, and that they choose to make this a personal contest, the best candidates will not emerge and our country has problems far more serious than politicians.

SELECTION DAY
ARRIVAL

- Participants are to arrive at the designated location at 8:30 a.m. (local time zone), introduce themselves to the other can-

didates, verify each others driver's licenses/passports and ensure they have agreement on who is which number.

- Each candidate is to wear a name tag that has their assigned
  number (1 to 10), initials, and name (e.g., #5, TC, Tim Cox).
- Candidates should be seated (or standing if there are no
  seats) in numerical order (1 to 10) no later than 9:00 a.m.
  Any candidate not in their place at the designated start time
  is immediately eliminated, with no exceptions.
- If at 9:00 a.m. six or more of the candidates agree, the group
  can move to an alternate location (within five miles) and start
  one hour later.
- The moderator should be agreed upon.
- Visitors are welcome as long as they remain silent and are not
  disruptive. Any candidate may ask any spectator to leave.

INTRODUCTIONS (VOTE 1)

- It is expected that every candidate will have printed and stud-
  ied the other candidates' responses in advance of the meeting.
- Each candidate will have three minutes or less to introduce
  himself. He can use the time however he likes, but it is suggested that he use the following template. The process will
  start with candidate #1 and proceed numerically until all candidates are done (thirty minutes). The following candidate
  should begin his introduction at the exact time, interrupt-
  ing the prior candidate mid sentence if required (we all know
  how long winded some can be, and this could become a long
  day if the allotted times are not followed). Here is the recommended template for the opening speech.
  o Name;
  o Report if you have ever had a family member hold any
    federal office, have ever passed the bar, or if your family
    has ever had assets valued at more than $11.5 million;
  o Family information;
  o Education;
  o Daytime job/activities;

- o Extracurricular activities/hobbies;
- o Why you are interested in this process;
- o Why you would be a good candidate;
- o What your key message is;
- Beginning with candidate #10, and going in reverse order, each candidate can then take three minutes to discuss their top three issues (thirty minutes).
- Vote 1, per the rules outlined above, will be taken followed by a short break that will last for fifteen minutes. Scorecards should be placed facedown when complete.

INTERVIEWS (VOTE 2)

- In round robin fashion per the schedule that follows each candidate will spend eight minutes with each of the other candidates, and then have two minutes to locate the next candidate on the Round Robin schedule.

1x1s								
A	B	C	D	E	F	G	H	I
1...2	1...3	4...8	5...8	5...10	1...9	8...9	6...8	2...8
3...4	2...4	2...6	6...10	4...6	6...7	2...7	2...10	1...10
5...6	5...7	7...10	7...9	2...9	2...5	4...5	4...9	4...7
7...8	6...9	3...9	2...3	3...7	3...8	1...6	1...7	3...6
9...10	8...10	1...5	1...4	1...8	4...10	3...10	3...5	5...9

- The conversation during this time is entirely up to the two candidates. It is recommended that candidates prepare their questions in advance. Here are examples of questions you may want to ask:
- o Why do you feel so strongly about x?
- o Help me understand why you are against y.
- o Let me explain why you may want to reconsider z.
- The interviews are expected to take one hour and thirty minutes. If all is on schedule, a twenty minute break may be taken.
- Once each candidate has interviewed all of the others, the pool will reconvene. Beginning with candidate #6, and ad-

vancing forward to candidate #10, then to #1, and then proceed until candidate #5. Each candidate may ask any three candidates to answer a single question that is twenty words or less. Each respondent will have one minute to reply. This process should take thirty minutes. As an example, if candidate #1 asks candidates #8, #9, and #10 if they agree with xyz, each of the three will be required to answer in front of all participants. This will expose any deceitful answers given during the private interviews. It is recommended you vote against those who change their stories. Questions may be directed to any three candidates, but you will most likely want to ask your top three candidates. It will become obvious which candidates are being most seriously considered.

- Vote 2 will be made on the same scorecard as Vote 1 per the rules above. Two different candidates must be eliminated (assuming a full pool), and the two top choices selected. The candidates will have fifteen minutes to submit their vote and take a short break. Scorecards should be placed facedown when complete.

FINAL INTERVIEWS (VOTE 3)

- In the same round robin fashion as above but in the reverse order, each candidate will have four minutes to interact with each of the other candidates. You and the other candidate will of course determine what to discuss, but it is suggested that you use a portion of the time to campaign for yourself or one of the other candidates. There will be two minutes to move from one interview to the next (sixty minutes).
- A ten minute break should be taken.
- Each candidate is allowed to write a single question, directed to no more than two candidates (in order) on an index card. The question must be a simple question that can be answered with yes, no, or a number. The card should be placed in a stack and the stack shuffled by the moderator once all cards

are submitted. The candidate to whom the question is directed must answer yes or no, provide a number if appropriate, and then take no more than one minute to comment. All candidates are encouraged to ensure consistency in the answers with what they have heard throughout the day.

- Closing statements: each candidate will have two minutes to make a closing statement. Closing statements will begin with candidate #5 go down to #1, around to #10, and then down to #6 (twenty minutes). It is recommended that each candidate have a draft of this statement prepared in advance of the session.

- Vote 3: Each candidate will record their top choice. The choice may be the same or different from the other top choices on their card, but cannot be one of the five candidates they eliminated in Vote 1 or 2.

SCORING

Once Vote 3 is complete, the moderator will tally the scores with all other candidates present. In the final round, the candidate with the most points will be declared the nominee. In all other rounds, the top two candidates, even if tied, will both advance to the next round.

If there is a tie between exactly two candidates for first place in the final round, or second place in all but the final round, the tie will be settled based on the following prioritized tie breakers:

- The candidate (or candidates if there is also a tie for third) with the next most points will award all of his points to one of the candidates in the tie. Unless there is a tie for third place, the decision will be final. If those tied for third assign their points to different candidates, the next tie breaker will be used.

- Of the tied candidates, the candidate who received the most first place votes in the final round will be declared the winner. If equal, the next tie breaker will be used.

- Of the tied candidates, the candidate who received the fewest "eliminate points" in the first round will be declared the winner. If equal, the next tie breaker will be used.
- Another vote will be taken between the two tied candidates by all candidates still present. If equal, the next tie breaker will be used.
- Another vote will be taken by all candidates still present, excluding the one(s) who had the lowest point total. If equal, the next tie breaker will be used.
- The system moderator will decide between the tied parties.

If there is a tie between three or more candidates for first place, in any round, those tied for first will vote amongst themselves to determine the first place candidate. Note that no candidate can ever vote for himself. If A votes for B, and B for A, C would have the deciding vote for first place. If a settlement is not reached, with A voting for B, B for C, and C for A, as an example, the tiebreaker process for two candidates will be used until one candidate is eliminated, and then the eliminated party will name the first place finisher.

After first place is settled, and if there had been a tie between three or more candidates, the first place candidate will determine second place by choosing from the tied candidates. If the candidate refuses to cast a tie-breaking vote, he will be eliminated from the process entirely and the process to determine first place will start anew. This should never happen.

A post selection session blog will be created for each selection session so that those who participated in the process can voice their opinion of the other candidates. Their comments and identification will become public information.

THE FINAL SELECTION SESSION

The final selection session for each district will occur on the same day, two Saturday's after the last district has selected its final ten candidates. The following changes to the process will be made for the final round:

- Each of the ten candidates will be given ten minutes to make a speech prior to the beginning of the selection session. The speech will be made at the host location (school, church, etc.), and is open to the public and the media.
- There will be a five-minute break between speeches. The other nine candidates are expected to collectively interrupt any candidate who goes longer than his ten-minute allotment.
- The public speeches will be made by Candidates #1 through #10, in order, and will begin at 9:00 a.m., 9:15, 9:30, etc.
- All candidates must deliver their speech from the same location with the same audio and video equipment that all have agreed on. If there is no agreement by 8:30 a.m. that morning, no equipment may be used by any candidate.
- GOOOH will register each of the 435 nominees with the appropriate authorities as soon as possible after the final round.

ELECTION DAY

No later than ninety days before the election we will have identified our 435 nominees. It is of course impossible at this time to say who they will be, what they will stand for or what they will have done in their life to that point, but a few things will be certain. They will not be actively affiliated with either party. They will not have taken any money from special interest groups. They will have documented their position on over a hundred issues and bound themselves to resign from office if they violate their stance on any of those issues. They will not be a member of a political family, a lawyer, or someone with more than $11.5 million dollars in assets. They will have been selected by the very best people within your district, the ones who were willing to run for Congress themselves without party affiliation or special interest money. You are not committed to voting for the nominee of your district, but I am willing to bet everything I own, in fact some say I already have by quitting my job and embarking on this journey, that you will be impressed, perhaps thrilled, with the quality of our candidates.

I have seen no other way to break the political gridlock that has captured our country. There is absolutely zero risk with following this plan and identifying the 435 nominees. Whether or not you vote for the one who bubbles to the top of the process in your district is entirely up to you, and is not a decision you have to make until after the nominee is named. I hope you will enter the process and help us select the very best person your district has to offer. If you do not participate, you have little reason to ever again complain about our politicians.

Election Day 2008 will be one of the greatest moments in our nation's proud history. It will be the first step on a journey that will restore our country in our own eyes as well as the eyes of the world. Those who participate in the process will be as great of patriots as those who battled for our freedom over two hundred years ago. Now is the time to do your part for our posterity.

RECLAMATION DAY

The voice of the people will be clear on November 4, 2008. We the people will have taken control of our House. The first ninety days in office will focus on drafting the legislation and amendments that our 435 nominees have documented they will support. We will seek approval so that on day ninety, April 3, 2009, we will have every document on the president's desk ready for signature. We will of course be dependent on approval by the Senate, but any senator who disagrees with the clear mandate given to the House on Election Day 2008 might as well resign. If they do not support the voice of the people, we will remove them the next time their name appears on the ballot.

It is impossible to say what issues will obtain consensus without actually going through the process, but here are the bare minimum, no-brainers, that I hope all candidates will have agreed to. Your list may very well be different than mine. As we go through this process, I strongly discourage you from supporting any candidate who would not support all of the following items:

- Term limits of four years or less for members of the House of Representatives.

- Redefinition of who can run for the House of Representatives.
- Amending the Constitution with the Law of Predominant Majority.
- Amending the Constitution with the Law of Common Sense.
- Creating a balanced budget Amendment, with exceptionally limited exclusions.
- Passing a line-item veto that ensures the president has the ability to cut any "pork" project that somehow slips through Congress.
- Amending the Constitution to clarify that religion is a core principle of our country, and while we cannot and will not force a specific religion or religious activity on anyone, we will also not prevent anyone from practicing religion in a reasonable manner.

I personally hope that the following are also passed, based on my personal values and beliefs, but this list and even the list above will of course be up to the will of the people:

- Index the retirement age to "life expectancy" minus five years for those fifty and younger.
- Only apply the Endangered Species Act to animals larger in mass than a golf ball (i.e., no more endangered bugs).
- Abolish federal government programs for health, education, and welfare, returning control of the programs to each individual state. This does not necessarily mean to cut spending.
- Pass a law to ensure punitive damages go to a cause that improves the affected parties, not lawyers.
- Amend the Constitution with a specific moment after conception at which abortion becomes illegal—I prefer twelve weeks—and end the debate.
- Put an end to judicial activism by requiring Supreme Court and Appellate Court judges to require the House of Repre-

sentatives to vote on issues not clearly written in law, with their vote becoming the basis for all cases thereafter, and an indicator of how judges should rule.

- Deem that the rights of a person found guilty of a crime are considered rescinded from the moment they committed their crime (though the rights could not actually be rescinded until after they are found guilty).

- Initiate a program that seeks alternatives from private industry that will supplement or replace our existing highway transportation system and cut our dependency on foreign oil by 50 percent within ten years.

- Enact laws capping the size of the federal government (as a percent of GDP) and requiring annual reductions in the number of government employees by at least 5 percent year over year for the next twenty years.

- Enact a Guest Worker Program for immigrants wishing to work in America that ensures we can control the number of immigrants, who is allowed to enter, and the rules by which they will be taxed, insured, and returned to their homeland.

- Create a deterrent for those who enter the United States illegally (outside of the Guest Worker Program), initiating the building of a Great Wall of Mexico that requires all people found in our country illegally to labor on the wall for 365 days, with no pay, and then be returned to their homeland.

- Reduce the number of countries in which we have military troops deployed and the amount of money we are spending on total military expenses by 5 percent year over year.

- Replace the current income tax with a consumption tax as defined in the FairTax plan, eliminating 90 percent or more of the IRS.

- Require the adoption of an .xxx Internet domain for all pornographic sites and require that software vendors provide parental controls on all software that can access the Internet.

- Terminate all current subsidies, including those to foreign countries, businesses, farms, and ranches, and establish dollar caps on any future subsidies as well as two-of-ten year limits.[269]

SENATORS

We will monitor senators closely, report those behaving like the representatives we have just replaced, and campaign aggressively against any who continue to abuse the system: taking money from lobbyists, attempting to add riders to the budget, or trying to manipulate the system. If necessary, we will begin a national campaign for two-term (twelve years) senatorial term limits, or even use a variation of the GOOOH process to replace the thirty-three senators up for reelection in 2010.

BEYOND NINETY DAYS

Each of our nominee's will be required to meet for three hours, on the first Monday of February, May, August, and November, with all candidates who made it to the final selection session. Each of the final ten candidates are requested to submit how they would have voted on each past and pending issue so that their selected representative is hearing, firsthand, the input of key members of his district. It is expected that each of the final ten will also meet quarterly with those who participated in the round before, the final fifty.

FUNDRAISING

Candidates are not to participate in any fundraising activities. The GOOOH organization will perform all fundraising, marketing, and campaigning for all of our candidates. Candidates will not raise or spend funds for their personal campaign. This most specifically applies to the nominee selected to compete against the Democratic and Republican politicians.

The Web site will allow for online donations, and an address will be provided for those who wish to send contributions via local mail.

However, for this effort to work we will need some very large donors, individual or corporate, to make donations of significance. It is expected that we will need to raise $50 million to have a 50-percent chance of being successful and $200 million to give us a 90-percent probability of success. We expect to reach that total from the following composite of donors: twenty donors of $5 million or more; one million donors with average donations of one hundred dollars. Ideally, we will find an angel, a single multi-millionaire businessman who will step forward. A Ross Perot or Steve Forbes who will understand the value in investing in a system that selects 435 representatives of the people instead of one long shot for president. Whether that person is Warren Buffet, Bill Gates, Michael Dell, an heir of Walton or Bass, or any one of the three hundred billionaires in this country remains to be seen, but it is certain that a chance like this, to redirect the course of our country, will not present itself very often, if ever again. Not only are we looking for the twenty-first-century versions of George Washington, Ben Franklin, Thomas Jefferson, and James Madison, we are looking for men of wealth who can help launch this effort. I hope you will step forward!

SUMMARY

It goes without saying that this plan is far from perfect. What I am proposing is not a simple undertaking, and the method I'm proposing is certainly expected to improve with time. I've worked with dozens of exceptionally intelligent people to get the idea to this point. I've received feedback from peers who lean way left, those who lean way right, and some who are perfectly in the middle. I've canvassed as many people as I could find that would provide feedback, a wildly diverse set of characters that all seem to have one thing in common: an aching dissatisfaction with politics, politicians, and the destruction of our country.

I am certain there are things I have missed, and that many of my ideas can be improved upon, but the plan outlined in the pages of this book will allow us to make sweeping changes immediately. This book is intended to explain the concept. The final plan will be documented on the Web site. We cannot wait for the politicians forced upon us to fix what is broken. They will not. We cannot wait for the political process to fix itself. It will not. Things will get worse, the debt will grow, and taxes will increase. We will soon reach a point from which we cannot recover, assuming we have not already reached it. We cannot wait for the perfect plan; it will not materialize. Our country is not at risk of being attacked by an outside enemy; it is being destroyed by a cancer within. We all know it. Do we have the courage to act?

XII The Call to Action

We are blessed to have been born in America. We have freedoms not even considered in most of the 192 other countries. We can choose our God, our mate, and where we live. We can own as much land as we can afford. We can own our homes. We are able to choose whatever profession we desire in an economy that is second to none. How much money we make is entirely up to us.

Our family is safe, though our bullish ways have lessened our security. Our children have access to a respectable education, we have a network of medical professionals ready and able to take care of us, and we can travel when and where we desire. We would not move to any other country in the world. There are so many things to be grateful for that it is difficult, at times, to understand why the vast majority of us are so dissatisfied. We are not completely unhappy—admitting so would be un-American—but we are not satisfied either. We know we can do better.

A survey I conducted found that over 80 percent of people "absolutely agree" that our country is the greatest in the world, today. Less than 10 percent believe that will be the case fifty years from now. Just as views of Congress have become somewhat more negative, so too have opinions about the federal government. Barely a third of us believe we can trust the government to do what's right "just about always" or "most of the time," while 66 percent say we trust the government "only sometimes" or "never." Those are horrible results. Back in the 1960s, the number that trusted government was close to 80 percent.[270] What has happened to our government?

Trust is a strong word. We are generally trustworthy people, and not trusting someone is an exceptionally strong statement. In my entire life, I can think of only a few people I have known whom I did, or do not, trust. It's not like we are electing Saddam Hussein or Adolf Hitler to run our country, so it is hard to imagine that today 66 percent of us don't trust our government. The more basic questions are: do you believe those running our country represent the people, and do you trust them to fix the things that are wrong? When I issued my surveys, I found that only 5 percent of the respondents actually thought we had the right people in place. It is time to confront the enemy.

Do we want to continue doing what we have been doing, or is it time to consider a change? Do we want career politicians or true representatives to do the work that must be done? Do we believe that politicians and the two political parties will fix, or even address, what is wrong with our country?

THIS IS OUR PROBLEM

In Jim Hightower's book, *Thieves in High Places*, he closes with the hypothetical Bob announcing his run for president. Bob says, "I want my country back. Probably, you do too. But who's going to bring it back for us? Republicans? Democrats? Wall Street? Corporate executives? Media pundits? Or any of those other wax dummies sealed in their glass cages?" The only answer, of course, is you and me.

The thing that keeps me up at night is my concern that our generation is dumping this problem on our children. Imagine the state of our country twenty or thirty years from now, the mess that our grandchildren will be forced to live with and in. We are spending their money and destroying their future, and I cannot live with myself for doing so. Look once again at the founding words of Mr. Paine. First he said, "But to expend millions…is unworthy the charge, and is using posterity with the utmost cruelty; because it is leaving them the great work to do, and a debt upon their backs from which they derive no advantage. Such a thought is unworthy a man of honor, and is the true characteristic of a narrow heart and a peddling politician."[271] The situation is different, but the sentiment is as true now as it was then. Are we men of honor if we leave the country in this condition, or worse, the condition we are all predicting twenty or thirty years from now? He goes on to describe the Londoners of the time, the ones who put up with what the Americans would not: "London, notwithstanding its numbers, submits to continued insults with the patience of a coward. The more men have to lose, the less willing are they to venture. The rich are in general slaves to fear, and submit to courtly power with the trembling duplicity of a Spaniel."[272] Why do we accept the behavior of today's politicians?

Alexis de Tocqueville wrote, "I do not assert that men living in democratic communities…are forever altering, and restoring secondary matters; but they carefully abstain from touching what is fundamental. They love change, but they dread revolutions."[273] You may dread the inconvenience of having to revolt, but can you live with yourself if you do not?

Dreading revolutions is a good thing, but ignoring them because of complacency or fear is dishonorable. The words of Paine hurt, not because they are harsh, but because they hit so close to home. We have been lulled to sleep by the success of our economy, but our House is built of cards. We have time to recover, but we must act soon. To date, we have not had a legitimate way to revolt. Now we do. Patriotism and commitment are all that we need; they will become the forces that drive us.

Act or Ignore?

Remember the boat ride earlier in the book? It was describing life in America. We've paid a trivial courtesy to those who built and stocked the ship for us, benefiting from their more than two hundred years of blood, sweat, and tears. We have had it relatively easy for a long, long time, certainly for all of my lifetime. But the waterfall is roaring, and if you don't hear it, you are deaf, naive, or blissfully both. The noise you hear will soon be a scream, and if we do not do something soon, it will be too late. If we do not start rowing before the fall can be seen, we will fail.

Do you question if it is there? Are you not convinced that we must grab the oars now? Do you honestly believe we can wait any longer? As the water nears the fall, the current grows stronger. There is a point at which, no matter how hard you row, the power will be too great. Gravity never tires; it cannot be denied. This is your wakeup call. We must get to shore before it is too late. We cannot wait. Now is the time to *row like hell*!

Are you willing to engage, to do your part? Are you willing to enlist the help of others? You and I can paddle like madmen, but the more oarsmen we can find, the easier it will be. Unfortunately, getting others to acknowledge the situation and put their weekend soccer games on hold (or turn *American Idol* off) is not as easy as it sounds. Too many people become bored with this conversation after only a few minutes, and that is indicative of the biggest challenge we will have. Most people do not care enough or pay enough attention to what is happening to get involved, and they are unlikely to put forth the effort in what will be a long and difficult battle. If you read this book, you are not typical. You are commended for making the time, but the hard work is ahead. The success of GOOOH will depend entirely on how many people you are personally willing to enlist in the effort.

I believe in writing down goals. I have found that if you do so they will be accomplished. When my wife and I receive a high school graduation announcement from a friend, we send them a check that has one string attached: the graduate must create a list of one hundred things they want to do in life. They don't have to show anyone the list, but they have to create it. Many do not, but those who do, five or ten years later, will always tell me about the things they did from their list that year. I encourage you to make such a list if you have never done so, and I encourage you to put "kick the politicians out of our House" near the top.

For GOOOH to become successful, I suggest an additional list. Get a blank sheet of paper and write the numbers one to one hundred on the paper, with enough room to add a person's name or initials at a later time. Then, make a personal commitment that you will tell one hundred people about GOOOH by the end of the next month. Keep the paper on the counter where you will see it every day. Write a date by the number ten, when you will have that slot filled. Do the same with numbers twenty-five, fifty, seventy-five, and one hundred. Write down your goals, remind yourself of them every single day, and you will reach them. Once you have written them down, you are half way there.

Every day find two or three people and ask them, "What do you think about GOOOH?" If you want variety in your life, ask them, "I'm in, are you?" If they do not know what you are talking about, tell them. E-mail your friends and send them a message with a link to the Web site, or just ask them what they think about GOOOH. Ask people standing in front of you in whatever line you are in. When you go to a restaurant, ask the couple sitting in the booth next to you. When you go to a ballgame or a concert, ask a few more. "Never doubt that a small group of thoughtful, committed citizens can change the world. Indeed, it's the only thing that ever has." [274]

If you really want to make a difference, try starting a conversation on this topic with a group of friends. Watch how quickly many of them will completely disengage. Challenge them to join us. If you really want to change the country, find ten acquaintances who will spread the word. It is predicted that this book will sell over a million copies. If each of you will ask one hundred people the question, one hundred million people will be aware of GOOOH, one-third of the country (yeah, I know there will be overlap, but let's keep the math simple). If you will do your part, we can make this happen.

Do you recall the Samuel Adams quote? He said, "If ever a time should come, when vain and aspiring men shall possess the highest seats in Government, our country will stand in need of its experienced patriots to prevent its ruin." The time has come. We are the experienced patriots. If we wish to prevent the ruin of our country, the demise from within, we must act and we must act now. The good news is that we do not need swords or rifles and we must not risk our life or even our livelihood. All we need is a little of your time.

This book is our blueprint, the master plan that will lead us to victory. This is a peaceful revolution. All that we need is to light that fire of desire that you feel yearning in your heart. Doing so will send our enemies, the politicians and the two parties, scurrying for cover. They will regroup and come out firing, but it will be too late. We need to bury our apathy, end our dependence, and unleash the passion and energy that makes our country great. It is time to repair the damaged House of our once proud and mighty nation. If you do not take advantage of this opportunity, you have no right to ever complain about politicians or the state of our country again. Take action or bear the consequences.

Over two hundred years ago Thomas Jefferson said, "God forbid that we should ever be twenty years without such a rebellion." Our rebellion is long overdue. We have been too comfortable to speak up. Our complacency has led us to this point. Will we rise up and take charge, or cower in the comfort of our living room and cross our fingers that the politicians will turn the country around?

The problems before us sound amazingly similar to the situation in 1776. The English took no action while America battled for freedom. How many Brits do you think now wish they had fought with us against their government? Listen to the words of Thomas Paine from over two hundred years ago. Don't they sound familiar to the complaints you hear today? "But the constitution of England is so exceedingly complex, that the nation may suffer for years without being able to discover in which part the fault lies, some will say in one and some in another, and every political physician will advise a different medicine."[275] Isn't that exactly what is happening today?

See if this quote from George Washington hits home: "The time is near at hand which must probably determine whether Americans are to be freemen or slaves; whether they are to have any property they can call their own....The fate of unborn millions will now depend, under God, on the courage and conduct of this army....Let us therefore rely on the goodness of the cause and the aid of the Supreme Being, in whose hands victory is, to animate and encourage us to great and noble actions." We are the army, but we need not swords, and lives need not be lost. Our actions will decide if we are to remain freemen or become slaves. If you think being called a slave is an overstatement, tell the IRS you are not going to pay the portion of your taxes designated for any item you disagree with. Half of your income is already taxed, and the number is going up. Once the government takes over the Health Care system as much as 70 percent of our money will be controlled by Big Brother. The government has made so many rules that we must follow, that while we are not yet slaves, we become more like one every day.

Confucius said, "To put the world right in order, we must first put the nation in order; to put the nation in order, we must first put the family in order; to put the family in order, we must first cultivate our personal life; we must first set our hearts right." That we can do. Is your heart in it? Then we must focus our minds on the problem at hand. With the right focus we have the intelligence to do whatever we desire. It is only inaction that will allow our mighty House to crumble to the ground.

George Hegel, pointing out the shallowness of mankind and the vanity of man said, "What experience and history teach is this—that people and governments have never learned anything from history, or acted on principles." Is this true? Are we not willing to stand up for the principles that are important to us? Are we really unable to learn from the fall of every empire before us, unable to recognize what happens to government when politicians take control? Will we ignore the words written not just here, but the ones screaming in your mind, throbbing in your heart, and reverberating through your soul? This book probably did not tell you many things that you did not already know, but until now we have not had a way to respond. Will we ignore history? Are you ready to act on the principles that are important to you?

John Gardner told us, "The citizen can bring our political and governmental institutions back to life, make them responsive and accountable, and keep them honest. No one else can." He is right. It is our job, yours and mine, to make the changes that will redirect our country. If you and I don't, no one else can.

"In our age there is no such thing as keeping out of politics. All issues are political issues, and politics itself is a mass of lies, evasions, folly, hatred, and schizophrenia."[276] It is time for every one of us to join the political fray and retake control from the inmates running the asylum. John Adams said, "I must study politics and war that my sons may have liberty to study mathematics and philosophy." We can no longer ignore the messy mess of politics, or the country we leave behind will be one that our children, regardless of their commitment or effort, will never be able to restore. There is still time for us to act, but we must commit!

THE EVILS OF GOVERNMENT

We have been warned of the evils of government since our country was founded. Can you guess who said the following? Do any surprise you?[277]

- "Government, even in its best state, is but a necessary evil; in its worst state, an intolerable one."
- "The scope of government must be limited, and the power dispersed."
- "Government is not reason, it is not eloquence, it is force; like fire, a troublesome servant and a fearful master. Never for a moment should it be left to irresponsible action."
- "The function of government must be to favor no small group at the expense of its duty to protect the rights of personal freedom and of private property of all its citizens."
- "That government is best which governs least."
- "The essence of Government is power; and power, lodged as it must be in human hands, will ever be liable to abuse."

George Orwell wrote vividly of his concerns with big government and where our society might end up if we do not keep government in check. His leading character, Winston, rightly feared Big Brother.

Even O'Brien, an official he had mistakenly trusted, turned against him. Winston was being "trained" by O'Brien who asked, "What is two plus two?" Winston replied, "How can I help seeing what is in front of my eyes? Two and two are four." To which O'Brien replied, "Sometimes, Winston. Sometimes they are five. Sometimes they are three. Sometimes they are all of them at once. You must try harder. It is not easy to become sane."[278] Once the government controls all the power, it is hard to predict what it might do. Orwell satirically wrote about helplessness under an all-powerful government. How much control do you feel you have over the government today? Don't you see the government getting bigger? Don't you see power consolidating in the hands of fewer and fewer people? Does the government belong to you or the politicians?

There are some who seem to want the government to take care of them. Without saying it, perhaps even without knowing it, they are asking that we convert to socialism. Those asking have not yet found personal success and evidently do not have dreams of being successful. Should they throw in the towel? Are they suffering from Stockholm syndrome? Do the pied-piper politicians simply have them under their spell, living as hostages for so long that they have begun to sympathize with the very ones who hold them prisoner? Have they fallen prey to the handouts, not fully understanding where the process leads? Or do they simply enjoy redistributing the wealth of others because it makes them feel like they are somehow helping?

What I don't understand is how many Americans have fallen into the trap. Is socialism what the country wants? Juan Enriquez in *The Untied States of America* leads you to believe that we may soon be discussing whether or not the states in the Northeast and the ones on the West Coast should break away and form their own countries, becoming the next iterations of France and Sweden. Is that where all this is heading? Will America soon be three distinct countries: the Left Coast, Middle America, and the Northeast?

The growth of government brings more than just death to a re-public; it brings demise, and demise is worse than death. Death you do not see or feel or hear or smell. When it arrives you depart. Demise rapes while you watch. It cuts like a sharp knife, screams with hysterical pain, and rots even a living corpse. It advances like darkness and pulls like gravity. At some point, demise cannot be stopped or reversed. Are we in the earliest stages of demise?

WE MUST ACT NOW

In 300 B.C., Plato said, "Those who do not take an interest in public affairs are doomed to be ruled by evil men." Thomas Paine said, "If there must be trouble, let it be in my day, that my child may have peace." Thomas Jefferson told us, "Dissent is the highest form of patriotism." John Kennedy said, "Ask not what your country can do for you, but what you can do for your country." Dick Armey, Speaker of the House in 1995, said, "The voters have had it. Had it with profligate federal spending. Had it with the endless array of federal regulations. Had it even with the entitlement programs that account for most of the federal program."[279] We had enough then and now we've had it for twelve more years, yet nothing changes. Will we speak up, or will we be ruled by evil men?

Jim Hightower pointed out, "Those who came before us risked all of their property, their reputations, their freedom, and their lives to push the boundaries of democracy for us…What are you doing that is more worthy of your efforts than trying to establish the moral principles of fairness, justice, and equality for all in our America?"

Reverend Martin Niemoller, a Pastor in Germany in 1945, recounted the events as Hitler rose to power: "In Germany, they first came for the Communists, and I didn't speak up because I wasn't a Communist. Then they came for the Jews, and I didn't speak up because I wasn't a Jew. Then they came for the trade unionists, and I didn't speak up because I wasn't a trade unionist. Then they came for the Catholics, and I didn't speak up because I was a Protestant. Then they came for me, and by that time there was nobody left to speak up."

I find Niemoller's quote eerie; when I read it today, this is what it says to me. Your-name-here, a citizen of America in 2008, recounted the events as America self-destructed: In America, they first came for our republic, and I didn't speak up because I didn't know that a pure democracy was a bad thing. Then they threw out our guiding principles, and I didn't speak up because the lawyers threatened me with lawsuits. Then they came for equal rights, and I didn't speak up because I had compassion for those who had suffered. Then they discarded common sense, and I didn't speak up because I was a law-abiding citizen. Then they came for God, and I didn't speak up because I could still worship at my church. Then they came for my country, and by that time there was nothing left to take.

We cannot afford to wait. Two hundred and fifty years ago, a leading member of the British Parliament, Edmund Burke said, "All that is necessary for evil to prevail is for good men to do nothing."[280] Thomas Jefferson said, "If a nation expects to be ignorant and free…it expects what never was and never will be." Frederick Douglass said, "Those who profess to favor freedom, and yet deprecate agitation, are men who want crops without plowing up the ground. They want rain without thunder and lightning." "It is a common defect of men in fair weather to take no thought of storms."[281] If we continue to ignore the obvious, to take no action, our children and theirs will bear the consequences.

Lou Dobbs recently wrote a compelling piece titled "Middle Class Needs to Fight Back Now." He makes many excellent points in the article, and I strongly encourage you to read it. Dobbs said, "Our so-called representatives in both parties have been working against the interests of the middle class for so long that they take our votes for granted, or they take advantage of the fact that a sizable number of us don't vote at all." He goes on to say, "Hardworking Americans have not spoken out about their increasingly marginalized role in this society, and as a consequence they've all but lost their voice. Without that strong, clear and vibrant voice, all the major decisions about America and our future will be made by the elites of government, big business and the dominant special interests."[282] It is obvious what is happening. Those in power want us to remain silent.

We cannot wait for someone else to do what must be done. We cannot allow the two parties and the politicians to run our country into bankruptcy. We cannot allow our education system to fail any longer and our health care costs to soar any higher. We cannot continue lazily drifting down the river and ignoring the mighty fall that lies ahead. We must address the pending Social Security crisis and take control of our borders. We need to rebuild the foundation of our country, reestablishing our religious roots and raising our morals so that our children will do the same. The country is nearing the tipping point.

Joseph Farah tells us, "It's time to ignite the Second American Revolution. It's time to celebrate virtue and knowledge again. It's time to wake up your neighbors so they can once again smell the sweet aroma of freedom....Let's take America back."[283]

WILL THE PLAN WORK?

Do yuo qetusoin if scuh a paln cna scueced? Cosinder teh pheeomnnal pweor of the hmuan mnid. Aoccdrnig to rscheearch at Cmabrigde Uinervtisy, it deosn't mttaer in waht oredr the ltteers in a wrod are plcaed, teh olny iprmoetnt tihng is taht the frist and lsat ltteer be at teh rghit pclae. The rset can be a tatol mses adn yuo can sitll raed it wouthit porbelm. Tihs is bcuseae the huamn mnid deos not raed ervey lteter by istlef, but the wrod as a wlohe. We cna do wtaheevr we dciede to do. Scucses is in raech.

In *Taking America Back*, Farah outlined many of the problems we face today. Yet he stopped short of providing a solution. He said, "Nor am I vain enough to suppose that I could come up with an entire agenda for redirecting the course of a nation." I understand his sentiment, but some of the greatest inventions in history have come from a seed planted by a single person. Ben Franklin, one of the greatest inventors of all time said, "I was not discouraged by the seeming magnitude of the undertaking, as I have always thought that one man of tolerable abilities may work great changes and accomplish great affairs among mankind if he first forms a good plan, and cutting off all amusements or other employments that would divert his attention, makes the execution of that same plan his sole study and business."

Ben Franklin was a patriot just like you and I. He changed the world, not by himself, but with an idea and the support of many around him. I may be proven wrong, but I do believe this plan can and will redirect the course of our mighty nation. This plan will work, if people like you will step forward and join the revolution.

The most important thing we can do is put everyday citizens in office who are committed to a specific platform, people who are truly average, everyday, citizens. The platform these citizens are committed to should be their own, not one defined by a party or paid for by a lobbyist. It must be a platform that they live and breathe and believe every single moment of their waking life, not one that they have been told to believe. But how do we get these people elected?

Orwell wrote, "The people need only to rise up and shake themselves like a horse shaking off flies. If they choose, they could blow the Party to pieces by tomorrow morning. Surely sooner or later it must occur to them to do it."[284] Yet he saw the problem, and went on to say, "Until they become conscious they (the people) will never rebel, but until after they have rebelled they cannot become conscious."[285]

Are we conscious? Will we rebel? If we do, en masse, we can blow the parties to pieces. But will we make the commitment to do what we need to do? Will we retake the Power that rightfully belongs to the people? Power can be a scary thing. It attracts men of a different stamp and changes the very essence of the person who has it. Those with Power always want more; it is a thirst they cannot quench, it is a cup that is never full. Those with Control hold fast; it is a vice that only tightens. Neither Power nor Control will be relinquished willingly. Power grows with its good friend Time, positioning its weapons, stockpiling its munitions, and relishing its strength. Control fortifies as Power grows, strengthening its walls, deepening its moat, and discouraging would-be attackers. The politicians have all the power. They have complete control. A battle with weapons of convention, a war abiding by their rules of engagement, has no outcome other than defeat. A frontal assault is destined to fail. Brawn and bravado will not suffice, but commitment, intelligence, bravery, and action will.

"In the beginning of change, the patriot is a scarce man, and brave, and hated, and scorned."[286] The most difficult step is making the commitment. "All truth passes through 3 phases: First, it is ridiculed. Second, it is violently opposed, and third, it is accepted as self-evident."[287] Are you brave enough to join the revolution early, or will you sit on the sidelines, ridicule or oppose the idea, hesitate to get your hands dirty? "The electorate is the source of strength for a revolutionary idea, because the people, en masse, will support an idea that makes sense, although unconventional, while the elites will support it only when they see they have no choice."[288] "Truth will be proven by the consensus of millions."[289] "Destiny is not a matter of chance, it is a matter of choice; it is not a thing to be waited for, it is a thing to be achieved."[290]

Once again we can look to the words of Thomas Paine. He said, "These proceedings may at first appear strange and difficult...until an independence is declared, the Continent will feel itself like a man who continues putting off some unpleasant business from day to day, yet knows it must be done, hates to set about it, wishes it over, and is continually haunted with the thoughts of its necessity." He added, "We have it in our power to begin the world over again."[291]

There are those who will say we cannot do many of the things suggested in this book because we will be infringing on the special rights of minorities. I am willing to bet that the ones making this argument are the ones abusing the system. I say this is our country and we can do whatever the hell we want to do. If we want to put God back into our Constitution, let's do it. If we want to take away the "rights" of drug dealers, NAMBLA, and the KKK, let's take them. If we want to operate on guiding principles instead of technicalities, then let's do so. If we want to apply common sense instead of the judiciary interpretations of ambiguous words, who can tell us that we cannot? If we want to limit the power that lawyers and activist judges have in our society, let's limit them.

It is my strongest desire that we contemplate every change in earnest and that each change is made with caution and wisdom, but if we want to change, let us change. It is one thing to control lunatics, but quite another to constrain liberty. We must be careful not to destroy what is left of the legitimate foundation of our country. It is time to redefine the meaning of checks and balances. Separating the judiciary and the legislature is a first step. Our Nation has tilted out of balance. Every fringe behavior has charged to the center, and the center has been forced to scramble to the fringes. The scale is out of whack. It is time to recalibrate.

Notes to Specific Groups

I have held nothing back, and it is certain that I have likely offended some by writing what I felt must be written, but this story must be told. If everybody would speak honestly and say everything they believed should be said, our country would be a better place. We have been politically correct for far too long and kept too much bottled inside.

This system proposes excluding a few specific groups of which you may be a member. We will debate on the Web site if anyone in fact will be turned away, but I ask that you support the process either way. In your eyes, I am absolutely wrong on a few things and out of line on a couple of others, but so are you. Our desires, however, should hopefully be the same: to put the country back on track. The current system is not working, and there is no other plan in sight. We can allow the politicians to debate and politic, to advise different medicines, but they have no cure. It is up to us to treat the ailment.

Support this plan with your heart, your mind, and your actions. Debate the issues with your peers and let the process identify the best representatives. We can adjust the plan as we move forward, and we will debate the topics until our death, but today is the day we join forces, and November 4, 2008, is the day we wage war.

For the vast majority of you, the ones who believe in God, whatever God, do not try to use this effort to force religion on those who are not interested or ready. Now is not the time to try to save every last soul. You will turn off those who do not believe and scare away those who are in between. Those who do not believe will step forward when they are ready. Give them space. I do hope that we can restore religion and morality as the basis for our laws, exactly as was intended when the country was founded, and I do hope to push back the atheist influence that has invaded our space, but we must do so based upon principles. We cannot behave in the same way that the Murray followers have, but we can reestablish the importance of religion in America while we take our country back.

I ask that the lawyers of America not hastily chastise this plan because I have proposed excluding them in this initial iteration. This plan will have a much better chance of succeeding if you will support the process. We can debate if you should be included in the forums, but give thought to why the plan is laid out this way. The truth is, as a group, lawyers hold too many of the seats in the House and no longer seem to represent the common man.

Given that lawyers provide 25 percent to 50 percent of all political funding, excluding lawyers may cause this plan to fail, but for now, I'll take that chance. Once the system is established and we are electing true representatives, we should consider removing this restriction. For now, in order to effect change, I ask that lawyers still support this plan as is. Do it for the country.

Excluding the wealthiest people from this system is also going to create a potentially devastating conflict. I am counting on a few very wealthy people to fund GOOOH, and at the same time I am excluding them from the process. The proposition will be problematic for many, but I trust some will understand. We have a real problem today in that Congress is dominated by wealthy people. And let's be real—a wealthy person is not experiencing the same problems as a couple whose husband is a mechanic and whose wife is a school teacher. A wealthy person leads a different, more privileged life. That does not mean they did not bust their butt to get where they are, and it does not mean they do not make tremendous sacrifices every day. But for now, there are too many exceptionally wealthy people in Congress, and the voice of the average Joe is not being heard. I considered going a step further and setting the bar even lower by excluding any person who has a net worth of more than a million dollars, but for now have drawn the line at 250 times the median income. It is a nice round number, and I am attempting to minimize the number of people who are excluded. We'll see if I have drawn the line in the right place based on public reaction, and we do of course have the option of changing the number or allowing lawyers in before we start the selection sessions.

I have criticized some specific black men, not the entire race, but specific individuals who I called out by name. Please understand the difference. We must make an attempt to change the current system that is so clearly failing. The numbers do not lie. We can all do better, but the current system is only making things worse. Quit listening to Sharpton, Jackson, and those like them. Further, Al, Jesse, and anyone else playing the same self-serving games—try giving someone else a chance. You guys are the root cause of one of the most fundamental things wrong with our country today. Try shutting up for a few years!

This is a full frontal attack on politicians, yet I still ask for politicians to support this plan. You know better than anyone that what is written is the truth. Will you help iron out the wrinkles in the plan, or will you turn them into mountains? Will you accept that you really are not in a position to solve the problems of our day and give the people a chance by stepping out of the way?

I expect those of you who intend to fight our system to argue that the questionnaire is not a viable solution. You will say that issues are not so black and white, and that nailing you down on issues will prevent you from negotiating or compromising. You will not understand the value of the line. While I admit that there are shades of gray on every issue, not having a definitive position that can be clearly articulated is not working. I honestly have no idea how anyone I vote for is going to vote on any issue, and I think most of the population agrees with me. You say you will not raise taxes, and then you do. You say you will vote for term limits, and then you don't. You insist on trying to solve problems that we do not want or need solved. You debate a minimum wage for three months. Who asked you to do that? Are the people making $5.15 an hour writing you letters or calling your office? Of course not! You debate illegal immigration for another three months and again accomplish nothing. You offer an expensive prescription drug plan for a system facing bankruptcy. Was that done for any reason other than the purchase of votes? Of course not! You give oil companies tens of billions of dollars in tax credits while they are making record profits. Do they really need incentives to drill for oil? Give me a break! You insist on policing a civil war in the Middle East between fanatics who have been fighting for a thousand years while we have 16,000 people being murdered on our own streets every year. You provide aid to Columbia while their cocaine is handed out in the hallways of our schools. You pay multi-million dollar corporations and millionaire aristocrats not to farm their land so they will support your campaign. In the end, too many of you do not care about our country or our freedom. You will not stand up for what you know is right unless it will get you votes. All most of you care about is power and the status and money that come with it. Forget about yourself, for once, and think about the country.

To the few politicians that are trying to use the system honestly, I do sincerely applaud you. But, I ask that you consider the flaws in the current process as I have discussed and support this system. It will deliver a solution that is 435 million times better than what the current system possibly can. Be a patriot. Step aside voluntarily. Support the people.

There are a few other groups that should be offended. The ACLU, NAMBLA, and the KKK, please let me know how much you disagree with me. I will consider your rebuttal a ringing endorsement of the plan.

WHEN THE BOOK HITS THE STREETS

Sales of the book will be modest at first. There will be valid questions, some will debate the merits of the plan, and others will blast not the idea but my personal opinions. But the word will spread.

I need you to call the local radio shows, and convince the audience and the host to investigate GOOOH. Help convince the hosts that I am not just another mad quack, the next in a long line of raving lunatics, but a reasonable person with a sensible plan. In time, a single national talk show host, one who is not vested in the two-party system, will want to ask a few questions. Perhaps Neal Boortz, or someone like him, will want to talk. Others will follow, questioning, but not endorsing. Traffic at the Web site will begin to pick up. A few of you will be persistent in your effort, talking to friends, handing out GOOOH cards, calling the talk shows, writing the editors. Book sales will begin to pick up.

A television talk show will see the novelty in the plan, and not having any particular affiliation with either party, will extend an invitation to discuss it on the air. Conan O'Brien, Maury Povich, Craig Ferguson, or some other will take an interest. Most of the major outlets will continue to ignore us, but it will not be long until a select few news organizations will acknowledge the possibility. Maybe Bill O'Reilly, Greta Van Susteren, or Sean Hannity, hosts who tend to consider the views of others, will entertain the thought and help the plan gain momentum.

A low buzz will begin to spread across the land. The voice of the people will grow louder. Sales of the book will accelerate. Local radio shows will start talking about the plan because those supporting it have insisted on talking about it. They will become champions because they are the ones outside the system who have the exact same exasperated concerns you and I have, and they are the ones who will ignite the revolution. They will recruit the extra oars we need.

A few people from the Entertainment industry will step forward next. Tired of the same old same old with the current system and leaders, and tired of being associated with the radical left-wing liberals like Streisand, Sarandon, and Fonda who garner so many headlines, they will begin to speak out. More oars in the water.

And then the rocket will launch. Oprah, Rush, Dobbs, King, Regis and Kelly, Letterman, or Leno will consider the plan. One or two will decide they are willing to give the idea more air time. *60 Minutes*, *20/20*, or one of the other national news outlets will do a story. They'll take the idea under their wing and silently endorse it. They will emphasize the need for change, and they will acknowledge that the two parties and the politicians are the problem. They'll give the idea air time, putting muscle behind the oars.

At that point, the revolution is primed. The first GOOOH Day will be a national event. People from all over the country, on April 15, 2008, will man the oars.

The concept, barely acknowledged by more than a handful of politicians in public, will become the story. Having ignored it as just another independent, libertarian, radical idea from a "non-player" with no hope, they will now be forced to respond. A single politician, a patriot, tired of the shenanigans, will admit the truth. Public support will be clear as signs, stickers, and symbols begin sprouting across the land. As the press gives the idea attention, the oars will begin to move. Slow, precise, steady, and persistent, like soldiers marching in formation, the oars will pull, lift, advance, and drop. Pull, lift, advance, drop. And again. And again and again and again.

The devil will let his presence be felt once the book can no longer be ignored. One of two things will happen. The ship will turn to shore or it will be pushed into the strengthening current. Will an all-out attack on the author, the book, and the concept be launched by a few or by many? I do not know. Will I be censured and chastised, labeled a racist and a bigot, or called an impractical idiot and a delirious dreamer?

Or, will I be considered an American patriot recognized for telling the Emperor he has no clothes? Will those with power attack the idea, and me, in the same way a shark attacks bloody flesh in the water? Will the smear of my family, my life, my effort, or who-knows-what threaten to become the topic? Will we lose focus on the process, the only thing that should matter at that point? Will talking heads feel compelled to discuss the flaws and the failings, emphasizing whatever chum momentarily surfaces, or will they grab an oar? The ride could become unpleasant, or the ship could turn.

The media has the hammer. Will they admit that they too are fed up with the parties and the politicians? Will they pledge their allegiance to the people instead of the power? Will they tell the politicians to Get Out of Our House? Or will they tell the people to shut up? Will they help the plan develop or will they ensure that it dies? Time will reveal if their allegiance is with the people or the power.

If the media sides with the people, the boat will turn. Those who have been hiding in the dark will begin to show themselves, commanding the oarsmen with orders that will not be followed. We can expect to hear from those who will want to modify the system. They will seek changes that enhance their chances, or try to take control of the system itself. Manipulation of the new system will be attempted before the first child is delivered. Lawyers will litigate. Aristocrats will spend. Politicians will slander. We will choose our representatives.

WHEN PEOPLE CRITIQUE THE PLAN

There will be many who seek to sink our ship. Some will say the plan has no legitimate chance and attempt to convince you not to waste your vote. Others will argue our point publicly while sabotaging privately. Seek out the naysayers and ask them these questions:

- Is it okay to pass this massive debt to our children?
- What are politicians doing to solve the pending Social Security crisis? What are they doing to address medical costs, welfare, incarceration, or any of the other problems I have discussed?
- Do they prefer that we become a socialist country?
- How do they justify the expansion of government and the redistribution of wealth?
- Do they want a career politician elected instead of a common man?
- Do they want God expelled forever from our lives?
- Do they have examples of what the two parties have made better that did not involve spending money we do not have?
- Do they believe our country is improving or declining?
- Do they have a better idea?

Listen to what they say. Do not try to convince them—you cannot. Do not argue with them, but let them explain their view. Ask them questions, but do not tell them the answers. Teach them how you fish, but do not feed them. When you go your way ask them only to consider what they said before sleep comes that night. Ask them again tomorrow and the day after that. Even liars know when they lie. The truth will sit on the tip of their tongue, but do not expect it to kiss their lips immediately. Their hearts and souls will know. Conversion will come with time. Plant the seed and let patience bring fruit.

CALLING ALL ANGELS

The future of America depends on angels. Not just the heavenly kind, but the wealthy, earthly ones. I am referring to those who are sitting on 100,000 or more Grover Clevelands. Your talents, your mind, and your labor have earned you personal success. You have been blessed. It is no accident that almost 50 percent of all billionaires live in our country. We have less than 5 percent of the world's population but 95 percent of the wealthiest people. You deserve everything you have, but now is the time to reflect on all that this great country has offered. It is time to consider giving back in a way that will keep the dream alive for the 300 million citizens who pray for the opportunity to follow in your footsteps. Warren Buffet or Bill Gates, will you support this system? Michael Dell or Steve Jobs, I'd love a chance to talk. Ross Perot or Steve Forbes, this is a solution that can make a difference. A single person running for president will have nowhere near the impact that 435 representatives will. Actors and actresses, sports superstars, heirs, and heiresses, this is your opportunity to leave a legacy. Give me a call.

WHAT SHOULD YOU DO?

There are only a few things that you need to do. None are complicated.

- Visit the GOOOH Web site.
- Register to vote—as an Independent.
- Sign the GOOOH petition—on the Web site.
- Write the word GOOOH on anything and everything that you legally can.
- Every day, ask two or three people about GOOOH.
- Place GOOOH cards, stickers, and stamps everywhere there are people.

- Donate time and money to the cause—until it hurts.
- Run for the House of Representatives. Even if you do not want to win, be a part of the selection process.
- Vote.

Between now and Election Day, there is zero risk in this approach. Supporting the system as it launches will send a clear signal to the politicians. Registering for the system commits absolutely nothing. Running for office at most will cost you a month or two of Saturdays and a hundred dollars. If we do nothing more than debate the issues and select our nominees, we will have won. I am confident you will be amazed with the quality of the people who bubble to the top of our system, but identifying them changes nothing.

On Election Eve, you will know exactly where we stand. Until the moment you vote, you are not committed to this system. Until your vote is cast you can always decide to support the same old Democrats or Republicans who you have always supported. By supporting the system, up until the very last minute, you will have changed the direction of our country, for the better. I hope you will follow through with that commitment because you are convinced our nominees are the better choice, but until Election Day, put your heart, your mind, and your soul behind this idea with all the energy and passion you can muster, regardless of your belief on any issue. You owe this to your children and theirs. This is our revolution. Charge!

SUMMARY

David Brooks of the *New York Times* wrote an article titled "In the Midst of Budget Decadence, a Leader Will Arise." It says what we all hope, "There's going to be another Ross Perot, and this time, he's going to be younger. There's going to be a millionaire rising out of the country somewhere, and he or she is going to lead a movement of people who are worried about federal deficits, who are offended by the horrendous burden seniors are placing on the young, and who are disgusted by a legislative process that sometimes suggests that the government has lost all capacity for self-control."[292]

I believe where Ross Perot, Steve Forbes, and others continue to go wrong is in trying to win the Presidency. Our focus should be on first ensuring we have the appropriate representation in our House, and the most pragmatic way to secure that representation is to kick the politicians out. If we must, then we can address the Senate and the Presidency.

One of my favorite musical verses comes from a Jeremy Camp song. The line asks, "Would you take the place of this man; would you take the nails from his hands?" Christians believe a single man once willingly accepted the pain of the entire world so that we all could live. The question before us is not as profound, but it is of more importance than any other we will answer in our day. Will you fight for our country? Will you bear the pain, or will you leave the battle for our children and grandchildren? My oar is in the water. I am rowing as hard as I can. Will you join me?

Notes

TODAY

1.   Bill O'Reilly, *Who's Looking Out for You* (Random House: Broadway Books, 2003), 7.

2.   University of Michigan: National Poverty Center, "Poverty in the United States," http://www.npc.umich.edu/poverty/ (accessed July 19, 2007).

3.   Gail Russell Chaddock, "US notches world's highest incarceration rate," The Christian Science Monitor, August 18, 2003, http://www.csmonitor.com/2003/0818/p02s01-usju.html (accessed July 19, 2007).

4.   U.S. Dept. of Justice—Bureau of Justice Statistics Press Release, May 21, 2006.

5.   American Academy of Allergy, Asthma, and Immunology, "Asthma Statistics," http://www.aaaai.org/media/resources/media_kit/asthma_statistics.stm (accessed July 19, 2007).

6.   Jude Wanniski, *The Way the World Works* (Regnery Gateway, 1998), 3, 34.

7.   Thomas Paine, *Common Sense* (Dover Publications, 1997—originally published by William and Thomas Bradford, 1776), 2.

8   Consideration is being given to allow non-litigating lawyers to participate in the system, but we have not seen a valid proposal on how to draw the line to support this position. As a lawyer might say, this is under advisement at this time...

9   It is unlikely that we will actually keep all lawyers out of the system, but I want them to pause and think that many would like to. My personal perspective is clear, but this will ultimately be decided by members of GOOOH.

TIME TO ACT

10 Robert Putnam, *The Beliefs of Politicians* (Yale University Press, 1973), 1.

11 In the 2010 election we will need to determine if we want to relax the "no politician" rule to allow those selected to run a second time.

12 We are considering allowing members to participate offline, but cost and logistics suggest we will not be able to make this happen.

13 See the other footnote on lawyers...

14 There is an override clause discussed later.

15 Estimation based on formula for calculating number of children of incarcerated parents, Denise Johnson, "Effects of Parental Incarceration," in *Children of Incarcerated Parents*, edited by Katherine Gabel & Denise Johnson (New York, NY: Lexington Books 1995), 62; "Prison and Jail Population Statistics," (U.S. Department of Justice: 2000), "Prison and jail inmates at midyear 1999," Bureau of Justice Statistics Bulletin.

16 U.S. Census Bureau, "Income Climbs, Poverty Stabilizes, Uninsured Rate Increases," August 29, 2006, http://www.census.gov/Press-Release/www/releases/archives/income_wealth/007419.html (accessed July 19, 2007).

17 Ted Halstead, "The American Paradox," in *The Real State of America*, ed. Ted Halstead (Perseus Book Groups: Basic Books, 2004), 9.

18   Bill Bradley, *The New American Story* (Random House, 2007), 154.

THE DECLINE OF AMERICA

19   Calculated as follows: The top 10 percent of taxpayers pay the bulk of all taxes ((8.7t / (300m * 10 percent)) * 4).

20   Gail Russell Chaddock, "US notches world's highest incarceration rate," The Christian Science Monitor, August 18, 2003, http://www.csmonitor.com/2003/0818/p02s01-usju.html (accessed July 19, 2007).

21   Maya MacGuineas, "Radical Tax Reform," in *The Real State of America*, ed. Ted Halstead (Perseus Book Groups: Basic Books, 2004), 60.

22   Larry Elder, *The Ten Things You Can't Say in America* (St. Martins Griffin, 2000), 212.

23   These numbers do not include those who receive a GED, a token document that confirms you have basic reading and writing skills but were not able to stay in school and graduate.

24   Bill O'Reilly, *Who's Looking Out for You* (Random House: Broadway Books, 2003), 8.

25   U.S. Census Bureau, "Older Americans Month Celebrated in May," from Facts for Features, April 25, 2005, http://www.census.gov/Press-Release/www/releases/archives/facts_for_features_special_editions/004210.html (accessed July 19, 2007).

26   David Wallechinsky, "Parade," *Austin-America Statesman*, January 14, 2007.

27   William Finn Bennett, "Divorce rate down in county; but national figure holds steady—about half of all marriages," *North County Times*, May 28, 2007, http://www.nctimes.com/articles/2007/05/29/news/top_stories/1_02_405_28_07.txt (accessed July 19, 2007).

THE FALL OF EMPIRES

28   Daniel McGraw, "Demolishing Sports Welfare," ReasonOnline, May 2005, http://www.reason.com/news/show/32180.html (accessed July 19, 2007).

29   Bill Bradley, *The New American Story* (Random House, 2007), 76.

30   AP, "ACLU to defend group against charges its Web site incited murder," FreedomForum, August 31, 2000, http://www.freedomforum.org/templates/document.asp?documentID=3922 (accessed July 19, 2007).

31   Niall Ferguson, "Empires with Expiration Dates," Foreign-Policy.com, September/October 2006, http://www.foreign-policy.com/story/cms.php?story_id=3550 (accessed July 19, 2007).

32   Rabi Daniel Lapin, *America's Real War* (Multnomah Publishers, 1999), 350.

33   John F. Kennedy, *Profiles in Courage* (Harper and Brothers, 1956), 7.

34   David Wallechinsky, "Parade," *Austin-America Statesman*, January 14, 2007.

35   Stephanie Cragun, "Voter Apathy, Why Its a Big Problem," AssociatedContent, August 24, 2006, http://www.associatedcontent.com/article/53439/voter_apathy_why_its_a_big_problem.html (accessed July 19, 2007).

36   Elliott Fulmer, "Remember Those Term-Limit Pledges?" PRWatch.org, October 10, 2006, http://www.prwatch.org/node/5275 (accessed July 19, 2007).

37   Robert Longley, "Congress Votes • Itself a Pay Raise," About.com, http://usgovinfo.about.com/cs/agencies/a/raise4congress.htm (accessed July 19, 2007).

38   I was not able to confirm that the $7.9 million figure was accurate. Most of the sites that comment on these type of numbers, for some reason or another, choose not to give the actual figure, which is interesting in itself. http://www.randalee.com/bbs1/index.cgi?noframes;read=2776&quote=1, http://urbanlegends.about.com/library/blcongress.htm (accessed July 19, 2007).

39   Newt Gingrich, *Winning the Future* (Regnery Publishing, 2005), 218.

40 "America's Lawyers and Lawyers by Specialty," AmericasList. com, http://www.americaslists.com/business/alls.htm (accessed July 19, 2007).

41 Bureau of Labor Statistics, "Occupation Report: Total Employment in 2004," U.S. Department of Labor, http://data. bls.gov/oep/servlet/oep.noeted.servlet.ActionServlet?Acti on=emprprt&Occ=XXXXXXXXXX&Number=All&S ort=emp_base&Base=2004&Proj=2014&EdLevel=&Sea rch=List&Type=Occupation&Phrase=&StartItem=0 (accessed July 19, 2007).

42 Power-of-Attorneys, "Are there too many lawyers?" Power-of-attorneys.com, http://www.power-of-attorneys.com/are_ there_too_many_lawyers.htm (accessed July 19, 2007).

43 David Watkiss, "The Litigation Explosion and the Trial Lawyer's Changing Role," International Academy of Trial Lawyers, 2005, http://www.iatl.net/deans/83_litigation_1.asp (accessed July 19, 2007).

44 David Watkiss, "The Litigation Explosion and the Trial Lawyer's Changing Role," International Academy of Trial Lawyers, 2005, http://www.power-of-attorneys.com/are_there_ too_many_lawyers.htm (accessed July 19, 2007).

45 Alexis de Tocqueville, *Democracy in America* (Mentor Books: New American Library, 1956), 125.

46 Bill O'Reilly, *Who's Looking Out for You* (Random House: Broadway Books, 2003), 164.

47 Allen Breed, "Paternity test ordered on baby of Duke accuser," Boston.com, December 16, 2006, http://www.boston. com/news/nation/articles/2006/12/16/paternity_test_or dered_on_baby_of_duke_accuser/ (accessed July 19, 2007).

48 Wendy McElroy, "Dancer's Suit Puts Corrupt Lawyers on Their Toes," Foxnews.com, August 1, 2006, http://www.foxnews. com/story/0,2933,206615,00.html (accessed July 19, 2007).

49 Ronald Bibace, "The Federalist, (107)," ConstitutionalGuardian.com, July 17, 1997, http://www.constitutionalguardian. com/federalist_papers/fed107.htm (accessed July 19, 2007).

50   Diane Dew, "Revealing Facts on the ACLU: from its own writings," DianeDew.com, http://www.dianedew.com/aclu. htm (accessed July 19, 2007). References George Grant, *Trial and Error American Civil Liberties,* (Word Publishing, 1989).

51   Chris Banescu, review of "The ACLU vs. America: Exposing the Agenda to Redefine Moral Values," by Alan Sears and Craig Osten, Orthodoxnet.com, September 12, 2005, http://www.orthodoxnet.com/articles/Banescu/Review_ACLU_vs_America_2005.php (accessed July 19, 2007).

52   Bill O'Reilly, *Who's Looking Out for You* (Random House: Broadway Books, 2003), 114.

53   Michael Bates, "The ACLU and what war on Christmas," Renew America, December, 13, 2005, http://www.renewamerica.us/columns/bates/051213 (accessed July 19, 2007).

54   Alan Sears and Craig Osten, "The ACLU vs. America," Great Commission Center International, http://www.gcciusa.org/English/publications/eBooks/ARTG/I-08.pdf   (accessed July 19, 2007).

UNDERMINING ISSUES

55   John DiIulio, introduction to "Jeremiah Project Report—Religion: The Forgotten Factor in Cutting Youth Crime and Saving At-Risk Urban Youth," David Larsen and Byron Johnson, Manhattan-Institute for Policy Research, No. 2, 1998, http://www.manhattan-institute.org/html/jpr-98-2.htm, (accessed July 19, 2007).

56   Larry Elder, *The Ten Things You Can't Say in America* (St. Martins Griffin, 2000), 164.

57   Mark Goldblatt, *National Review Online,* March 29, 2002.

58   National Institute on Drug Abuse, "High School and Youth Trends," U.S Department of Health and Human Services, December 2006, http://www.nida.nih.gov/Infofacts/HSYouthtrends.html (accessed July 19, 2007).

59   Greater Dallas Council on Alcohol and Drug Abuse, "Malignant Neglect: Substance Abuse & America's Schools,"

The National Center on Addiction & Substance Abuse at Columbia University, September 2001, http://www.gdcada. org/dii/l/l.htm (accessed July 19, 2007).

60   Thomas Hallberg, "Restrictive drug policy is better than liberal drug policy," European Cities Against Drugs, http:// www.ecad.net/svnet/akt/TH_Speech_EU2006.pdf (accessed July 19, 2007).

61   University of Michigan: National Poverty Center, "Poverty in the United States," http://www.npc.umich.edu/poverty/ (accessed July 19, 2007).

62   Black: a person with skin color that is generally considered black. Also referred to as African-American, etc.

63   Brown: a person with skin color that is generally considered brown. Also referred to as Hispanic, Spanish, Mexican, etc.

64   Larry Elder, *The Ten Things You Can't Say in America* (St. Martins Griffin, 2000), 144.

65   These numbers do not include those who receive a GED, a token document that confirms you have basic reading and writing skills but were not able to stay in school and graduate.

66   Jay P Greene, "High School Graduation Rates in the United States, Manhattan- Institute, April 2002, http://www.man-hattan-institute.org/html/cr_baeo.htm (accessed July 26, 2007).

67   Goldwater Institute, http://www.goldwaterinstitute.org/ar-ticle.php/602.html (accessed October, 2006). Unable to confirm the link in July of 2007. The *Washington Times* reported similar data in a November, 2003, article that was verified in July of 2007, http://findarticles.com/p/articles/mi_go1637/ is_200311/ai_n9348221).

68   U.S. Department of Education, http://www.ed.gov/pro-grams/find/title/index.html?src=fp (accessed July 19, 2007).

69   U.S. Census Bureau, "Income Climbs, Poverty Stabilizes, Uninsured Rate Increases," August 29, 2006, http://www.

census.gov/Press-Release/www/releases/archives/income_
wealth/007419.html (accessed July 19, 2007).

70 Douglas Besharov, *Family and Child Well-Being After Welfare
Reform* (Transaction Publishers, 2003), 35.

71 Manning Marable, "Along the Color Line," August, 2000,
PeaceworkMagazine.com ("Racism, Prisons, and the Future of Black America"), http://www.afsc.org/pwork/1200/
122k05.htm (accessed July 19, 2007).

72 Charles Sykes, *Dumbing Down Our Kids* (St. Martin's Griffin, 1995), 220.

73 "United States: Uniform Crime Report – State Statistics
from 1960 to 2005," The Disaster Center, http://www.disas-
tercenter.com/crime/ (accessed July 19, 2007).

74 "Crime in the United States," Answers.com, http://www.answers.
com/topic/crime-in-the-united-states (accessed July 19, 2007).

75 "United States: Crime Rates 1960 to 2005," The Disaster
Center, http://www.disastercenter.com/crime/uscrime.htm
(accessed July 19, 2007).

76 Mona Charen, *Do-Gooders* (Penguin Group, 2004), 29.

77 Victor Davis Hanson, "Eye of the Beholder," in *The American
Enterprise Online*, May 2006.

78 "United States: Uniform Crime Report—State Statistics
from 1960 to 2005," The Disaster Center, http://www.disas-
tercenter.com/crime/ (accessed July 19, 2007).

79 Margaret Talbot, "Overflowing Jails," in *The Real State of
America*, ed. Ted Halstead (Perseus Book Groups: Basic
Books, 2004), 191.

80 Paige Harrison & Allen Beck, "Prisoners in 2005," Washington DC: U.S. Department of Justice (November 2006): 1.

81 Glaze, Bonczar & Bonczar, "U.S. Department of Justice, Bu-
reau of Justice Statistics, Probation and Parole in the United
States, 2005," Washington DC: U.S. Department of Justice
(November 2006): 1.

82 Christopher Hartney, "U.S. Rates of Incarceration—A Global Perspective," National Council on Crime and Delinquency,

November 2006, http://64.233.167.104/search?q=cache: LHjtRMfsuC4J:www.nccd-crc.org/nccd/pubs/2006nov_ factsheet_incarceration.pdf+incarceration+rates&hl=en&c t=clnk&cd=20&gl=us (accessed July 19, 2007).

83   Roy Walmsley, "World Prison Population List—Sixth Edition," *International Centre for Prison Studies* (2006): 1.

84   The Sentencing Project, "New Incarceration Figures: Thirty-three Consecutive Years of Growth," SentencingProject.org, December 2006, http://www.sentencingproject.org/Admin/Documents/ publications/inc_newfigures.pdf (accessed July 19, 2007).

85   T.P. Bonczar & Allen J. Beck, "U.S. Department of Justice, Bureau of Justice Statistics, Lifetime Likelihood of Going to State or Federal Prison," Washington DC: U.S. Department of Justice (March 1997): 1.

86   Estimation based on formula for calculating number of children of incarcerated parents. Denise Johnson, "Effects of Parental Incarceration," in *Children of Incarcerated Parents*, ed. Katherine Gabel & Denise Johnson (New York, NY: Lexington Books 1995), 62; "Prison and Jail Population Statistics," (U.S. Department of Justice: 2000), "Prison and jail inmates at midyear 1999," Bureau of Justice Statistics Bulletin.

87   "Mentoring incarcerated youth to reduce recidivism," Corporation for National & Community Service, NationalServicesResources.org, http://www.nationalserviceresources. org/epicenter/practices/index.php?ep_action=view&ep_ id=1009 (accessed July 19, 2007).

88   "Crime in the United States—2005," U.S. Department of Justice: Federal Bureau of Investigations, September 2006, http://www.fbi.gov/ucr/05cius/data/table_32.html (accessed July 19, 2007).

89   Howard Snyder and Melissa Sickmund, "Juvenile Offenders and Victims: 2006 National Report," Office of Juvenile Justice and Delinquency Programs: National Center for Juvenile Justice, March 2006, 235, http://ojjdp.ncjrs.gov/ojstatbb/ nr2006/downloads/NR2006.pdf (accessed July 19, 2007).

Oil Dependence

90   *Round Rock Leader*, January 27, 2007.

91   Ricard Bayon, "The Fuel Subsidy We Need," in *The Real State of America*, ed. Ted Halstead (Perseus Book Groups: Basic Books, 2004), 78.

92   Nelson Schwartz, "Ready for $262 a barrel oil?" CNNMoney.com, April 11, 2006, http://money.cnn.com/2006/01/27/news/international/pluggedin_fortune/index.htm (accessed July 19, 2007).

93   Ricardo Bayon, "The Fuel Subsidy We Need," in *The Real State of America*, ed. Ted Halstead (Perseus Book Groups: Basic Books, 2004), 78.

94   Republican National Committee, "First Iraq, Now Energy, Hillary Proposes 'Strategic Energy Fund' By Echoing Kerry's Out Of This World Rhetoric," GOP.com, http://www.gop.com/News/Read.aspx?ID=6808 (accessed July 19, 2007).

95   Richard Heffner, introduction to *Democracy in America* by Alexis de Tocqueville, (Mentor Books: New American Library, 1956), 22.

96   Rabi Daniel Lapin, *America's Real War* (Multnomah Publishers, 1999), 35.

97   Ibid, 270.

Failure
Big Government

98   Alexis de Tocqueville, *Democracy in America* (Mentor Books: New American Library, 1956), 22.

99   Michael Hodges, "Grandfather Economic Report Series," March 2007, http://mwhodges.home.att.net/mwhodges.htm (accessed July 19, 2007).

100   Jan Malcolm, "Spending more and getting less for U.S. health care," *MN Journal* 23, no. 2 (March 2006), Citizen's League, http://citizensleague.org/publications/journal/archives/2006-3.pdf (accessed July 19, 2007).

101   Bill Bradley, *The New American Story* (Random House, 2007), 76.

102   "Relative Size of Federal Spending, 1940–2003," Truthand-Politics.org, http://www.truthandpolitics.org/outlays-per-gdp.php (accessed July 19, 2007).

103   Tom Curry, "Ten things to know about the federal budget," MSNBC, February 7, 2005, http://www.msnbc.msn.com/id/6910217/ (accessed July 19, 2007).

104   Bill O'Reilly, *Who's Looking Out for You* (Random House: Broadway Books, 2003), 36.

105   U.S. Department of Energy, "U.S. DOE starts Freedom Car, retires PNGV," DieselNet.com, January 12, 2002, http://www.dieselnet.com/news/2002/01doe.php (accessed July 19, 2007).

106   Ibid.

107   AP, "Fannie Mae profit shrinks by $6.3 billion," The Daily News, December 7, 2006, http://www.tdn.com/articles/2006/12/07/biz/news02.prt (accessed July 19, 2007).

108   Dick Armey, *Freedom Revolution* (Regnery Publishing, 1995), 89.

109   Maya MacGuineas, "Radical Tax Reform," in *The Real State of America*, ed. Ted Halstead (Perseus Book Groups: Basic Books, 2004), 61.

110   Jim Hightower, *Thieves in High Places* (Penguin Group: Viking Penguin, 2003), 82.

111   "Forbes 400 Richest in America," *Forbes*, http://www.forbes.com/lists/home.jhtml?passListId=54&passYear=2000&passListType=Person (accessed July 19, 2007); "World's Richest People: 691 Billionaires on Earth," Kahsoon.com, June 11, 2005, http://www.kahsoon.com/2005/06/11/worlds-richest-people-691-billionaires-on-earth/ (accessed July 19, 2007).

112   "What Former IRS Commsionners Say," Geocities.com, http://www.geocities.com/cmcofer/commish.html (accessed July 19, 2007).

SPENDING

[113] Thomas Paine, *Common Sense* (Dover Publications, 1997), 34.

[114] Robert Scott, "International Picture: Increases in foreign liabilities financed through sale of government securities," Economic Policy Institute, June 30, 2006, http://www.epi.org/content.cfm/indicators_intlpict_20060630 (accessed July 19, 2007).

[115] Dick Armey, *Freedom Revolution* (Regnery Publishing, 1995), 90.

[116] Reported in *Austin-American Statesman* et al., January 20, 2007.

[117] Michael Calabrese and Maya MacGuineas, "Spendthrift Nation," in *The Real State of America*, ed. Ted Halstead (Perseus Book Groups: Basic Books, 2004), 34.

[118] *USA Today*, Cauchon & Waggoner, October 4–5, 2004, http://www.usatoday.com/news/nation/2004-10-03-debt-cover_x.htm; Sugi Sorenson and Stephen Cobb, "The U.S. Income Tax Burden," Allegromedia.com, April 17, 2000, Dennis Cauchon and John Waggoner, "The looming national benefit crisis," *USA Today*, October 5, 2004, http://www.allegromedia.com/sugi/taxes/ (accessed July 19, 2007).

[119] Philip Howard, *The Death of Common Sense* (Warner Books, 1996), 183.

[120] "The coming financial collapse of the U.S. government: Fed papers reveal what's in store for Americans," Counterthink.org, July 17, 2006, http://www.counterthink.org/z019659.html (accessed July 19, 2007).

[121] Reported in *Austin-American Statesman*, January 20, 2007.

TAX SYSTEM

[122] Harry Brown, *Why Government Doesn't Work*, (Liamworks, 1995), 227.

[123] Larry Elder, *The Ten Things You Can't Say in America* (St. Martins Griffin, 2000), 212.

124 Neil Boortz and John Linder, *The FairTax* (Harper Collins: Regan Books, 2005), 16.

125 "What Former IRS Commsionners Say," Geocities.com, http://www.geocities.com/cmcofer/commish.html (accessed July 19, 2007).

126 Neil Boortz and John Linder, *The FairTax* (Harper Collins: Regan Books, 2005), 118.

127 John Walker, "U.S. Tax Code Online," Fourmilab.ch, http://www.fourmilab.ch/uscode/26usc/ (accessed 7/19/2007).

128 Chris Edwards, "Tax Code Kills Civil Liberties," Cato Institute, April 15, 2004, http://www.cato.org/pub_display.php?pub_id=2613 (accessed July 19, 2007).

129 The story that explained this in detail was cut during the edit process. Perhaps we will post it on the web.

130 Paul Krugman, "The Tax-Cut Con," *New York Times*, September 14, 2003, Health.

131 Rabi Daniel Lapin, *America's Real War* (Multnomah Publishers, 1999), 234.

Health System

132 Rong-Gong Lin II and Juliet Chung, *Los Angeles Times*; reported in the *Austin American- Statesman* July 9, 2006. Cost estimates for breastbone and naval separation are from the Children's National Medical Center in Washington, D.C.; cost estimates for head separation are from the University of California, Los Angeles.

133 VOA News Now, "U.S. Health Care: World's Most Expensive," NewsVOA.com, February 28, 2006, http://www.voanews.com/english/NewsAnalysis/2006-02-28-voa59.cfm (accessed July 19, 2007).

134 Charles Masenas, comment on "Barbados Kids Learn With Methods U.S. Shuns," by David Beard, *Sun-Sentinel*, June 6, 1997, Mathforum.org, http://mathforum.org/kb/thread.jspa?forumID=206&threadID=477072&messageID=1461805#1461805 (accessed July 19, 2007).

135 President George Bush (Forward), "Transforming the Federal Role in Education So That No Child is Left Behind," Whitehouse.gov, http://www.whitehouse.gov/news/reports/no-child-left-behind.html (accessed July 19, 2007). (Emphasis mine.)

136 These numbers do not include those who receive a GED, a token document that confirms you have basic reading and writing skills but were not able to stay in school and graduate.

137 Calculated by the $9,000 average per student times the 47 million students.

138 U.S. Department of Education, "The Federal Role in Education," February 4, 2006, http://www.ed.gov/about/overview/fed/role.html?src=ln (accessed July 19, 2007).

139 U.S. Department of Education, http://www.ed.gov/programs/find/title/index.html?src=fp (accessed July 19, 2007).

140 Dick Armey, *Freedom Revolution* (Regnery Publishing, 1995), 196.

141 http://www.lacriminaldefenders.com/CM/Custom/TOC-RepresentativeCases.asp (accessed July 19, 2007).

142 http://www.statesman.com/news/content/news/stories/local/06/14bigelow.html (accessed June 14, 2006).

143 Boyd A. Byers, *Mandatory Arbitration of Employment Dispute*, 67 J. Kan. B.A. 18.

144 President George Bush (speech), "President Signs Class-Action Fairness Act of 2005," Whitehouse.gov, February 8, 2005, http://www.whitehouse.gov/news/releases/2005/02/20050218-11.html (accessed July 19, 2007).

145 "Equal Employment Opportunity Commission ," Answers.com, http://www.answers.com/topic/equal-employment-opportunity-commission (accessed July 19, 2007).

146 Mona Charen, *Do-Gooders* (Penguin Group, 2004), 4.

147 Ibid., 28.

148 Ibid.

149   Philip Hagar, "U.S. Plans No Prosecution of Dan White," *Los Angeles Times*, November 22, 1983.

150   Randy Shilts, *And the Band Played On: Politics, People and the Aids Epidemic* (St. Martin's Press, 1987), 147.

151   Ronald Sullivan, "Ex-Inmate Wins Award in Bias Case," *New York Times*, August 6, 1992.

152   Mike DuPre, "Burglar pursues suit against doctor who shot him," GazetteXtra, June 13, 2007, http://www.gazetteextra.com/prochaska061307.asp (accessed July 19, 2007).

153   Bill O'Reilly, *Who's Looking Out for You* (Random House: Broadway Books, 2003), 164.

154   The White House, "Legal Reform: The High Costs of Lawsuit Abuse," Whitehouse.gov, January 5, 2005, http://www.whitehouse.gov/news/releases/2005/01/20050105-2.html (accessed July 19, 2007).

155   Liz Kowalczyk, "Rising doctors' premiums not due to lawsuit awards," Boston.com, June 1, 2005, http://www.boston.com/business/articles/2005/06/01/rising_doctors_premiums_not_due_to_lawsuit_awards/ (accessed July 19, 2007).

156   Manhattan Institute, "The New Billionaires: Top officers of Trial Lawyers, Inc. haul in sky-high fees for little work," TrialLawyersInc.com, 2006, http://www.triallawyersinc.com/html/part03.html (accessed July 19, 2007).

157   Philip Howard, *The Death of Common Sense* (Warner Books, 1996), 140.

158   "Win Big! Lie in Front of a Train," Overlawyered.com, http://www.overlawyered.com/archives/02/jun3.html, referencing *New York Law Journal*, June 26–27, 2002 (accessed July 19, 2007).

159   Thomas Sowell, *The Vision of the Anointed* (Harper Collins: BasicBooks, 1995), 160.

160   Center for Individual Freedom Foundation, "U.S. Supreme Court Keeps a Watchful Eye on the 9th Circuit," http://www.centerforindividualfreedom.org/legal/9th_circuit.htm (accessed July 26, 2006).

161 George Will, "Supreme Court Cleans up after 9ᵗʰ Circuit," Real Clear Politics, November 16, 2006, http://www.realclearpolitics.com/articles/2006/11/supreme_court_cleans_up_after.html (accessed July 19, 2007).

162 Walter Olson, "Courting Stupidity: Why smart lawyers pick dumb jurors," ReasonOnline, January 2003, http://www.reason.com/news/show/28630.html (accessed July 19, 2007).

163 Walter Olson, "Courting Stupidity: Why smart lawyers pick dumb jurors," ReasonOnline, January 2003, http://www.reason.com/news/show/28630.html (accessed July 19, 2007).

164 Philip Howard, *The Death of Common Sense* (Warner Books, 1996), 11.

165 Mona Charen, *Do-Gooders* (Penguin Group, 2004), 145–148.

166 Robert Kennedy Jr., *Time Magazine*, May 19, 1967; and Michael Bates, "Edwards Takes Page from RFK's Book," NewsBusters, July 12, 2007, http://newsbusters.org/node/14047 (accessed July 19, 2007).

167 Douglas Besharov, *Family and Child Well-Being After Welfare Reform* (Transaction Publishers, 2003), 35.

168 U.S. Census Bureau, "Income Climbs, Poverty Stabilizes, Uninsured Rate Increases," August 29, 2006, http://www.census.gov/Press-Release/www/releases/archives/income_wealth/007419.html (accessed July 19, 2007).

169 Larry Elder, *The Ten Things You Can't Say in America* (St. Martins Griffin, 2000), 234.

170 The White House, "Achievements of the Welfare Reform Law of 1996," Whitehouse.gov, February 2002, http://www.whitehouse.gov/news/releases/2002/02/welfare-book-02.html (accessed July 19, 2007).

171 Robert Rector, "Means-Tested Welfare Spending: Past and Future Growth," The Heritage Foundation, March 7, 2001, http://www.heritage.org/Research/Welfare/Test030701b.cfm (accessed July 19, 2007).

172 Philip Howard, *The Death of Common Sense* (Warner Books, 1996), 156.

173   Robert Rector, *Wall Street Journal*, September 25, 1990.

174   Joseph McNamara, "When in Trouble, Don't Call the Feds," *Wall Street Journal*, August 24, 1994, A10. Reported in Thomas Sowell, *The Vision of the Anointed*, 154.

175   Paige Harrison & Allen J. Beck, "U.S. Department of Justice, Bureau of Justice Statistics, Prisoners in 2005," Washington DC: U.S. Department of Justice (November 2006): 1.

176   Christopher Hartney, "U.S. Rates of Incarceration—A Global Perspective," National Council on Crime and Delinquency, November 2006, http://64.233.167.104/search?q=cache: LHjtRMfsuC4J:www.nccd-crc.org/nccd/pubs/2006nov_factsheet_incarceration.pdf+incarceration+rates&hl=en&ct=clnk&cd=20&gl=us (accessed July 19, 2007).

177   Glaze, Bonczar & Bonczar, "U.S. Department of Justice, Bureau of Justice Statistics, Probation and Parole in the United States, 2005," Washington DC: U.S. Department of Justice (November 2006): 1.

178   "Who's Who in U.S. Prisons," CBSNews.com, July 31, 2002, http://www.cbsnews.com/stories/2002/07/31/national/main516966.shtml (accessed July 19, 2007).

179   "Costs of Incarceration and Supervision," *The Third Branch* 36, no. 5 (May 2004), http://www.uscourts.gov/ttb/may04ttb/costs/index.html (accessed July 19, 2007).

180   Mike Ward, "As prisons fill, state hunts for scarce beds," *Austin-American Statesman*, July 24, 2006.

181   Bay City News, "Convicted Murder Mastermind Seeks Execution Stay," CBS5.com December 14, 2005, http://cbs5.com/deathrow/local_story_348212624.html (accessed July 19, 2007).

182   "U.S. Prisons Overcrowded and Violent, Recidivism High," Infoplease.com, http://www.infoplease.com/ipa/A0933722.html (accessed July 19, 2007).

183   Chris Buell, "Rights groups sue Rumsfeld over prisoner abuses," University of Pittsburg School of Law: Paper Chase Newsburst, March 1, 2005, http://jurist.law.pitt.edu/

paperchase/2005/03/rights-groups-sue-rumsfeld-over.php
(accessed July 19, 2007).

184 "ACLU of Rhode Island Files Appeal on Behalf of Christian Prisoner Barred from Preaching at Religious Services," ACLU, January 12, 2006, http://www.aclu.org/religion/frb/23445prs20060112.html (accessed July 19, 2007).

185 http://urbanlegends.about.com/library/bl_sheriff_joe_arpaio.htm (accessed July 19, 2007).

186 *Lowell v. Brown*, 280 F. 193, 196 (1922); Mark Knutson, "Charles K. Ponzi Website: The Remarkable Criminal Financial Career of Charles K. Ponzi," March 15, 2007, http://www.mark-knutson.com/ (the scheme) (accessed July 19, 2007).

187 Usually prosecuted under the FTC Act, though most states have specific laws as well.

188 Heather Williams, "Florida alleges $117 million Ponzi scheme based on viatical sales," Insure.com, March 30, 2001, http://info.insure.com/states/fl/viaticalfraud301.html (accessed July 19, 2007); "California Police Make Arrests In Alleged Ponzi Scheme," ConsumerAffairs.com, May 17, 2006, http://www.consumeraffairs.com/news04/2006/05/ca_ponzi.html (accessed July 19, 2007).

189 Ronald Lee and John Haaga, "Government Spending in an Older America," *Population Reference Bureau: Reports on America* 3, no. 1 (May 2002), http://www.prb.org/pdf/ReportonAmericaGovtSpendng.pdf (accessed July 19, 2007).

190 "The Future Growth of Social Security: It's Not Just Society's Aging," Congressional Budget Office: Long-Range Fiscal Policy Brief, no. 9, July 1, 2003, http://www.cbo.gov/showdoc.cfm?index=4380&sequence=0 (accessed July 19, 2007).

191 James Pinkerton, "What Would Kirk Do?" NationalReviewOnline, November 26, 2003, http://www.nationalreview.com/comment/pinkerton200311260919.asp (accessed July 19, 2007).

192 *Investor's Business Daily*, Friday January 5, 2007. A7; http://news.yahoo.com/s/ibd/20070105/bs_ibd_ibd/200714issues01 (accessed August 2006).

193   The White House, "Strengthening Social Security," Whitehouse.gov, http://www.whitehouse.gov/infocus/social-security/ (accessed July 19, 2007).

194   Life expectancy is projected to increase from 77 years today to 82.6 in 2050.

ENVIRONMENT

195   "Air Pollution, Heart Disease and Stroke,"AmericanHeart. org, http://www.americanheart.org/presenter. jhtml?identifier=4419 (accessed July 19, 2007).

196   Bernie Fischlowitz-Roberts, "Air Pollution Fatalities Now Exceed Traffic Fatalities by 3 to 1," Earth Policy Institute, 2002, http://www.earth-policy.org/Updates/Update17.htm (accessed July 19, 2007).

197   "Dishonorable Discharge: Toxic Pollution of America's Waters," Environmental Working Group, http://www.ewg.org/ reports/dishonorable/ddrivers.html (accessed July 19, 2007).

198   Robert Kennedy Jr., "Crimes Against Nature," in *The Best American Political Writing 2004*, ed. Royce Flippin (Avalon Publishing Group: Thunder's Mouth Press, 2004), 213.

199   http://www.doh.wa.gov/ehp/oehas/EHA_fish_adv.htm (accessed May 2006). The Report could no longer be found in July of 2007.

200   "Pork Power: Are Hog Farmers Creating A Waste Hazard?" CBSNews.com: 60 Minutes, June 22, 2003, http://www.cbsnews.com/stories/2003/06/19/60minutes/main559478. shtml (accessed July 19, 2007).

201   "Superfund: A National Commitment to Prevent Toxic Threats," BeSafeNet.com, http://www.besafenet.com/Superfund.htm (accessed July 19, 2007).

202   Patrick Michaels,"Opposing View: Live with climate change," USAToday.com, February 2, 2007, http://blogs.usatoday. com/oped/2007/02/post_4.html (accessed July 19, 2007).

203   AP, "Global Warming 'To Continue For Centuries,'" CBSNews.com, February 2, 2007, http://www.cbsnews.com/

stories/2007/02/02/tech/main2425536.shtml (accessed July 19, 2007).

204 Philip Howard, *The Death of Common Sense* (Warner Books, 1996), 26.

205 Ibid., 32.

206 Virginia Postrel, *The Future and Its Enemies*, (Simon & Schuster: The Free Press, 1998), 113.

207 NOAA Fisheries: Office of Protected Resources, www.nmfs. noaa.gov/pr/species/esa.htm (accessed July 19, 2007).

208 "Delisted Species," National Endangered Species Act Reform Coalition, March 18, 2003, http://www.nesarc.org/delist. htm (accessed July 19, 2007).

IMMIGRATION

209 WorldNet Daily, "Cop murder spotlights crisis of killer aliens," September 28, 2006, WorldnetDaily.com, http://www.wnd. com/news/article.asp?ARTICLE_ID=52198 (accessed July 19, 2007).

210 Predatory Aliens, "News: January to June 2005," Predatory-Aliens.com, http://www.predatoryaliens.com/html/news/ news05a.htm (accessed July 19, 2007).

211 Deborah Schurman-Kauflin, "The Dark Side of Illegal Immigration: Nearly One Million Sex Crimes Committed by Illegal Immigrants in the United States," Violent Crimes Institute, 2006, http://www.drdsk.com/articles.html#Illegals (accessed July 19, 2007).

212 Lou Dobbs, "Border Fence will leave Texas-size hole," CNN.com, October 26, 2006, http://www.cnn.com/ 2006/US/10/24/Dobbs.Oct25/index.html (accessed July 19, 2007).

213 "Overview—Illegal Aliens in the United States," The American Resistance, http://www.theamericanresistance.com/ref/ illegal_alien_numbers.html (accessed July 19, 2007).

214 Chuck Hanrahan, "Stop Illegal Immigration—Arrest Illegal Employers," WatchBlog, comment posted August 26, 2005,

http://www.watchblog.com/thirdparty/archives/002618.html (accessed 7/19 2007).

215 Congressman Steve King, "Biting the Hand that Feeds You," KingforCongress.com, April 26, 2006, http://www.kingforcongress.com/clippings/desk-immigration4-06.htm (accessed July 19, 2007).

216 Ibid.; AmericaOne, "What is the bigger threat to Americans today, terrorist thugs or illegal aliens?" May 15, 2001, FreeRepublic.com, http://www.freerepublic.com/~americaone/ (accessed July 19, 2007).

217 Congressman Ted Poe, http://www.house.gov/poe/remarks/immigration71205.htm (accessed April 2006).

218 Chuck Hanrahan, "Stop Illegal Immigration - Arrest Illegal Employers," WatchBlog, comment posted August 26, 2005, http://www.watchblog.com/thirdparty/archives/002618.html (accessed July 19, 2007).

ABORTION

219 Heinrich Von Staden (Translation), "Hippocratic Oath," *Journal of the History of Medicine and Allied Sciences* 51 (1996) 406–408, http://www.indiana.edu/~ancmed/oath.htm (accessed July 19, 2007).

220 Williard Cates Jr. et al., "The Public Health Impact of Legal Abortion: 30 Years Later," *Perspectives on Sexual and Reproductive Health,*Volume 35, no. 1 (2003), 25–8.

221 Steven Levitt and Stephen Dubner, *Freakonomics* (HarperCollins: William Morrow, 2005), 138.

222 Susanne Pickler, "Medical and Social Health Benefits Since Abortion Was Made Legal in the U.S.," Planned Parenthood, December 2006, http://www.plannedparenthood.org/files/PPFA/fact-health-benefits.pdf (accessed July 19, 2007).

223 Lilo Strauss et al., "Abortion Surveillance, United States, 2003," Center for Disease Control, November 24, 2006, http://www.cdc.gov/mmwr/preview/mmwrhtml/ss5511a1.htm?s_cid=ss5511a1_e (accessed July 19, 2007).

224 Walter Larimore, "The Abortifacient Effect of the Birth Control Pill," Eternal Perspectives Ministries, June 21, 2005, http://www.epm.org/articles/larimore_list.html (accessed July 19, 2007).

225 Randy Alcorn, "Does the Birth Control Pill Cause Abortions?" Eternal Perspectives Ministries, 2006, http://www.epm.org/articles/bcp5400.html (accessed July 19, 2007).

Gun Control

226 Kristine Favreau, "Impact of Luby's gunmen still felt," *Killeen Daily Herald*, September 17, 2006, http://www.kdhnews.com/docs/stories/story.aspx?sid=11857&cid=4 (accessed July 19, 2007); "Luby's Massacre," Wikipedia, April 2007, http://en.wikipedia.org/wiki/Luby's_massacre (accessed July 19, 2007).

227 This quote is credited to Jefferson, but influenced by Beccaria. Thomas Jefferson, *Commonplace Book* (Princeton University Press, 1989); http://www.criminology.fsu.edu/crimtheory/beccaria.htm (accessed July 19, 2007).

228 Larry Elder, *The Ten Things You Can't Say in America* (St. Martins Griffin, 2000), 281.

229 Steven Levitt and Stephen Dubner, *Freakonomics* (HarperCollins: William Morrow, 2005), 131.

230 "Guns and Crime in the United States: Gunsafe Fact Sheet," Gunsafe, http://gunsafe.org/position%20statements/Guns%20and%20crime.htm (accessed July 19, 2007).

231 Larry Elder, *The Ten Things You Can't Say in America* (St. Martins Griffin, 2000), 294.

232 David P. Kopel, "Rowan Case and the Need to Bear Arms," *Wall Street Journal*, November 11, 1988, reported by Elder, 298.

233 "CCW License Holders: 'Law-Abiding Citizens?'" BradyCampaign, http://www.bradycampaign.org/facts/research/?page=incident&menu=gvr (accessed July 19, 2007).

Internet

234 "CCW License Holders: 'Law-Abiding Citizens?'" BradyCampaign, http://www.bradycampaign.org/facts/research/?page=incident&menu=gvr (accessed July 19, 2007).

235   "Federal Bureau of Investigations: Operation Candyman," FBI.gov, March 18, 2002, http://www.fbi.gov/pressrel/ pressrel02/cm031802.htm (accessed July 19, 2007).

236   "Child Porn Ring Smashed," CBSNews.com, March 19, 2002, http://www.cbsnews.com/stories/2002/03/18/national/main503982.shtml (accessed July 19, 2007).

237   John Oates, "FBI arrest 65 in P2P child porn raids," The Register, May 17, 2004, http://www.theregister.co.uk/2004/05/ 17/peer_porn/ (accessed July 19, 2007).

238   Jerry Ropelato, "Internet Pornography Statistics," TopTenReviews, http://internet-filter-review.toptenreviews.com/internet-pornography-statistics.html (accessed July 19, 2007).

239   "Internet Gambling: An Overview of the Issues," General Accounting Office, December 2002, http://www.gao.gov/new. items/d0389.pdf (accessed July 19, 2007).

240   Bruce Schneier, "Why Spam Won't Go Away," *Forbes*, December 12, 2006, http://www.forbes.com/home/security/ 2006/12/11/spam-security-email-tech-security-cz_bs_ 1212spam.html (accessed July 19, 2007).

241   "What is Spam?" Strategis, May 25, 2005, http://e-com. ic.gc.ca/epic/internet/inecic-ceac.nsf/en/h_gv00170e.html (accessed July 19, 2007).

242   "Learn IT: Defeating Spam in the Enterprise," Whatis.TechTarget.com, January 27, 2006, http://whatis.techtarget. com/definition/0,,sid9_gci931780,00.html (accessed July 19, 2007).

MILITARY

243   Jude Wanniski, *The Way the World Works* (Regnery Gateway, 1998), 329.

244   *James Madison, Political Observations, 1795.*

245   Baker Spring, "Defense FY 2008 Budget Analysis: Four Percent for Freedom," The Heritage Foundation, March 5, 2007, http://www.heritage.org/Research/Budget/bg2012.cfm (accessed July 19, 2007).

246   Anup Shah, "World Military Spending," GlobalIssues.org, February 25, 2007, http://www.globalissues.org/Geopolitics/ArmsTrade/Spending.asp (accessed July 19, 2007).

247   "U.S. Forces Order of Battle," GlobalSecurity.org. April 13, 2007, http://www.globalsecurity.org/military/ops/iraq_orbat.htm (accessed July 19, 2007).

248   "Military of the United States," Wikipedia, http://en.wikipedia.org/wiki/Military_of_the_United_States#Overseas (accessed July 19, 2007); Department of Defense, "Base Structure Report: Fiscal Year 2003 Baseline," DefenseLink.mil, http://www.defenselink.mil/news/Jun2003/basestructure2003.pdf (accessed July 19, 2007).

249   Robert Longley, "Database Tracks U.S. Troop Deployment Since 1950," USGovInfo.About.Com, 2007, http://usgovinfo.about.com/od/defenseandsecurity/a/troopdeploy.htm (accessed July 19, 2007).

250   Bill Bradley, *The New American Story* (Random House, 2007), 76.

251   Heather MacDonald, "Have We Crossed the Line?" *City Journal* (Winter 1993).

252   Stanley Czerwinski, testifying to the Senate Housing and Transportation Subcommittee, March 6, 2002.

GLOBALIZATION

253   Joseph Farar, *Taking America Back*, (Thomas Nelson: WND Books), 164.

254   Larry Elder, *Investor's Business Daily*, June 1997, 205.

255   Curt Tarnoff and Larry Nowels, "CRS Report for Congress - Foreign Aid: An Introductory Overview of U.S. Programs and Policy," U.S. Department of State: Foreign Press Centers, April 15, 2004, http://fpc.state.gov/documents/organization/31987.pdf (accessed July 19, 2007).

256   Ibid.

257   Ibid.

258   Ibid.

TERRORISM

259 "U.S. Plants Open to Terrorists," CBS, June 13, 2004, http://www.cbsnews.com/stories/2003/11/13/60minutes/main583528.shtml (accessed July 19, 2007).

ECONOMY

260 Bureau of Labor Statistics, "Employment status of the civilian noninstitutional population, 1940 to date," U.S. Department of Labor, http://www.bls.gov/cps/cpsaat1.pdf (accessed July 19, 2007).

261 Stephen Rose, "What's (Not) the Matter With the Middle Class?" The American Prospect, September 4, 2006, http://www.prospect.org/web/page.ww?section=root&name=ViewWeb&articleId=11943 (accessed July 19, 2007).

THE CANDIDATE QUESTIONNAIRE

262 Life expectancy is projected to increase from 77 years today to 82.6 in 2050.

THE PLAN TO TAKE OVER OUR HOUSE

263 This is not a binding commitment to do so, but is the intended plan.

264 This rule is put in place to get past the idiotic, "What you did in high school or college?" issues. My belief is that without such a rule we will eliminate many worthy candidates who simply don't want to have to relive something stupid they did while young, inebriated, on Spring Break, or a combination of all three. If we can all admit that many of us did some incredibly dumb things as part of the growing up process, but really are decent people, we will be able to focus on issues of merit. While the age of twenty-five is admittedly arbitrary, and should perhaps be lower, let's give the candidates the benefit of the doubt and seek out those who have behaved properly throughout their adult life.

265 Other groups are likely to be added over time.

266   If legal.

267   The final logistical arrangements will be defined on the Web site.

268   There may also be a GOOOH 1-800 phone number where the results can be reported.

269   Meaning an entity cannot receive subsidies for more than two years in any ten year period.

THE CALL TO ACTION

270   Pew Research Center for The People and The Press, "Hillary Clinton Seen as Leader of Democratic Party; BUSH A DRAG ON REPUBLICAN MIDTERM PROSPECTS," directed by Andrew Kohut, February 9, 2006, http://people-press.org/reports/pdf/270.pdf (accessed July 19, 2007).

271   Thomas Paine, *Common Sense* (Dover Publications, 1997), 34.

272   Ibid., 40.

273   Alexis de Tocqueville, *Democracy in America* (Mentor Books: New American Library, 1956), 267.

274   Margaret Mead.

275   Thomas Paine, *Common Sense* (Dover Publications, 1997), 5.

276   George Orwell.

277   Thomas Paine, Milton Friedman, George Washington, Franklin Roosevelt, Henry David Thoreau, James Madison.

278   George Orwell, *1984* (Penguin Putnam: New American Library, 1950), 207.

279   Dick Armey, *Freedom Revolution* (Regnery Publishing, 1995), 6.

280   Rabi Daniel Lapin, *America's Real War* (Multnomah Publishers, 1999), 355.

281   Machiavelli.

282   Lou Dobbs, "Middle class needs to fight back now," CNN. com, October 18, 2006, http://www.cnn.com/2006/US/10/10/Dobbs.Oct11/index.html (accessed July 19, 2007).

283 Joseph Farah, *Taking America Back* (Thomas Nelson: WND Books, 2003), 16.

284 George Orwell, *1984* (Penguin Putnam: New American Library, 1950), 60.

285 Ibid., 61.

286 Mark Twain.

287 Arthur Schopenhauer.

288 Jude Wanniski, *The Way the World Works* (Regnery Gateway, 1998), 360.

289 Erich Fromm, afterword to *1984* (Penguin Putnam: New American Library, 1950), 264.

290 William Jennings Bryan.

291 Thomas Paine, *Common Sense* (Dover Publications, 1997), 44, 51.

292 David Brooks, "In the Midst of Budget Decadence, a Leader Will Arise," *New York Times*, February 19, 2005, Section A, page 15.

Bibliography

Armey, Dick. *Freedom Revolution.* Regnery Publishing, 1995.

Bayon, Ricardo. "The Fuel Subsidy We Need." In *The Real State of America,* edited by Ted Halstead, 78–84. Perseus Book Groups: Basic Books, 2004.

Besharov, Douglas. *Family and Child Well-Being After Welfare Reform.* Transaction Publishers, 2003.

Boortz, Neil and John Linder. *The FairTax.* Harper Collins: Regan Books, 2005.

Bradley, Bill. *The New American Story.* Random House, 2007.

Brown, Harry. *Why Government Doesn't Work.* Liamworks, 1995.

Calabrese, Michael and Maya MacGuineas. "Spendthrift Nation." In *The Real State of America,* edited by Ted Halstead, 34–42. Perseus Book Groups: Basic Books, 2004.

Charen, Mona. *Do-Gooders.* Penguin Group, 2004. de Tocqueville, Alexis. *Democracy in America.* Mentor Books: New American Library, 1956.

Elder, Larry. *The Ten Things You Can't Say in America.* St. Martins Griffin, 2000.

Enriquez, Juan. *The Untied States of America.* Crown Publishing, 2005.

Farah, Joseph. *Taking America Back.* Thomas Nelson: WND Books, 2003.

Friedman, Milton. *Capitalism and Freedom.* University of Chicago Press: Phoenix Books, 1982.

Gingrich, Newt. *Winning the Future.* Regnery Publishing, 2005.

Halstead, Ted. "The American Paradox." In *The Real State of America,* edited by Ted Halstead, 7–14. Perseus Book Groups: Basic Books, 2004.

Hightower, Jim. *Thieves in High Places.* Penguin Group: Viking Penguin, 2003.

Howard, Philip. *The Death of Common Sense.* Warner Books, 1996.

Kennedy, John F. *Profiles in Courage.* Harper and Brothers, 1956.

Kennedy, Robert Jr. "Crimes Against Nature." In *The Best American Political Writing 2004,* edited by Royce Flippin, 213–234. Avalon Publishing Group: Thunder's Mouth Press, 2004.

Lapin, Rabi Daniel. *America's Real War.* Multnomah Publishers, 1999.

Levitt, Steven and Stephen Dubner. *Freakonomics.* HarperCollins: William Morrow, 2005.

MacGuineas, Maya. "Radical Tax Reform." In *The Real State of America,* edited by Ted Halstead, 51–62. Perseus Book Groups: Basic Books, 2004.

O'Reilly, Bill. *Who's Looking Out for You.* Random House: Broadway Books, 2003.

Orwell, George. *1984.* Penguin Putnam: New American Library, 1950.

Paine, Thomas. *Common Sense.* Dover Publications, 1997. Originally published by William and Thomas Bradford, 1776.

Postrel, Virginia. *The Future and Its Enemies.* Simon & Schuster: The Free Press, 1998.

Putnam, Robert. *The Beliefs of Politicians.* Yale University Press, 1973.

Sowell, Thomas. *The Vision of the Anointed.* Harper Collins: Basic-Books, 1995.

Shilts, Randy. *And the Band Played On: Politics, People and the Aids Epidemic.* St. Martin's Press, 1987.

Sowell, Thomas. *The Vision of the Anointed.* Harper Collins: Basic-Books, 1995.

Sykes, Charles. *Dumbing Down Our Kids: Why American Children Feel Good About Themselves But Can't Read, Write, or Add.* St. Martin's Griffin, 1995.

Talbot, Margaret. "Overflowing Jails." In *The Real State of America,* edited by Ted Halstead, 191–191. Perseus Book Groups: Basic Books, 2004.

Wanniski, Jude. *The Way the World Works.* Regnery Gateway, 1998.